STRAIGHT TALK
On Canadian Unity

Organized around four central themes, *Straight Talk*, a collection of Stéphane Dion's speeches from 1996 to 1998, shows the breadth and strength of Dion's convictions. He believes that Canada is first and foremost a nation of caring people, in contrast to the image projected by the endless, dry constitutional debate. He argues that the melding of diversity and unity that is the basis of this nation is possible only because of the particular federalism that Canadians have invented. This federalism, however, is far from perfect and it is the responsibility of government to continue to work to improve it, always remembering that its core must be the quality of service it provides to Canadians.

Dion believes that the Quebec question is not a constitutional question but one that concerns identity: many francophones believe that their identity and culture are not respected in the rest of Canada and see the anglophone majority as a force for assimilation, while many in other provinces feel that separatists do not share the same values of openness and tolerance. He believes strongly that the secession process the Parti Québécois had proposed – effecting independence on the basis of incorrect legal theory, an unclear referendum question, and a majority of fifty percent plus one – is difficult to reconcile with democracy and raises questions that must be discussed openly and resolved democratically.

Straight Talk is a refreshingly honest and frank discussion about a matter that has been at the forefront of Canadian's thoughts for too many years.

THE HONOURABLE STÉPHANE DION is minister of Intergovernmental Affairs.

D1444853

STRAIGHT TALK

On Canadian Unity

Stéphane Dion

McGill-Queen's University Press
Montreal & Kingston · London · Ithaca

© McGill-Queen's University Press 1999
ISBN 0-7735-1853-3 (cloth)
ISBN 0-7735-1856-8 (paper)

Legal deposit fourth quarter 1999
Bibliothèque nationale du Québec

Published simultaneously in French under the title
*Le Pari de la franchise: discours et écrits
sur l'unité canadienne*
ISBN 0-7735-2039-2 (broché)

Printed in Canada on acid-free paper

McGill-Queen's University Press acknowledges the
financial support of the Government of Canada through
the Book Publishing Industry Development Program
(BPIDP) for its activities. We also acknowledge the
support of the Canada Council for the Arts for our
publishing program.

Canadä

Canadian Cataloguing in Publication Data

Dion, Stéphane
Straight talk: on Canadian unity
Collection of speeches delivered 1996–1998.
ISBN 0-7735-1853-3 (bound)
ISBN 0-7735-1856-8 (pbk.)
1. Federal government – Canada. 2. Federal-provincial
relations – Canada. 3. Federal-provincial
relations – Quebec (Province) I. Title.

FC98.D565 1999   321.02'091   C99-900603-7
F1034.2.D565 1999

This book was typeset by Typo Litho Composition Inc.
in 10/12 Sabon.

CONTENTS

Preface by Peter Russell / vii

Introduction / xiii

SECTION 1   THE SPIRIT OF FEDERALISM

Regaining Confidence in Canada / 3

Canada's Communities and the Hope for Canadian Unity / 6

Speech to the American Council for Quebec Studies / 14

The Ethic of Federalism / 25

Our Two Federations: Contrasting Evolutions and
Common Challenges / 36

Canada: A Fair Federation / 45

SECTION 2   A CHANGING FEDERATION

Federalism: A System in Evolution / 59

History and Prospects of the Canadian Social Union / 68

Amendment of Section 93 (Education) of the Constitution Act,
1867 / 80

Amendment of Term 17 of the Terms of Union of Newfoundland
with Canada (Newfoundland Schools) / 86

The Decentralized Nature of the Canadian Federation / 93

Zero Déficit: Our Common Objective / 103

My Praxis of Federalism / 114

Social Union: Canadians Helping Canadians / 121

SECTION 3 CANADIAN IDENTITY AND THE
QUEBEC SOCIETY

The Canada We Share / 131

Fears About "Distinct Society" Status Are Unfounded / 138

Quebec's Reasonable Request / 141

Canadian Diversity and the Recognition of Quebec / 143

Francophone Communities Outside Quebec: At the Heart
of the Canadian Ideal / 150

Renewal and the Role of the Métis / 159

Respecting the Balance of Equality and Diversity / 166

On the Harmonization of Federal Legislation with Quebec
Civil Law / 169

The Canadian Ideal / 174

SECTION 4 THE DANGERS OF SECESSION
IN DEMOCRACY

Speech on a Motion by the Opposition / 185

Letter to Mr. Lucien Bouchard, Premier of Quebec / 189

Letter to Mr. Bernard Landry, Deputy Premier of Quebec and
Minister of State for the Economy and Finance / 194

Letter to Mr. Bernard Landry, Deputy Premier of Quebec and
Minister of State for the Economy and Finance / 198

Why a Quebecer Wants to Keep British Columbia as Part of
His Country / 200

Letter to Mr. Jacques Brassard, Quebec Minister for Canadian
Intergovernmental Affairs / 208

Beyond Plan A and Plan B: The Two Debates on Canadian
Unity / 214

Letter to Mr. Claude Ryan / 222

Respect for Democracy in Canada / 225

The Practical Difficulties of a Unilateral Secession / 233

Statement in Response to the Ruling of the Supreme Court / 239

Letter to Mr. Lucien Bouchard, Premier of Quebec / 243

The International Community and the Secessionist Phenomenon / 248

PREFACE

I happily confess to being the instigator of this book.

Early in 1996, soon after Stéphane Dion left his position as professor of political science at the University of Montreal to become federal minister of Intergovernmental Affairs, I began to receive a steady stream of grey envelopes bearing the ponderous return address of Office of the President of the Queen's Privy Council for Canada and Minister of Intergovernmental Affairs. Academics, journalists, politicians, and government officials across the country were receiving the same grey envelopes, containing copies of the speeches Stéphane was giving and the letters he was publishing as he discharged his responsibilities as the Chrétien government's point man on national unity and the constitution. Their contents were anything but ponderous or grey.

At first in reading Stéphane's speeches and letters I was simply interested to see how a good friend and academic colleague was adapting to political life. I had first known Stéphane through his father, the late Professor Leon Dion of Laval University, one of Canada's greatest political scientists. After 1984, when Stéphane returned from Paris with his doctorate and joined the Department of Political Science at the University of Montreal, I came to know him much better, first through his academic publications on public administration, nationalism, and Canadian politics, then through his participation in the Canadian Political Science Association as a member of its Board of Directors and as co-editor of the *Canadian Journal of Political Science*. In the 1990s we travelled together in China as part of a Royal Society of Canada team discussing democracy with scholars from the Chinese Academy of Social Science. Through these contacts I could see that Stéphane was a talented and engaged scholar – every inch the rigorous political scientist but also a very committed democrat and federalist. I was curious to see how these talents and beliefs would translate into his performance as a leading player in the central drama of Canadian politics.

As I read the ever-widening file of his ministerial products I found a marvellously focused combination of Dion's scholarly rigour and passionate appreciation of his country. In his day-to-day engagement with what for a generation has been the dominant preoccupation of Canadian politics, the so-called national unity issue, Stéphane was expounding an understanding of the genius of this country, Canada. It became increasingly clear to me that no one in Canadian public life today came close to articulating what Canadians have achieved together since the founding of their federation in 1867 – and what they are capable of achieving together in the future. The contribution he was making to our public life was, in my view, too valuable, too significant, to simply accumulate in filing cabinets. It deserved publication in a form that would be both more accessible and more enduring.

In January 1998 I wrote Stéphane suggesting that a selection of his speeches and letters be prepared for publication as a book and offered my services to approach scholarly presses about the project. Stéphane replied that he thought this was a useful suggestion, providing the book was published in both French and English. With that encouragement, I approached several publishers of academic and scholarly works.

I felt strongly that a scholarly press was the appropriate publisher of this collection of Stéphane's speeches and writings. These were not, after all, the usual after-dinner musings of a political leader, put together by staff writers with a distinctive phrase or two tossed in by the speaker. In these writings we see the practical application of a brilliant intellect to the affairs of state. The arguments advanced, the theories and presentations of facts that buttress them, are those of a sophisticated and accomplished political scientist. Though their first objective was, and is, to advance the federalist cause in an immediate popular political sense, they contain ideas and put forward positions that fully merit the attention of those whose interest in Canada's national unity struggle is as much academic as political. So I was delighted when McGill-Queen's agreed to publish the collection.

It is not easy for an academic with the intellectual brilliance of a Stéphane Dion to make the transition to politics. The very things that academics like myself most admire may not go down as well with the general public or with their political opponents. Clear, logical arguments, supported by an impressive mastery of the relevant facts, while impressive to the intellectual to others, especially those strongly committed to the cause being denounced, may appear professorial, even arrogant. It is not that the language used is pedantic: readers will not find Stéphane's speeches or letters cluttered with technical jargons or obscure words. It is more a matter of tone – the very clear, analytical way their "straight talk" disposes of propositions advanced by the sovereignist side – that is so devastating. For those accustomed to more rhetorical and less cerebral forms of political communication, it is like being hit with a bucket of cold water – and they do not always appreciate the treatment.

No problem

Entering into politics is always problematic for the scholar and intellectual. That is why so few take the plunge and so very few are asked to "volunteer" – and why even fewer are successful. It is fascinating to watch the progress of someone who dares to take up the challenge – especially when his academic accomplishments are in the very field of his political assignment.

The closest parallel with Stéphane Dion is, of course, Pierre Trudeau. Both men were recruited into politics by Liberal prime ministers anxious to bolster their government's position in Quebec. In 1965 Lester Pearson invited Trudeau, with his fellow-Quebecers Jean Marchand and Gérard Pelletier, to join the Liberal caucus in Ottawa. In 1996 Jean Chrétien issued a similar invitation to Stéphane Dion and Pierre Pettigrew. In both cases Trudeau and Dion were neophyte politicians recruited for their intellectual strength on the constitutional and unity issues. Both men accepted the invitation not because they sought a career in politics but because they believed they could make a significant contribution to preserving and strengthening the Canadian federation. Both faced the challenge of countering the mainstream of political opinion among their own people in Quebec. At first, and in Trudeau's case overall, their ideas about Canada and its future found much more support in English Canada and outside Quebec than among French-speaking Quebecers.

Striking as the Trudeau/Dion parallels are, the differences between them are just as interesting – and instructive. These are differences of character, context, and, above all, their understanding of the kind of political community Canada at its best can be.

While both Trudeau and Dion were well published and respected scholars, their professional careers followed very different patterns. Trudeau was fully engaged in political action and debate long before his formal entry into politics in 1965. Besides his work as a law professor and academic, he had a lively legal practice, was a man of letters, a founder of a leading journal of opinion, *Cité Libre*, and a left-wing political activist. Dion, in contrast, followed a much narrower path, indeed the only career path a person of his generation could take toward a professional academic career in a discipline like political science. These days, becoming a tenured academic at a major university is a bit like joining the priesthood. A demanding program of graduate studies culminating in a Ph. D. must be completed and then immediately followed by publication of a series of learned articles in leading academic journals. Meeting these tests for entry into the academy requires an almost monastic discipline, leaving little scope for outside activities. So, unlike Trudeau, Dion came to politics with far less experience in public life and accustomed to a much quieter, more conventional life-style.

Nor did he bring with him, nor has he cultivated those eccentricities of behaviour that can add up to the charisma that came to be such a vital part of Trudeau's political success. Dion must rely instead primarily on the strength and clarity of his thinking to achieve his political objectives. In a political era that so often seems to value style over substance and celebrity over integrity, this presents a formidable challenge.

There are also important differences in the intellectual formation of these two scholar-statesmen. Trudeau, though formally a lawyer, drew mainly from his strong background in western political philosophy and history in his writings and speeches. The reader will find much of the same grounding in philosophy and history in Dion's writing – though in Dion there is much more of Tocqueville and his appreciation of national cultures than of the more individualistic liberal thinkers, like Locke and Mill, who inspired Trudeau. Dion, however, is much better versed in the policy sciences. In his discussion of social and economic policy issues we find a mastery of technical and statistical detail that was absent from Trudeau's writing. In the vernacular of our day, Dion, much more than Trudeau, is "a policy wonk". Yes

Trudeau was propelled into politics by the very beginning of the constitutional crisis inaugurated by Quebec's "quiet revolution". Dion entered politics after a generation of constitutional struggle. This difference in political context accounts, I believe, for the very different ways in which these two men define and execute their political projects.

Trudeau, as an intellectual leader of Quebec's "quiet revolution," feared that the democratic energies unleashed by that revolution were being captured by a narrow, ethnic-based Quebec nationalism. In taking up a position of political leadership in Ottawa, Trudeau's aim was not to reach an accommodation with Quebec nationalism. Rather the task he set himself was to convert the adherents of that nationalism to what he saw as the larger, and morally more legitimate, goal of making all of Canada a political community in which French-speaking Canadians, competing on equal terms with English-speaking Canadians could fulfil themselves. It was for this end, this kind of conversion, that Trudeau championed constitutional change.

By the time Dion came to Ottawa it was clear that Trudeau's project of conversion had not worked. The "Trudeau vision" may have captured hearts and minds in English Canada, but it had not come to define the constitutional aspirations of francophone Quebec. In *la belle province*, Quebec nationalism remains alive and well. And so Dion's project is not one of conversion but of reconciliation. In many of the writings in this volume the reader will find Dion advocating and setting out the conditions for a reconciliation – a reconciliation of Quebec nationalism with a highly decentralized and multi-national Canadian state.

Dion's understanding of Canada, of what at our best we Canadians can be, is much closer to the vision of George-Étienne Cartier, and to the thinking of Henri Bourassa, than Trudeau's vision ever was. He sees our multiple identities not as a problem to be overcome by conversion to some new common definition of ourselves but as "an incomparable collective richness." Dion has no difficulty accepting that Quebec, as the homeland of a founding people and the one jurisdiction in North America with a French-speaking majority, must have a special place in the Canadian federation. This view of Quebec, however, does not exhaust his understanding of that province. He sees also that Quebec has cultural and ethnic minorities who enrich it and who possess collective rights that cannot be ignored. His appreciation of Canada as a union of peoples who, rather than assimilating into a dominant culture, seek by their very diversity to enrich one another is wider than either Cartier's or Bourassa's in that it accommodates the claims of Canada's Aboriginal peoples for recognition and self-government.

The reconciler's approach to constitutional change is very different from the would-be converter's. Dion is no advocate of the constitutional status quo. But neither is he an advocate of efforts at "big bang," mega constitutional change in which we try to settle all our constitutional issues at once. The constitutional amendments made under his watch, the on-going adjustments in the way our federal system operates, the new self-government arrangements Canada is negotiating with its native peoples, the recognition by Ottawa and the provincial premiers of Quebec as a distinct society, all of which are analysed and defended in these writings, are part and parcel of an incremental and evolutionary kind of constitutional growth. Unfortunately, Canadians have become so conditioned by a generation of big-bang efforts that detractors of his approach can get away with calling it the status quo.

The path Dion has chosen to take as reconciler of our national differences is not an easy one. It promises no grand resolution of the "national unity" issue. His instruments of persuasion are essentially those of the brilliant intellectual, not the charismatic politician. Difficult though his project may be, Canada's future depends very much on its success. For if we Canadians – English, French, Aboriginal, multicultural – cannot eventually embrace Stéphane Dion's understanding of this country's genius, I believe we cannot have Canada.

Peter H. Russell
University Professor
University of Toronto
November 1998

INTRODUCTION

At the invitation of Prime Minister Jean Chrétien, I entered the federal Cabinet on January 25, 1996, without any direct political experience, but driven by my convictions on Canadian unity and determined to defend them in complete frankness and in all circumstances.

These convictions have become stronger and clearer over the course of my dialogue with Canadians. They have guided my actions as Minister of Intergovernmental Affairs and have nourished my writings and speeches on national unity. I have submitted them for public debate throughout the country, in both official languages, even in places where I knew full well that they would be unpopular.

This book is a compilation of some of my speeches and my writings, organized into four themes: the spirit of federalism, the practice of federalism, identity, and secession. Each of these four sections centres on one of my main convictions regarding Canadian unity.

The spirit of federalism

The first conviction that I express in this book is that our country, Canada, is first and foremost a principle of caring, one of the best ever invented by the human spirit. And yet, this is not at all how Canada was most often defined in the years prior to my entering politics. It was too often perceived as an endless constitutional dispute, and it was after years of such constitutional obsession that Quebecers were called on to express themselves on sovereignty-partnership on October 30, 1995. There was one country in the world where the debate on unity had been reduced to a dry discussion on the Constitution, and it happened to be my country.

It was time to say and to demonstrate, openly and unashamedly, that the fact of being together gives us one of the best qualities of life in the world. The main strength and the true greatness of Canada is its capacity to unite different populations around common objectives. This melding of unity and diversity could not be maintained without the federalism that we have invented. That is why I have called the first section "the spirit of federalism."

In short, I proposed a change of perspective. Rather than seeing the separatist threat as proof that our federation is a failure, I maintained that the federation is an undeniable success, and that we will be able to improve it even more once we have resolutely decided to stay united.

I felt the need to talk about the spirit of federalism in the first section because my views on this theme give rise to the three others: the practice of federalism, identity, and secession. In effect, our federative culture 1) helps our governments to adapt to new economic and social conditions, 2) calls on our populations to unite their identities within one political unit, and 3) founds our citizenship on a principle of caring which secession could not break without making us commit a grave moral error.

The first section comprises six speeches which, each in its own way, talk about federalism here and elsewhere. It opens with the statement I made upon my appointment to the Cabinet. Because it sets out the reasons why I entered politics, this first statement is in itself an introduction to all the themes that will be dealt with later in this work. It is followed by a speech I gave to the Canadian Federation of Municipalities, where I pointed out that federalism is a system that favours experiences at the local level and encourages governments to be inspired by them. My speeches to the American Council for Quebec Studies and at the Ideas in Action symposium in honour of Professor Peter Russell talk about the federal system's capacity to foster the harmonious cohabitation of cultures. In my speech to senior state officials in Cleveland, Ohio, I compared the Canadian federal experience with the American federal experience, while my speech to the Calgary Chamber of Commerce, as well as a similar speech to the Chambre de commerce de Trois-Rivières (which is not included here), talked about the quest for regional equity which is specific to Canadian federalism.

Evolving federalism

Our federalism, however valuable, is far from perfect. We must continually seek to improve it. We will succeed in doing so all the better if we put an essential value at the core of our initiatives for reform: quality of services to citizens. This is the second conviction I set out in this work.

To improve our federation, it is necessary to make an effective diagnosis of how it works now. I find inaccurate the belief that Canada will work only at the cost of constitutional upheaval. Here again, constitutional obsession is an error, because frankly, although its Constitution can always be improved, Canada already "works" admirably in comparison with other countries. Also false is the belief that our system is a centralizing straitjacket controlled by the federal government. In fact, our federation is one of the most decentralized in the world. But the opposite diagnosis, likening our decentralization to balkanization, is also completely erroneous. In fact, only a flexible, decentralized federalism can hold together such a vast and diversified country.

Improving our federation will not be achieved by a blind, abstract bias in favour of the provinces or, conversely, in favour of the federal government. Instead, it must be achieved by consistently and honestly assessing the real capacity of our governments to provide citizens with high-quality services that are adapted to current realities and future challenges.

Thus, one of the myths I resolved to debunk in the debate on unity is that of the so-called "status quo". In point of fact, Canadian federalism is continually evolving, and major changes have been made to it in recent years, especially since the Throne Speech of February 27, 1996, with the goal of better adapting it to citizens' needs.

The second section opens with a speech given to an audience of federal public servants. It highlights the flexibility and dynamism of Canadian federalism. The second speech deals mainly with the changes made to Canada's social union. It is followed by my two speeches in the House of Commons that launched the debates on the bilateral constitutional amendments on the denominational education systems of Quebec and Newfoundland. The next speech in this section, given at the University of Ottawa, outlines at least 17 major changes implemented or underway within the federation, mainly after the Throne Speech of February 27, 1996. It is followed by a speech dealing with the economic advantages of Canadian federalism and the costs of political uncertainty. The next speech examines the principles that are guiding the Chrétien government's initiatives for change to make the federation more harmonious and more efficient. The final speech shows how incorporating these principles, which are centred on the quality of services to citizens, has led the federal government to negotiate with the provinces improvements to Canada's social union.

Canadian identity and Quebec society

The Quebec question is above all a matter of identity, not the Constitution. I felt the need to state and re-state this third conviction that inspires me, because it goes to the very heart of the debate on Canadian unity.

What makes so many Francophone Quebecers susceptible to arguments in favour of independence is neither the supposedly over-centralized nature of our federation nor its ostensible balkanization. It is the feeling that their own identity, their language and their culture are not respected elsewhere in Canada, that they are seen as a nuisance rather than one of the intrinsic components of the Canadian identity. They see the Anglophone majority as a force of assimilation, rather than an ally. This is why the difficulty of having Quebec recognized as a distinct society has greatly tarnished Canada's image with many Quebecers.

In the face of the separatist threat, many citizens in the other provinces, and in Quebec, made a misdiagnosis. They concluded that the reason so many Francophone Quebecers were falling prey to separatism was that Quebec society did not share the values of tolerance and openness that are the hallmark of Canada. Some thought that it was xenophobia that was driving part of Quebec society to separatism. For this reason, the close result of the referendum of October 30, 1995, in no way disposed the rest of the country to recognizing Quebec's distinct character. On the contrary, the stronger separatism appears in Quebec, the less other Canadians see Quebec society as a positive and essential component of their country.

So what could be done to counter this feeling of mutual rejection? Certainly not getting back into constitutional obsession and presenting recognition of distinct society as an essential condition of Canadian unity. Instead, Quebecers and other Canadians had to be shown how much they need one another, and how the Canada they have built together is based on an admirable principle of caring, and that this country works and can be improved. In other words, they had to reacquire their taste for Canada. Second, they needed to be shown that the specificity of Quebec society is an essential component of Canada and that recognizing that specificity is in keeping with the values that unite us and with the other realities of our country. Third, the whole debate on explicitly recognizing Quebec as a distinct society in the Constitution needed to be toned down, by showing how absurd it is to make Canadian unity hinge on this issue.

In other words, it was a question of getting out of this false dichotomy between the concept of distinct society and that of the equality of the ten provinces. Quebec is obviously in a distinct, or unique, situation in North America. The ten provinces are equal in the sense that there is only one status of province in Canada. And these two concepts – unique character of Quebec and equality of the provinces – can be reconciled the moment it is admitted that equality is not synonymous with uniformity in Canada. Equality must go hand in hand with a deep-rooted respect for everything that makes up Canadian diversity: the provinces and territories, regional realities, the Aboriginal and Métis peoples, the two official languages, and the multicultural character of the population. And this respect for diversity also goes hand in hand with the unique character of Quebec society. I believe that this is what the premiers and territorial leaders wanted to express through the Calgary Declaration: a commitment to draw on the best of Canadian diversity, including the unique character of Quebec society, while respecting equality and fairness.

I do not know whether a legal text inspired by the principles of the Calgary Declaration will one day find its way into the Canadian Constitution. In any event, I do not believe that what is essential in this matter is of a constitutional or legal nature. As will be seen from reading this section, my objective was for Canadians in the other provinces and territories to make a gesture of good will toward Quebecers and call on them to do likewise. There was a need to counter mutual rejection and promote reconciliation.

This is what I wanted to express in my speeches and writings on Canadian identity and Quebec society, some of which are included in the third section of this work. The first of these is a speech I gave in British Columbia on the values that we share as Canadians. In the two articles that follow, which appeared in the *Calgary Herald*, I defended distinct society. The first was a response to an article in which Peter Menzies, Editorial Page Editor, reproached me with defending a concept that was unoriginal and did not enjoy public support, at least in Western Canada. The second was a response to an open letter in which the Reform MP Stephen Harper criticized my first article. The speech that follows was given to representatives of the Jewish, Italian and Greek communities of Toronto and Montreal. In that speech, I stated that Quebec's specificity is not only compatible with Canada's cultural diversity, but is the logical result of it. Another speech, to members of the Institut franco-ontarien, highlighted the importance of linguistic duality as an essentially Canadian value and that duality's contribution to Canada's economic and social success as well as on the international scene. In a speech to the Métis National Council, I suggested that taking account of Canada's diversity must also lead us to demonstrate greater respect for the country's Aboriginal and Métis peoples. That speech is followed by a letter I wrote to the editor of the *Financial Post* in response to an article that columnist Rafe Mair had written opposing the Calgary Declaration. In the next speech, given at a symposium on harmonizing federal laws with Quebec civil law, I talked about the richness of Canada's bijuralism. This section concludes with a speech given to the Hebrew University of Jerusalem, in which I looked at the values that unite Quebecers with other Canadians and give Canada its universal character.

The dangers of secession in democracy

In one of Canada's provinces – mine – there is a government that intends to effect secession and is announcing a procedure to that end. In my opinion, simple politeness demands that one tell this government frankly what one thinks not only about its plans for secession, but also about the procedure it intends to use. And if that government's only response to the objections raised is attempts at intimidation and a barrage of insults, seeking only to discredit those who made the objections, one must repeat the same objections, just as frankly and just as politely. I believe I have done just that. I was not the only one, but my role as a minister has put me at the centre of this debate.

I believe very strongly that a secessionist process is very difficult to reconcile with democracy, and that in that connection, the process proposed by the PQ government poses grave problems, which we need to talk about frankly, among democrats. This is my fourth conviction on Canadian unity, which I set out in the last section of this work.

I believe it is contradictory for a government to claim that it can exempt from the rules of law a secession that it could only effect in reality by having recourse to rules of law. I believe it is irresponsible for a government to claim that it can effect independence on the basis of an unclear referendum question and a slim majority, without ensuring that secession is the clearly expressed choice of the population. I believe it is immoral for a government to want to impose its secession on populations that indicated very clearly that they wanted no part of it. Finally, simply from a practical point of view, I believe it is unrealistic for a government to think that it can unilaterally break up a modern democratic state.

I raised these objections first and foremost as a Quebecer who does not want to see his society divided in circumstances that are unprecedented in democracy. For I am fundamentally opposed to the procedure for secession proposed by the PQ government because I deeply support Quebec society. And I know that Quebecers are never as deeply divided as when they are asked to give up Canada. However serious the difficulties an attempted secession would create between Quebec and Canada, I am convinced that the most complex problems would arise between Quebecers.

From that viewpoint, the real question is not whether Quebecers can decide their future: no one in Canada is proposing to hold them against their clearly expressed will. The real question is how, by what procedure, Quebecers who no longer want Canada could take it away from Quebecers who want to keep it. Above all, we must not find ourselves divided on such a serious issue in confusion, without having followed a decision-making process that is clear, legal and fair for all.

I would not have been able to conduct this debate on the procedures for secession without the strong support of Prime Minister Jean Chrétien. But I did not receive the same support from all federalists. Some of them openly reproached me with having initiated the debate along these lines. This is because, in their opinion, I broke two golden rules. The first is that one has to woo so-called soft nationalists and tell them what one thinks they want to hear – that is, engage in a discourse that gives a number of separatist theories more than their due, but does not advocate independence as such. It is thought that challenging these theories, on which there is believed to be a consensus, would risk provoking a backlash against federalism. I won't deny that this rule appears to have a certain logic. Undecided voters, who might be the decisive element in a referendum, are Quebecers who are proud of their Francophone identity but uncertain about the prospect of leaving Canada. It is feared that by highlighting the risks of an attempted secession, one will hurt their pride and push them into the independence camp.

The second golden rule consists of never publicly admitting that the opponents might win. It is feared that talking openly about the possibility of secession will make people come to think that it is less improbable. For a federalist, talking not only about the why of secession, but also about the how, is pushing the hypothesis of defeat too far. Thus, when I openly state the hypothesis of a victory by my opponents, I give it credibility in the eyes of the world, including my own supporters, and increase the risk of being defeated. At least, so goes a rule traditionally accepted in politics, which makes admitting the possibility of defeat a self-fulfilling prophecy.

I believe that both these rules are false. Admitting that one might lose is admitting at the same time that one might win. And if I believe in the merit of my cause and my convictions, I should never be afraid of clarifying all dimensions of the issue. Clarity and frankness are my allies, confusion and ambiguity my enemies. As for undecided voters, they are not "soft", they are citizens who are perfectly capable of revising their conception of things, as long as one is not afraid of presenting them with valid arguments. They are also susceptible to frankness and reason. In short, we must stop being inhibited by the dual fear of backlash and self-fulfilling prophecy.

This section begins with my maiden speech in the House of Commons, which talked about the difficulty of reconciling secession and democracy. It is followed by letters to Premier Lucien Bouchard and his ministers Bernard Landry and Jacques Brassard, which were also made public. I have also included a speech given in British Columbia opposing the use of the threat of separation as a means of blackmail. In my speech to the Montreal Press Club, I stated that all of the Government's unity initiatives are linked by a common effort of clarification, and that rather than seeing a plan "A" and a plan "B", a "soft" line and a "hard" line, these initiatives should be seen as a plan for clarity. The following text contains my response to criticism by Mr. Claude Ryan and others of the Chrétien government's decision to refer the legal aspects of a unilateral secession to the Supreme Court. After the Court rendered its opinion, on August 20, 1998, I expressed my admiration for the opinion in an official statement in the hours following its release. I subsequently wrote to Premier Bouchard, urging him to accept the Court's opinion in its entirety rather than making a selective reading of it. Before a group of foreign diplomats, I later examined the possibility of the Court's opinion being a useful inspiration for other countries experiencing unity problems similar to Canada's. The fourth and final part of the book ends with those reactions to the opinion rendered by the Supreme Court.

Why this book?

Patriotic oratory and sober economic analyses have their place in the debate on Canadian unity, and there are some examples of those in this book. But I felt that there were other issues that had not been sufficiently debated, at least not by politicians and the general public, before the 1995 referendum. I am thinking of the fundamental questions that secession raises regarding the nature of a political society, particularly with regard to democracy, citizenship, the rule of law, human rights, the nation, society, the people, the federal spirit, identity, self-determination and solidarity. We have too often set aside these questions, which are universal in scope. Our typically Canadian tendency of self-deprecation has often led us to belittle our debate on unity, seeing it as only a tiresome domestic fixation, of little interest to foreigners. In reality, we are facing an issue that may very well be the most crucial issue of the next century: how to maintain the unity of states made up of different populations.

I hope that I have helped to bring some of these issues out of the realms of academia and into the centre of the political arena, which is where they truly need to be debated. To be sure, political discourse is different from academic discourse. In active politics, I have had to learn to express myself on these issues differently from how I did in political science. My previous career had rather accustomed me to abstract reflections on political theory as well as to studies larded with footnotes on the evolution of public spending and government employees (as a specialist in public administration). As a politician, I have taken pains to express my convictions in a concise and, I hope, interesting way, with the passion of reason, without sacrificing rigour. The reader of these speeches will judge the extent to which I have succeeded. In any event, one cannot accuse me of trying to flatter my audiences. Yes, I did say that if Canada is divisible, so is Quebec. Yes, I did describe Bill 101 as a great Canadian law.

Of course, I have repeated myself. Political discourse necessarily contains central ideas and sound bites that are used over and over again, but each of the texts in this work adds to the others. I hope that readers of these speeches and writings will obtain a more complete idea of my opinions and actions, and of those of the Government as a whole in connection with Canadian unity.

This book does not have a conclusion, because it is much too early for conclusions. It will be understood that my hope is not just that Canada will win a reprieve of a few years. It is that my fellow citizens will decide resolutely to stay together. The driving idea that should convince us to do so, the one most often expressed in this book, is that of plural identities. In this global world, when we have the good fortune of having different identities, we accept them all. When we can count on our fellow citizens who open up other cultural dimensions for us, other experiences and assets than those we have ourselves, we accept their assistance and offer them ours. Therein lies the true greatness of Canada. For me, the real choice is not between Quebec and Canada. It is between being a Quebecer and a Canadian and being a Quebecer without Canada. That is why, fundamentally, beyond all the very real economic costs of separation, Canada will stay united, provided we have the courage to speak frankly.

I would like to express my heartfelt thanks to Professor Peter Russell, political science professor at the University of Toronto, for his suggestion of compiling these speeches and writings in a single volume. Professor Russell conceived and took the initiative on this project, and saw it through to its conclusion. I also thank McGill-Queen's University Press and the anonymous evaluators who deemed Professor Russell's project to be an initiative of interest to the academic community. It means a great deal to me that a university press is publishing my political writings, thus building a bridge between my two professional lives. I am also grateful to all the other people who have made this project possible: the capable researchers and writers in my office and in the Department of Intergovernmental Affairs, for their invaluable assistance at all stages in the preparation of these speeches, my parliamentary colleagues who initiated me in the art of politics as a complement to my political science studies, especially Prime Minister Jean Chrétien, and my many academic colleagues who have continued to write to me, sharing their ideas and debating them with me.

SECTION 1

The Spirit of Federalism

Regaining Confidence in Canada

Canada, a universal model of openness, tolerance and generosity, must not inflict on the world the spectacle of its break-up. On every continent, governments hesitate to grant their minorities rights and autonomy, because they suspect them, almost always incorrectly, of harbouring separatist ambitions. If Canada were to break up, worried majorities would hold it up as an example. It would be said that this defunct federation had died from an overdose of decentralization and tolerance – in short, from an overdose of democracy. Its demise would serve as an alibi for everything that one can expect from hardliners in the face of minorities' aspirations.

Rather than spreading mistrust between majorities and minorities in this way, we must instead show that different populations can live in harmony within a single state.

If Canada were unfortunate enough to split up, we, Quebecers and Canadians in the other provinces, would certainly be the first to pay the price. In Quebec, the majority would find it very difficult to obtain from its minorities the enthusiastic support that it, for its part, had denied Canada. It would never be able to give them the same high degree of autonomy that it had felt was not enough for itself as a Canadian province. As for the rest of Canada, it could by no means take for granted its unity without Quebec. There is no known example of a federation that has survived being cut apart at its centre.

The unemployment and poverty that afflict the industrialized world do not allow Canada to impose on itself, in addition, the costs of disunion. For the future of our children, for all Canadians, we must preserve Canada. It is through union, by staying together, that we will be able to make our lives easier.

A mere ten years ago, Canadian unity was solid. The vast majority of Quebecers no longer saw secession as a necessary recourse. To strengthen the Canadian union, the governments of the day undertook

---

Ministerial Statement

a constitutional round which did not work out. What some people called recognition, others understood to mean privilege. Since then, the understanding that Quebecers and other Canadians have of each other and of Canada has deteriorated to the point that a break-up has never been closer.

The saddest thing is that, out of resentment, out of frustration, many Quebecers are now ready to risk renouncing a country to which they nevertheless feel attached. That attitude ill prepares them for the costs and difficulties that secession will inflict on them. As for other Canadians, there are too many of them who, weary and exasperated, have resigned themselves or no longer want to make any attempt to preserve the unity of their country. This defeatism must be fought.

We have the means to do so. It consists of two strengths that have made our federation an admirable political system: linguistic duality and decentralization.

Democracies which are fortunate enough to have more than one official language, which enjoy through that fact a greater openness to a universe of cultures, make special arrangements to help their linguistic groups live together in harmony. Our Official Languages Act, and the recognition of language rights in the Constitution, constitute a model of that type of arrangement. We need only go further, and recognize as a strength, as an opportunity for Canada, that within this English-speaking North American continent, there exists a society that is functioning in French and takes the means to continue to do so while respecting its own linguistic minority. The Canadian provinces are all distinct from one another, but Quebec, with its French-language culture, introduces a special distinction which must be recognized as such. Such recognition, which leads neither to upheaval nor privilege, offers a guarantee that in the grey areas of the Constitution, those areas where the rules require some interpretation, Quebec's distinctiveness will be taken into account.

Our second strength lies in the fact that our federation is based on decentralization. A strong Canada must not be confused with a strong federal government alone, but must rather be based on a strong federative whole. Canada is lucky that its provinces have a high degree of autonomy. This favours creativity. It was the province of Saskatchewan that paved the way for our public health systems. It is thanks to decentralization that eight out of ten provinces have regained the path toward a balanced budget, each of them by focussing on their own resources and their own strategies.

It is also through a clearer distribution of roles and responsibilities between the two orders of government, more efficient forms of partnership, and through a more intelligent decentralization that is better designed for citizens, that we will find the path to unity, as Prime Minister Chrétien stated in his speech in Verdun on October 24, 1995.

The Swiss have the most powerful municipal system in the world, and from that extensive decentralization they derive a source of pride, an additional reason to feel Swiss. In the same way, we as Canadians have nothing to fear from decentralization. We know it well enough to make it our ally.

A strong federal government must not be confused with a centralizing government. Restricting itself to its own role will only make it more effective. Canadians understand this well. But Canadians will not accept provinces behaving like ten egotistical republics. Change is possible only if it is based on Canadian solidarity.

I have taken pains to demonstrate the relevance of these values and these principles, as an academic and as a researcher. I have defended them publicly by always saying the same thing in both official languages. The Prime Minister of Canada has invited me to better promote them by joining his Cabinet. I have accepted that honour.

Prime Minister Jean Chrétien is criticized a great deal in his native Quebec. But for my part, I see him as a leader who knows how to surround himself with capable people, how to listen and how to decide, and who is open to change. He has given me heavy responsibilities despite my political inexperience. I will do what I can to merit the confidence he has shown in me.

The federal government is also the government of Quebecers. It is important that Quebecers continue to bring to it their culture and their talents, because the truth is that we belong to a federation not only to profit from it, but also to help it with all our strengths. I am proud to be a Quebecer and a Canadian, and I will do everything I can to show how these two loyalties can complement each other well. I know that many of us will do so, through political action or through other democratic means. Together, we will help to bring about reconciliation. Quebecers and other Canadians must enter the next century united and stronger.

Canada's Communities and the Hope for Canadian Unity

CALGARY, JUNE 2, 1996

Too many of the people who believe in Canada are either passive or in despair towards the future of our country. Passivity and despair – we must free ourselves from these attitudes if we are to save Canada.

After the October 30 1995 referendum, many people throughout Canada hoped that the issue of national unity could simply be wished away, that the problem would disappear on its own. Many hoped that others would address the problem, and that it wouldn't involve them. To combat this passivity, I have travelled across Canada saying how much our country is in danger.

On the other hand, the voices of despair have been saying that the secession of Quebec is inevitable, that there is nothing we can do as governments or citizens to prevent it. To combat this despair, this resignation, I want to say that we must have hope, and that we have good reason to look to the future of Canada with hope.

One of the reasons I want to bring a message of hope today is that this audience gives me hope. You represent the level of government closest to the people in the towns, cities, and regions that make up this country. You speak for the local communities that form the fabric of Canada, where people live, work, and build their dreams together on a daily basis.

This is why I am here to discuss with you how Canada's communities are the hope for Canadian unity.

That is why I am so pleased that you have invited me to talk at this important gathering of the Federation of Canadian Municipalities. It is Canada's communities, from the small towns in isolated regions to the large cosmopolitan cities, that are its greatest strength. Federal and provincial politicians can learn much by looking to the strength of our communities.

The Toronto writer Jane Jacobs wrote a famous and insightful book called *Cities and the Wealth of Nations*. She argued persuasively that the economic strength of a country does not come from its natural resources or the economic policies of the central government. The true source of wealth and growth is the vitality of the cities, towns, and local communities that are at the base of the society and the economy.

It has been said that Canada is a country that works in practice, but not in theory. As Minister of Intergovernmental Affairs, I have the difficult task of convincing Canadians that their country can work despite pessimistic theorists. But as mayors, councillors and managers, you are privileged to speak for the grassroots of the Canada that works so well in practice, even in tough economic times.

In many ways, the problems that the country faces as a whole are similar to the problems that many of our towns and cities have dealt with successfully for many years.

Our communities in rural and remote regions of Canada have learned how to manage scarce resources and survive in tough economic times. Our large cities have shown us how people of many different backgrounds and languages can live together, reconciling unity with diversity.

These are the two lessons that federal and provincial governments should learn from our municipalities in dealing with the historic challenge to the unity of our country: how to follow a concrete, practical approach to solving problems, and how to bring together diverse communities.

Concrete approaches to problems

There is much the so-called higher governments can learn from you. We must avoid the temptation to try to solve all of our problems by appealing to abstract or technocratic solutions, by putting emotional symbolism above concrete substance, and by seeing constitutional change as the answer to every question. Instead, we must look to the practical wisdom of municipal governments, business, and community groups at the local level across Canada.

It seems to me that this is the approach that our government has taken to respond to the concrete needs of Canada's municipalities. The infrastructure program and the progress this government has made on crime and public safety are examples of the federal government working successfully to address the needs of communities, by responding to initiatives that emerged from the bottom up.

This is the same approach we should adopt in dealing with our national unity problems as well. This is exactly what the Government suggested in the February Throne Speech. Let me illustrate with a concrete example the practical approach we want to follow. In the Throne Speech the government committed to withdrawing from the field of manpower training in order to eliminate overlap and duplication.

Many of the provinces have demanded increased control over labour market training for many years, to integrate federal and provincial job training and job placement programs.

This Thursday, my colleague Doug Young, the Minister of Human Resources Development, sent all the provinces and territories a labour market proposal offering them responsibility for all active employment measures funded through the Employment Insurance fund.

The federal government is offering the provinces control of two billion dollars from the funds the federal government currently spends on active measures.

The provinces, if they choose, will be able to run their own employment measures programs such as wage subsidies, income supplements, and job creation partnerships and labour market services such as employment counselling and job placement.

This is an example of practical, flexible federalism at work. We are expressing our commitment to solidarity with unemployed workers across Canada, while respecting subsidiarity in allowing each province to design local programs to meet local needs.

It is in following your example, by taking a concrete approach, that we will improve our federation. We will have a strong federal government in its jurisdictions, strong provincial governments in their jurisdictions, strong municipal and local governments in their jurisdictions, and a strong partnership between all of them.

It is in following this spirit of concrete and flexible federalism that our federal and provincial Ministers of Environment, in their meeting last Friday, were able to bring about improvements in the field of environmental management.

This is the path we will follow in the upcoming First Ministers meeting, in order to show Quebecers and other Canadians that federalism is a powerful tool to improve their well-being.

Reconciling diverse communities

So our first lesson we learn from Canada's municipalities is the benefit of a concrete and practical approach. The second is how we can reconcile diverse groups within a single dynamic community.

Let me start with this simple question: why does Canada deserve to survive?

It is not only our economy and our wealth, although we all know that the United Nations and the World Bank consistently rate Canada as one of the most fortunate countries in the world.

wild

It is not because our flag is the most attractive, although it is well recognized and well regarded around the world. It is not because of the beauty and immensity of our land or the Rocky Mountains near here in Calgary, although it is hard not to be moved by all this natural beauty.

The reason we are so fortunate to be Canadians is not even what makes this country distinctive and particular, which would be cause enough to be proud.

No, the most important reason we have to make sure this country survives is that it has realized universal human ideals the rest of mankind can only dream of.

Canada is the best example of what the world must become in terms of tolerance, openness, and harmony between different communities.

Canada is perhaps the country where human beings, no matter where they come from, have the best chance of being treated as human beings. That, more than anything, is why I love this country, and why I don't want to see it torn apart.

As the Prime Minister said in his speech to the House on February 28, "... we have seen that when the world looks at Canada, what they see is the future. Or rather the best hope for the future of the world. Together, let's build that model of hope for the future of the world. Together, let's build that model of hope and confidence. That model for all mankind."

We have built a country that recognizes and celebrates linguistic duality, a country that recognizes the virtues of multiculturalism and the power of diversity, a country that recognizes the supremacy of individual rights but also the importance of protecting minorities.

And where do we see this tolerance, this openness, this diversity expressed more than in Canada's cities? Cities like Toronto, Montreal, Calgary, and Vancouver have all become rich cultural mosaics where people from many societies and many languages live together. Visitors from the United States and Europe are constantly amazed at the success of our cities in reconciling diversity.

Canadians are proud of their great cities, proud of the harmony that can still be found there, and are rightly calling on their municipal, provincial and federal elected officials to protect them from the spectre of discord and intolerance that has disfigured so many other beautiful cities throughout the world.

We must keep our cities safe and harmonious. We will succeed in doing so by relying on the great universal values of sharing, tolerance and hospitality. For nowhere on earth have those beautiful values been more effectively integrated into the collective culture than in Canada.

This is exactly what I said last February in my first speech as a Minister. I was in Vancouver, Canada's second most beautiful city – and I think almost every mayor here will agree that Vancouver is Canada's second most beautiful city after their own. What has been achieved in Vancouver and the Lower Mainland is a unique human accomplishment.

The encounter between Asian and European civilization has been troubled and war torn in history, and these cultures have often failed to understand each other. As Kipling said "East is East, and West is West, and never the twain shall meet."

But where else on earth but in those communities of Vancouver, and Richmond, and Surrey, is there such a wonderful chance to prove Kipling wrong? Where else do we see Asian and European cultures working together to create an even richer society.

It is much more because of this great human achievement than because of the Rocky Mountains that I want to leave British Columbia to my eight year old daughter as part of her country.

And that is why Vancouver, Calgary, Montreal and all the municipalities you represent, despite the immense geographic distances that separate them, are so close in spirit, and must remain in the same country, so that they can help one another always to pursue the same human ideal together.

Speaking of Montreal, let me tell you about that great metropolis where I live with my family. Every day, I see how much its citizens, whether Anglophones, Francophones, or Allophones, cooperate in community life and common projects in our city.

We share a love of Montreal's cultural life, its heritage, its parks and public spaces. We also share a common vision of Montreal's economic future. And within community organizations of all kinds, different cultural groups cooperate in close harmony.

Unfortunately, the threat of secession is hurting the vitality of Montreal. Montreal's economy is in decline. Too many Montrealers are leaving or thinking about leaving the city, all with sorrow and regret.

Recently, my colleagues Paul Martin and Martin Cauchon reached an agreement with Serge Ménard, Quebec's Minister responsible for Montreal, to adopt a common front in dealing with the economic problems of the city.

That is good news, because we all serve the same fellow citizens. And yet, despite all our efforts, it is indisputable that, until Quebecers and other Canadians have firmly decided to stay together within a united Canada, the social and economic health of Montreal will always be weakened by a harmful and unnecessary political uncertainty.

Montreal and Quebec as a whole form an admirable society of which all Canadians can be proud. And, apart from the problem of secession, it would be impossible to find a single issue that divides

Quebec society by pitting Francophones against non-Francophones. Even the language issue no longer does that, despite recent efforts by a few radical elements.

I have the honour to represent a riding in the Montreal region, Saint-Laurent-Cartierville, where some fifty communities from all over the world live together in harmony. That mini-United Nations, as I refer to it, is fully integrated into Quebec society and intends to stay in Canada.

In the House of Commons recently, a Bloc Québécois MP stated I had been elected, and I quote, "by the side door." He boasted that he had been elected by "the people," in a majority Francophone riding. In the Montreal and the Quebec that we love, that we admire throughout Canada, there are no side-door voters. We're all front-door citizens.

Quebecers share those great values of solidarity and openness with other Canadians. For those values, above all, they will take on the substantial challenges of the 21st century, together, within a united Canada.

To recap – a concrete, practical approach – reconciling different communities – these are the lessons I want to take from our municipalities to help solve our unity challenge. It will help make the federation work better, and it will also make us realize the importance of recognizing the different communities that make up our country, including recognizing the reality of Quebec.

Canadians from all provinces must not only accept, but celebrate Quebec's admirable effort to preserve its Francophone society within an Anglophone North America. They must say to Quebecers that they will support them, because the Francophone reality is part of the Canadian ideal.

Again, let us look at what we can learn from Canada's communities. In most cities and towns across Canada, there are areas that have been shaped by a particular cultural group. There are Italian or Portuguese areas in Toronto, Chinese areas in Vancouver, African-Canadian areas in Halifax. There are communities in Cape Breton that have a Gaelic identity and towns in Alberta with French or Ukrainian roots.

Often, the city councils of these communities will take special measures to recognize these historic cultural contributions, so you might see street signs in Portuguese in Toronto or Ukrainian community centres in Alberta.

Taking these measures not only helps to preserve the cultural heritage of an area, they can also be a great help to business and tourism in these communities by creating a unique and vibrant character in these towns or neighbourhoods.

Now nobody complains that in doing these things, these cities are undermining the rights of other groups, or that citizens from different cultural backgrounds would not be welcome in these communities. It is a recognition of a cultural heritage that is intended to improve the vitality of the entire community.

On a pan-Canadian level, this is exactly what recognizing Quebec's distinctiveness would do: it would recognize the historic cultural character of Quebec, unique by its French language, its culture, and civil law, and it would help preserve and promote a vibrant, dynamic identity to allow Quebecers to participate more confidently in Canada.

Recognizing Quebec is not a dangerous constitutional abstraction, nor a symbol that should divide the nation. It is a practical step which builds on the Canadian political tradition and the reality of the community in Quebec.

Conclusion

So here, then, is what we can learn from you in the process of national reconciliation. It is not a dramatic strategy, it is not a complete rewriting of the constitution.

It is a pragmatic approach, the same kind of approach you take as mayors and councilors.

Our Prime Minister, Jean Chrétien, probably knows more about this country than anyone else. His approach to questions of unity is not one of abstract constitutional visions, but one of pragmatic, concrete reform. He is open to almost any suggestion, if you can demonstrate that it is practical and workable, and will improve the lives of Canadians.

And I think on these practical questions we will find much common ground between all Canadians, whether French or English, easterners or westerners, aboriginals or recent immigrants.

In our towns and cities, we Canadians, better than so many others, have been able to reconcile our differences and work together on common initiatives. And if we bring that same wisdom to the larger Canadian community, we will succeed.

So please, participate in the debate in the coming months, help us through activities in your own communities to develop practical solutions that will allow us to improve and strengthen our federation. We need your voice as mayors, as councilors, as local officials, as people who are used to bringing your local communities together, as we try to bring our larger Canadian community together.

Tell us how you have achieved success in building unity in diversity in your own communities. Tell us the practical ideas and examples that have worked in your own towns and cities that could be applied by federal and provincial governments. Encourage your citizens to reach out and get to know their neighbours across Canada through such measures as twin cities and youth exchange programs.

We need your help to reconcile Quebecers and other Canadians. Ask your provincial and federal representatives to take risks for their country. All politicians want to leave their mark in history – tell them that history is now!

Canadian unity cannot be imposed from above. A deal among eleven first ministers on the constitution will not bring this country together. We cannot be reconciled on a piece of paper – we must be reconciled in our hearts. It is the communities of Canada that are at its heart, and unity must begin there.

Together, we can renew and restore our federal system. Together, we can save Canada, this model for all mankind. Ensemble, nous sauverons le Canada, ce modèle pour l'humanité tout entière.

Speech to The American Council for Quebec Studies

The American Council for Quebec Studies held its first Congress here in Quebec City in 1986; it was attended by 80 people. Here we are ten years later, with more than 300 participants and nearly 200 presentations on the various socio-cultural aspects of Quebec life: history, literature and poetry, theatre and cinema, economics and administration, the media, and, of course, politics.

I greatly envy your ability to look at Quebec from the outside, because our society must seem quite fascinating! I would like to thank your president, Richard Beach, for inviting me to take part in this "cultural immersion".

As I am speaking, Michel Tremblay's play *Les belles-soeurs* is playing in Romania; Céline Dion is performing in the Netherlands; the Ballets Jazz de Montréal is touring Germany; the Cirque du Soleil is putting on *Alegria* in Japan and premiering *Quidam* in the United States; the Carbone 14 dance company is giving a series of performances in Belgium; and the modern dance troupe La La La Human Steps is touring the United Kingdom. Quebec's artistic community has never had such international exposure, not to mention the whole intercultural dynamic it has developed within Canada in recent decades. Whether you are in Quebec City, Montreal, Toronto, or Vancouver, you can enjoy the Montreal Symphony Orchestra, a production by Robert Lepage or Denys Arcand, or a concert by the Aboriginal group Kashtin.

Music, painting, theatre, literature ... if I had the time, I would describe how far Quebec creativity is making its influence felt in every sphere of human activity, including our politics, which – as you know – traditionally produces some of the liveliest Canadian political personalities.

I would like to suggest today that this Quebec creativity is stimulated by its belonging to Canada and that, in return, Canada is enriched by the contribution of Quebec society. I want to show that Quebecers and other Canadians have every reason to stay together.

Attachment to the Quebec and Canadian identities

I am speaking to you as both a Quebecer and a Canadian who is very attached to both his identities and never wants to have to choose between them. I know that the vast majority of Quebecers feel the same. A poll conducted last February[1] showed that 21% of Quebecers appear to define themselves as Quebecers only, but that the rest, who represent the vast majority, identify themselves as Quebecers and Canadians, striking their own balance between those two identities. I confess that if it were the other way around, if 79% of Quebecers said that they didn't identify themselves as Canadians any more, I would be worried. But the fact is that Quebecers want to stay Canadian, and they are right to feel attached to Canada, since they have contributed a great deal to building it.

Nevertheless, many Quebecers who are attached to their Canadian identity responded in the affirmative to the question put to them by the Government of Quebec, on October 30, 1995, namely:

Do you agree that Quebec should become sovereign after having made a formal offer to Canada for a new economic and political partnership within the scope of the bill respecting the future of Quebec and of the agreement signed on June 12, 1995?

Quebecers rejected, by a majority of 50.6%, the option that the secessionist leaders had put forward for the second time in 15 years. Quebec and all of Canada came very close to being plunged into a crisis whose outcome would have been very uncertain.

Many Quebecers who are attached to Canada voted as the secessionist leaders wanted in the referendum because they didn't think that they were voting for secession. They wanted to affirm their Quebec identity, but did not think that they would have to give up their Canadian identity. That did not stop the leader of the secessionist forces, the then Premier of Quebec, calling their vote, on the night of his defeat, an endorsement for Quebec "independence," a term he'd never used during the referendum campaign! A poll conducted at the very end of the referendum campaign[2] showed that close to 80% of Quebecers who were planning to vote Yes believed that, if the Yes side won, Quebec would automatically continue its use of the Canadian dollar; 80% felt that Quebec's economic ties with Canada would remain unchanged; and 50% believed they would continue to use a Canadian passport. More than 25% believed that Quebec would continue to elect federal members of Parliament. Another poll[3] showed that almost one in five

Yes voters thought that a sovereign Quebec could remain a province of Canada.

Those who remind the secessionist leadership of these figures are accused of insulting the intelligence of Quebec voters, which is far from the truth. It's obviously not the voters' fault if the secessionists' strategy spreads confusion.

Secession is too grave a decision to be taken in confusion. Therefore one can understand why Canada's Prime Minister, in the February 27, 1996, Speech from the Throne, made a solemn commitment to see that what is at stake, secession, be made as clear as possible.

Those Quebecers who support secession must understand that this plan means they would lose their Canadian identity. They must find good reasons for giving it up. They must find even better reasons for uprooting the Canadian identity from the hearts of the many Quebecers who are attached to it. They must also think about the harm they would do to their fellow citizens from the other Canadian provinces. They must also realize that secession, once achieved, would likely be irreversible and therefore would affect not only their contemporaries, but future generations as well.

There is simply no valid reason to make such a grave decision. That is why we are very confident that Canada will remain united. The Government of Canada is demonstrating with more determination than ever before, in cooperation with all those citizens who believe in their country, in particular the Quebec federalist forces, to what extent the Quebec identity and the Canadian identity complement one another and why one should welcome them both rather than feel obliged to choose between the two. The threat of secession will then be averted and Quebecers, along with all other Canadians, will have found the road to reconciliation and unity.

When examined closely, none of the arguments that are brought forward in support of secession hold water, whether they be at the level of language and culture, that of political structure or that of the economy.

A bilingual federation united by shared universal values

Secession is tempting only among Francophone Quebec voters. The approximately 15% of non-Francophone voters cast their ballots overwhelmingly for Canadian unity, seeing no reason to choose between Quebec and Canada. Francophones must be shown that Canada in no way threatens their language and culture, but rather the contrary. The fact is that since the beginning of Confederation, in 1867, Quebec has never been as Francophone as it is today. The proportion of Quebecers capable of expressing themselves in French has reached the unprecedented level of 94%. In my Montreal constituency, while I must often speak in English to senior citizens of Greek, Italian or Jewish origins, their grandchildren automatically speak to me in French.

The advancement of French in Quebec is due in part to Canadian and Quebec language laws implemented in the 1960s and 1970s. These laws are now largely accepted, and, while some measures provided for in the Quebec legislation were struck down by the courts, none of them was of major importance. The issue of commercial signage is a case in point. In 1977, Quebec legislation imposed French-only commercial signage. In 1988, the Supreme Court of Canada ruled that a policy of French predominance was completely justified in this area, but that other languages could not be banned. That is the policy that now prevails in Quebec, and on which there is a consensus, with the support of more than 85% of Quebecers, according to public opinion.[4]

Quebec's language laws are more liberal than those in such irreproachable multilingual democracies as Switzerland or Belgium. Radical elements sometimes try to reignite linguistic tensions in Quebec, but they always fail. The solidarity between Quebec's Francophones and non-Francophones is admirable. Indeed, there is only one issue that can divide them along linguistic and ethnic lines: the issue of secession.

The solidarity displayed by Canada's other provinces and territories with regard to bilingualism and Quebecers' linguistic and cultural distinctiveness is also solid. A majority of Quebecers and other Canadians support bilingualism. The failure of constitutional reforms in recent years, which aimed, among other things, to have Quebec recognized as a distinct society within the federation, unfortunately created an utterly deplorable feeling of mutual rejection among too many Quebecers and other Canadians.

The truth is that the vast majority of Canadians want to recognize and celebrate as a fundamental characteristic of their country the fact that one of Canada's ten provinces, the second largest, has a Francophone majority, in an overwhelmingly anglophone North America.

Thus, a poll in March 1996[5] showed that 85% of Quebecers and 68% of other Canadians believed that "the Canadian constitution should recognize that Quebec, while equal to the other provinces, is different, particularly due to its French language and culture." As well, 82% of Quebecers and 84% of other Canadians felt that "Quebec is an essential component of the Canadian identity". The vast majority of my fellow citizens in the other provinces want to recognize Quebec's difference, and simply want some help in finding the words to express the support they have for their fellow citizens in Quebec.

In December 1995, the Government of Canada had a resolution passed in the House of Commons recognizing the distinctiveness of Quebec society, and an Act guaranteeing Quebec, and the four other major regions of Canada, that no constitutional change concerning them would be made without their agreement. The Prime Minister and the Government of Canada are continuing their efforts to see those measures entrenched in the Constitution.

The terrible misunderstanding surrounding recognition of Quebec's distinctiveness has convinced too many Quebecers and other Canadians that their values are incompatible. That belief is false. In fact, the very opposite is true. The main reason I am so attached to Quebec society is that it is completely imbued with the great universal values that make me love Canada. As a political scientist, I have always been struck by how much Quebecers and other Canadians strongly support the great universal values of tolerance, solidarity and justice. To cite one example among many, a poll this April[6] revealed that 74% of Canadians outside Quebec and 71% of Quebecers believed that "cultural diversity makes Canada stronger."

An international survey[7] comparing 118 cities in the world on the basis of 42 economic, social and environmental indicators ranked Montreal among the front runners (in 7th place), together with Vancouver (2nd), Toronto (4th) and Calgary (12th). Our large urban centres have their difficulties, their problems of unemployment and poverty, and face major challenges.

Nevertheless, they have succeeded in becoming models of cultural co-existence, and they provide their inhabitants with a level of security and a quality of life that are difficult to find elsewhere. This is one more reason why Montreal and Vancouver should stay together, in a united Canada, being so close in spirit despite the geographical distance that separates them.

Those universal values of tolerance and solidarity in diversity have taken root in Canada in large part because French and English people have had to learn to live together, which has prepared them to welcome new fellow citizens from all corners of the globe. Our history has not always been easy, and, like other countries, has its darker chapters. The result, however, is the Canada of today, an admirable human creation. Quebecers and other Canadians have built it together, which is why they will not give it up.

A decentralized, evolving federation

Canadians' spirit of tolerance has led them to understand, perhaps better than any other people, that equality is not synonymous with uniformity. It is that understanding that has guided them in putting in place a decentralized federation that is always striving for a balance between solidarity among all and respect for the differences of each.

Canada would never have been able to survive if it had not been a federation that ensures that Newfoundlanders can be Canadian the Newfoundland way, Manitobans can be Canadian in their way, and Quebecers can be Canadian the Quebec way.

The secessionist leaders claim that Canada is a centralized federation that leaves Quebec too little autonomy. They say our federation is rigid and incapable of evolving, and describe the federal government as a sort of foreign power in relation to Quebecers.

The truth is that one of our greatest strengths is precisely that our federation is based on decentralization. Experts in comparative federalism rank it among the most decentralized, alongside Switzerland. As a Canadian province, Quebec enjoys an enviable level of autonomy compared with the components of other federations. The flexibility of Canadian federalism has also meant that Quebec is differentiated from the other provinces through specific provisions in a variety of areas, including civil law, taxation, international relations, the pension plan, social policy, postsecondary education, and immigration.

Far from being rigid and immobile, our federation is constantly evolving, and that has not led to a bloated federal government. On the contrary, in the past four decades, we have seen a gradual and remarkable redistribution of the federal government's taxing and spending power to the provincial governments. For example, in 1950, the federal government collected $2.46 for every dollar of revenue collected by the provinces; in 1994, it collected only $0.96.

Today, faced with a danger that threatens our unity, we need more than ever to show Quebecers and all Canadians just how well their federation can serve them. We need a federal government that is more effective in its areas of jurisdiction, provincial and territorial governments more effective in theirs, Aboriginal administrations better-equipped to serve their populations, and a solid partnership uniting all of those institutions. That objective is broadly shared in Canada, which is why the federal government launched a vigorous plan to reform the federation in its Speech from the Throne in February 1996. This reform aims to clarify roles in sectors as varied as mining, forestry, recreation, the environment, social housing and the economic union. I will limit myself to describing briefly three key reforms: the federal spending power, labour-market training and the social union, issues which you Americans are also facing.

Concerning the federal spending power, the federal government made a commitment in the last Throne Speech to no longer use its spending power to create new shared cost programs in areas of exclusive provincial jurisdiction without the consent of a majority of the provinces. In so doing, we have taken a major step toward making federal-provincial relations more harmonious and consensus-driven. This commitment to limit the federal spending power has no equivalent in other federations; it responds to an historic grievance on the part of our provinces to the effect that the federal government has used its revenues to intervene too directly in their affairs, thus forcing them to change their priorities to satisfy the federal government.

As for labour-market training, the Government of Canada is launching a reform that gives the provinces greater autonomy in the area of job training and labour-market development, a public policy area that is very important in the new global economy, by giving them the opportunity to manage for themselves the approximately $2 billion a year the federal government currently spends on active employment assistance measures. The first agreements should be concluded shortly.

Finally, the Canadian social union is also changing. Financial transfers from the federal government to the provinces in the area of health and social programs now give the provinces greater flexibility in setting priorities and designing programs to meet local needs, while respecting the principles on which Canada's extensive solidarity is based. The Prime Minister and provincial premiers have formed a new federal-provincial council on renewing social policy, to study the implementation of more consensus-driven and efficient mechanisms, and examine more closely problems connected with child poverty.

It is noteworthy that these major reforms are being initiated with a strong Quebec presence in Ottawa. The Prime Minister is a Quebecer, as has been the case for 26 of the past 28 years. The Minister of Finance is currently a Quebecer, as is the President of the Treasury Board, the Minister of Human Resources and the Minister of Intergovernmental Affairs. The Chief Justice of the Supreme Court also happens to be a Quebecer, as is the country's most senior civil servant. Canada's ambassador to the United States is a Quebecer.

People belong to a federation not only because of what they can get out of it, but also to contribute their culture and their talents. Quebec men and women are contributing to the success and the evolution of the Canadian federation, and we must not lose the synergy they create through contact with their fellow citizens in the other provinces.

Canada's economic success

Secessionist leaders see justifications for their plans in every difficulty the Canadian economy experiences. Canada is going bankrupt, they said several years ago, looking at the heavy indebtedness of our federation. But Canadian institutions proved that they could handle these difficulties. In fact, Canada has got its finances in order to the point where its deficit next year will be one of the lowest in the OECD. Furthermore, seven out of ten provinces have balanced their budgets, or are recording surpluses, even though they were all in a deficit position a few years ago. Short term interest rates in Canada have dropped more than four-and-a-half points since the beginning of last year. The year prior to our government taking office Canada had, on a borrowing rates basis, the worst record of any G-7 country, with the exception of Italy. In 1997, according to the same criteria, Canada will have the best record in the G-7. In its recently released *World Economic Outlook*, the IMF predicts that Canada will outgrow all the other G-7 countries in 1997.

Therefore, the secessionist leaders have changed their target. In the October 1995 referendum, they claimed that English Canada had embraced a conservative culture incompatible with the Quebec values of social justice and compassion. They promised that a Yes vote would be a shelter against the cold wind of budget cuts blowing in from English Canada, and a lever for a new spirit of Quebec social democracy.

The federal government and the majority of the provinces have cleaned up their public finances, regardless of the political stripe of their governments. The same clean-up is now the order of the day for Quebec, one of the most indebted provinces in Canada. Because it is also less wealthy than the Canadian average, it receives assistance from the wealthier provinces. Canadian solidarity is expressed admirably in the principle of mutual assistance among wealthier and less wealthy provinces, through federal government transfers. That principle, which is likely carried further in Canada than in any other federation in the world, means that there are currently seven provinces that receive assistance from what are now the three wealthiest provinces: Ontario, Alberta and British Columbia.

In the 1930s, however, Alberta received assistance from the other provinces, including mine. That is what makes Canadian solidarity so great. Quebecers are currently benefitting from the assistance of their fellow citizens in the wealthier provinces, and will one day be able in turn to give special assistance to their fellow citizens in the less wealthy provinces.

For a number of months, the Government of Quebec has been following the lead of the other provinces in undertaking a courageous plan to put its fiscal house in order. We can look forward optimistically to the future, thanks to the resources of Quebec's economy, Quebecers' unique culture, cooperation among governments and solidarity among all Canadians. For example, the federal government has increased its support for Quebec business firms and public servants following the closure of the Quebec delegation offices in Boston, Atlanta, Chicago and Los Angeles. The federal government is also the government of Quebecers, but it is, in a way, also the government for American researchers, like most of you here today! The Canadian Embassy in Washington and our consulates across the United States are also at your service. The Government of Quebec can succeed in putting its fiscal house in order despite the costs of political uncertainty linked to its senseless plans for secession.

I am against secession not because I think Quebecers are incapable of managing their own independent state. I believe that we, Quebecers, are called to a greater ideal: that of continuing to improve the superb economic and social success that is Canada; that of fighting alongside our fellow citizens against the scourges of unemployment and poverty; that of continuing to ensure that comparisons by international bodies such as the UN or the World Bank continue to rank Quebecers so highly in so many areas of human activity.

The solidarity that unites Quebecers is exemplary, it is a strength that makes them greater and nurtures confidence in their economic and social future. And yet, their solidarity is complemented no less admirably by that which links them to their fellow citizens in the Atlantic provinces, Ontario, Western Canada and the North. Quebec and Canadian solidarity complement each other wonderfully, and it would be not only an economic absurdity, but, in particular, a moral error, not to keep both of them for ourselves and for our children. We need to take on the formidable challenges of the 21st century together.

Conclusion

Our country deserves to survive, and its chances of succeeding are excellent. Quebecers and other Canadians will stay together because we have achieved something irreplaceable in the world. We can be proud of our linguistic and cultural harmony, our economic success and the uniqueness of our institutions. We must improve our federation, and our government has launched major initiatives to that end. We can recognize, in complete confidence, Quebec's distinctiveness as a fundamental characteristic of our country.

That is what I believe I have shown you here today. I have done so by highlighting Canada's advantages, rather than the risks of secession. I have said almost nothing of the score of uncertainties, the clash of legitimacies, the economic and social upheaval, and the host of difficult negotiations we would be faced with if we undertook to choose among our fellow citizens rather than all staying together within Canada. I have not yet mentioned the important bone of contention between us regarding the legality or illegality of a unilateral declaration of independence and the request for clarification to that effect that has been addressed to the Supreme Court.

I will say about secession simply that it must not be seen as an opposition between Quebec and Canada, which would form two monolithic blocs. I am opposed to secession and want to fight against it with all the strengths democracy gives me because it would tear apart first and foremost my society, because it would pit Quebecers against Quebecers. Secession, with the uncertainties it generates, is the type of issue that can plunge the most tolerant populations into intolerance.

Secession is defined as a break in solidarity among fellow citizens. That is why, in its wisdom, international law extends to peoples the right of self-determination in its extreme form, that is the right to secede, only in situations where a break in solidarity is evident, such as in cases of military occupation or colonial exploitation. The secessions that have taken place to date have always arisen out of decolonization or the troubled times that follow the end of authoritarian regimes. It is not simply a matter of chance that no well established democracy that has experienced ten years of universal suffrage has ever faced secession. Such a break in solidarity appears very hard to justify in a democracy.

Canada, a universal model of openness, tolerance and generosity, is the last country in the world where identity-based fragmentation should be allowed to triumph. You Americans understand that instinctively. That is why you prefer that Canada remain united, while taking great pains not to interfere in Canadians' affairs. Your preference for Canadian unity is, of course, not due only to your economic interest. You, who have the heaviest international responsibilities, fear that the possible break-up of this great bilingual and multicultural federation would set a bad example for the rest of the world, at a time when identity-based tensions are raging in so many corners of the globe.

According to Professor Elazar of Temple University in Philadelphia, there are currently some 3,000 human groups who are conscious of a collective identity. And yet, there are currently only 185 states recognized in the UN, 86% of which are multiethnic in composition. The belief that any population with its own distinctive characteristics must have its own state is completely false. I do not want to see that belief triumph in my country. It is not only impractical, but also a moral error, because by learning to have their component cultures live together, states give their populations the opportunity of elevating themselves. By allowing them to experience tolerance, the cohabitation of cultures within the same state helps human beings to become better citizens.

Trying to ensure that everyone is part of a majority wherever he or she lives would be pointless and even destructive. We need to seek the means by which confident, flourishing minorities and cultures can live together within a single political structure. The presence and influence of the Quebec minority within Canada strengthens not only Canadians in the other provinces, but also Quebecers themselves, through the complementarity of their Quebec and Canadian identities.

Quebecers and other Canadians do not have the right to fail. They must move closer to one another and achieve reconciliation. They must succeed not only for themselves and for their children, but also – and why not? – for the other inhabitants of this poor planet, who see in Canada a source of hope and a country that has been blessed by fortune. President Truman said just that when he cited the Canadian experience as an example for all the peoples of the world: "Canada's eminent position today is a tribute to the patience, tolerance and strength of character of her people. Canada's notable achievement of national unity and progress through accommodation, moderation, and forbearance can be studied with profit by sister nations."

And, without wanting in any way to get involved in the American presidential campaign, I would like to conclude with a quotation from President Clinton, which I feel sums up the essence of what I wanted to say to you today: "In a world darkened by ethnic conflicts that literally tear nations apart, Canada has stood for all of us as a model of how people of different cultures can live and work together in peace, prosperity and understanding. Canada has shown the world how to balance freedom with compassion."

NOTES

1 CROP, February 1996.
2 Léger & Léger, October 1995.
3 Créatec +, October 1995.
4 CROP, May 1996.
5 Environics.
6 Ekos, April 1996.
7 Corporate Resources Group, January 1995.

The Ethic of Federalism

TORONTO, NOVEMBER 15, 1996

No one can appreciate the advantages of a federal system more than I. I hold it to be one of the most powerful combinations favouring human prosperity and freedom. I envy the lot of the nations that have been allowed to adopt it.

Alexis de Tocqueville, *Democracy in America*

They were placed like great families beside each other, and their contact produced a healthy spirit of emulation. It was a benefit rather than otherwise that we had a diversity of races.

George-Étienne Cartier, Confederation Debates,
February 7, 1865

Quebec nationalists cannot push their nationalist projects through to completion ... without abandoning the practice of mutual respect and tolerance that has been the essential condition for whatever the peoples of Canada have achieved together as citizens of a single state.

Peter H. Russell, "Can Quebeckers Be a Sovereign People?"

Peter Russell's work goes to the heart of the Canadian debate, reaching values beyond the inevitable constitutional squabbling. We Canadians do not want to choose between universal solidarity and respect for cultural diversities. We are strongly attached to both.

"I should regard it as a great misfortune for mankind if liberty were to exist all over the world under the same features," wrote Alexis de Tocqueville. That is the very misfortune the Canadian ideal intends to combat. Canadians know that the quest for what is right, just and good must be plural; they know that it is by drawing on the best part of each culture, each individual, regional or historical experience, that we come closer to what is best in civilization. Canadians know that equality must not be confused with uniformity. Or at least, those who do not know that yet should read and think about Peter Russell's work.

Paper presented to the Ideas in Action Conference, in honour of Professor Peter Russell, University of Toronto

That dual quest for the universal and for cultural diversity has been with us since the birth of our Confederation. We have often strayed from it since then, and committed grave mistakes and injustices, but the result is this admirable human achievement that is Canada.

One need only compare the thinking of George-Étienne Cartier with that of Peter Russell to gauge the continuity of the Canadian ideal. In his famous address on February 7, 1865, to the Legislative Assembly on the proposed confederation of the provinces of British North America, Cartier set out the principles which still define Canada today. He first stressed respect for cultures, using the terms of his era, those of "race" or "nation". Cartier identified four "races" which were then very much present: the French-Canadians, the Scots, the English and the Irish. Had there been others just as present, he would certainly have mentioned them, for there was nothing exclusionary in his thinking. Cartier did, however, commit the grave error of forgetting Aboriginals, an error which Peter Russell has ceaselessly sought to remedy.

Cartier also spoke of the Catholic and Protestant denominations, noted that there are many Catholics who are not French, and called again for tolerance and unity. "In our own Federation we should have Catholic and Protestant, English, French, Irish and Scotch (sic), and each by his efforts and his success would increase the prosperity and glory of the new Confederacy."[2]

Cartier ensured that the federal government would be strong, able to withstand the American threat – a threat which at that time was military – and also able to carry out large-scale common projects. The provinces, for their part, would be able to express the specific personality of their inhabitants. He predicted that the union with new provinces would help Quebec, because his province would thus be able to vary alliances rather than being merged into a united province with a rapidly growing Upper Canada. And thus, Quebec today allies itself on occasion with Ontario for industrial policy, with the Prairies and the Atlantic provinces for social policy, and with the Western provinces for international trade policy.

Finally, Cartier wanted Canada to be a "political nation," a nation of solidarity which transcends race, religion, history and geography, to ensure that the French in Quebec would never want to break their solidarity with other Canadians. If we seek a contract at the birth of our federal union, it is certainly the one expressed by Cartier, which has inspired all of Peter Russell's work. Quebecers of all origins have helped other Canadians a great deal to achieve that ideal; they must not renounce it.

The Canadian ideal seeks to guarantee the necessary cohabitation of cultures through an ethic of federalism. That is the idea I shall develop in the following text. Although I wrote this text wearing my new hat of minister of the Crown responsible for advising the Prime Minister on Canadian unity, I believe I have closely adhered to the academic rigour embodied by Professor Russell.

1. The necessary cohabitation of cultures

At a time when identity-driven aspirations are stronger than ever throughout the world, the idea that any population with its own distinctive characteristics should have its own state is completely false. "To each people its own state" is obviously an impractical idea, but it is also a moral error, because by learning to have their component cultures live together, states give their populations the opportunity of elevating themselves. The cohabitation of cultures within the same state helps human beings to become better citizens, by allowing them to experience tolerance.

According to Daniel Eleazar, there are some 3,000 ethnic or tribal groups in the world conscious of their respective identities. Of the over 180 politically "sovereign" states now in existence, over 160 are multiethnic in composition.[3] The idea of "one people, one state" would cause the world to explode.

This comment from a report by the Secretary-General of the United Nations is food for thought indeed: "Yet if every ethnic, religious or linguistic group claimed statehood, there would be no limit to fragmentation, and peace, security and economic well-being for all would become even more difficult to achieve."[4] I have met with my South African counterpart, the Minister of Intergovernmental Affairs of that brand new federation. South Africa does not have, as we do in Canada, two official languages – English and French – which are also international languages; it has eleven official languages, not to mention all sorts of languages that have been accorded some sort of political status. South Africa is coming out of the vilest possible experience ever invented by human beings for human beings, the nightmare of apartheid. Through reconciliation and striving for harmonious cohabitation of cultures, South Africa, with its eleven official languages, will gradually regain the strength it needs to take on the human and socioeconomic challenges it faces. The only solution for South Africa is unity, not fragmentation. It is surely not Canada, a country so blessed by fortune, that will be for South Africa and for the rest of the world an example of break-up.

Trying to ensure that everyone is part of a majority wherever he or she lives would be an exercise in futility. We need to seek the means by which confident, flourishing minorities and cultures can live together within a single political structure. The presence and influence of the Quebec minority within Canada strengthens not only Canadians in the other provinces, but also Quebecers themselves, through the complementarity of their belonging to Quebec and to Canada. Without sticking my nose into other countries' affairs, I believe that this is the same universal value that should be followed for the Scots in Great Britain or for the Catalans in Spain.

Canada, this country that has become a universal model of openness, tolerance and generosity, is the last country in the world where identity-based fragmentation should be allowed to triumph. That would be all the more regrettable because the reason that Canada is so open, so tolerant and so generous today is because the French and English, from the beginning, have striven to get along and to take advantage both of their respective identities and of the complementarity of their two great cultures. It has not always been easy; there have been some dark pages in our history, but the end result is this rich, tolerant society that is Canada.

Our large urban centres – Montreal, Toronto and Vancouver – are models of co-existence that have been able to avoid becoming racist cities, of which there are far too many examples, and for that very reason, they deserve to stay within the same state, being so close in spirit despite the geographic distance that separates them. In fact, a survey conducted by the Swiss Corporate Resources Group put them among the best metropolitan areas in the world in which to live – Vancouver finished second, Toronto fourth and Montreal seventh. These Canadian cities were ranked ahead of Brussels, London, Oslo and Paris, and way ahead of the highest-ranked American city, Boston, which came in at number thirty.[5] My own riding of Saint-Laurent-Cartierville is another example of a pluralistic, harmonious community, a veritable mini-United Nations, with more than 50 different, vibrant nationalities. I always find it to be an inspiration, because, for me, that is what Montreal, and Quebec, and Canada, are all about: an ideal of different cultures living together harmoniously within a single state.

I would like the Spanish to view the flourishing of Catalonia with confidence as a strength for Spain and not a threat to its unity. I would like the British to feel the same way about Scotland. I don't want my country, Canada, to serve as an example to be held up by the anxious majorities of Spain, the United Kingdom or elsewhere. My dream is that the American Congress, for example, instead of saying, as we have heard them say, "we don't want to create 'Quebec' within the United States, so we don't want to grant additional rights to our Spanish-speaking minority," will say instead, "let's take inspiration from what is happening in Canada, where Quebecers and other Canadians live together in harmony, because they accept one another with complete confidence." I'd like to hear the European Community stop saying, "Careful, let's not give our regions too much autonomy." I'd like Canada to be seen as an inspiration for the future, not only for Canadians, but also for other human beings who are experiencing the cohabitation of cultures within a single state.

2. The ethic of federalism

There are many ways to have populations live together, but the one I recommend and am going to discuss here is federalism. Federalism is often described as being efficient. In my society, Quebec, it is often depicted from that angle, in terms of profitability or profitable federalism: "Stay in Canada because we have a profitable federation", Quebecers are told. That's quite true, because four of the five richest countries in the world are federations: Canada, the United States, Germany and Switzerland.[6] I am sure that many readers will be aware of the UN or World Bank indicators that give Canada top marks in so many areas of human activity. Canada is a remarkable human achievement, a jewel on the planet, which gives its citizens among the best quality of life in the world. Nevertheless, we do have some serious problems, such as too much unemployment and too much poverty, especially among children. We need to rely on our strengths to tackle those problems, rather than turning our backs on them.

These positive international achievements are not the result of chance; in all likelihood, they stem from the fact that our federalism is profitable for all Canadians. Indeed, federalism as a universal ideal is more than profitable; it has an ethic which encourages cultures to live together.

More than ever, we need to reconcile the global and the local aspect of things, which Tom Courchene at Queen's University calls "glocalization", in other words, to reconcile extensive solidarity and desires for autonomy. Reconciling those two objectives, through federalism, has served humanity well in the past, and will be more necessary than ever in the years to come.

As far back as the 19th century, Tocqueville, that great liberal thinker and prophet of democracy, expressed that idea well: "The federal system was created with the intention of combining the different advantages which result from the magnitude and the littleness of nations."[7]

Isn't that idea still just as true today, at a time of market globalization and pressure for autonomy? Throughout the world, there are conflicting pressures both for larger political organizations and for smaller, more regional ones. The pressure for larger units has been generated by a growing awareness of worldwide interdependence and a need for greater influence in international decision-making. A demand for smaller, self-governing political units has arisen from a need to make governments more responsive to citizens and their primary attachments: linguistic and cultural ties, religious affiliations, historical traditions and social practices. These are the pillars of community.

Federalism helps to reconcile these dual pressures. It allows regional identities to be expressed both at home and abroad. For example, Francophone Canadians are represented in the Commonwealth, just as Anglophone Canadians are represented in the Francophonie. By being together, they form a vast, rich country; both groups have access to the G-7, which they would not have if Canada were to break up. People in Eastern Canada have as much access to the Asia-Pacific Economic Co-operation Forum (APEC) as Western Canadians do to the Northwest Atlantic Fisheries Organization (NAFO).

At the same time, however, Canada is a federation where each province can have its own perspective and solve its problems in its own way. We have experienced a situation where Canada's ten provinces had budget deficits; each of them has found its own way to resolve that situation, and seven of them have now balanced their budget or are showing a surplus. The method used by New Brunswick's premier was not the same as that used by Alberta, and will probably be different from the one Quebec will come up with, with its distinct society and its own culture. All provinces look to their own strengths, but that does not prevent them from helping one another through solidarity, which is something we need now more than ever; mutual assistance through larger entities and innovation through autonomy.

This leads me to some further comments about the ethic of federalism. The work of Alan Cairns, a recognized Canadian writer on federalism, clearly outlines that institutions not only enable us to do things; they also encourage moral principles. They contribute to the way in which we view the world and ourselves.

I believe that the two great moral principles that federalism encourages are tolerance and solidarity.

Tolerance

Federalism as a public philosophy encourages tolerance, which is expressed through our ability to understand different ways of doing things. Tolerance also encourages our ability to accept different ways of contributing to the life of a society. Charles Taylor talks about "deep diversity":[8] citizens recognize their citizenship in a number of different ways. In its most basic form, tolerance gives people the freedom to be themselves, so as to help one another more effectively.

Some people say that we must all be Canadian in the same way, or else our country is in danger. I believe that's a mistake. The Swiss, for example, have the most powerful municipal system in the world, and from that extensive decentralization they derive a source of pride, an additional reason to feel Swiss. It's the same thing in Canada, where we have strong provinces, as has been demonstrated in the comparative studies by Ron Watts of Queen's University.[9] Some Canadians see decentralization as a threat and feel that is why the country is threatened with break-up. I am convinced that the opposite is true. Canada would never have been able to survive if it had not been a federation that ensures that Newfoundlanders can be Canadian the Newfoundland way, Manitobans can be Canadian in their way, and Quebecers can be Canadian the Quebec way.

As Peter Russell observed, "The reality of Canadian citizenship is that at the psychic level it is extraordinarily heterogeneous. Aboriginal Canadians, Québécois Canadians, Canadians who identify with minority language communities or with ethnic or racial minorities as well as Canadians who yearn to identify with a unified Canadian nation have experienced their connection with Canada historically in very different ways."[10]

I'm a kid from Quebec City, now living in Montreal, and I have my own way of being Canadian; I don't have to be Canadian in the same way as someone from Winnipeg. I know instinctively, however, that sharing this same country with that person from Winnipeg makes both of us better human beings.

When I'm in my riding of Saint-Laurent-Cartierville and I'm talking with older people of Jewish, Italian or Greek origin, I almost always have to speak in English, because they have not been sufficiently integrated into Quebec society, for all kinds of historical reasons. When I talk to their 18- or 19-year-old grandchildren, however, I can speak in French; I can speak in English; I can even try my hand at Spanish. Those young people can express themselves in French, in English, and often in one or two other languages, and are thus wonderfully equipped for the next century. That's what the Montreal and the Quebec and the Canada of today are all about: a pluralistic society which must remain harmonious and tolerant.

It is sometimes said that federalism can work only in a homogeneous society, with the same religion and language. I could not disagree more. Federalism works well in a homogeneous society, but it is necessary in a heterogeneous society, because it promotes tolerance, which a heterogeneous society needs more than anything else. As Professor Russell has noted: "the practice of mutual respect and tolerance ... has been the essential condition for whatever the peoples of Canada have achieved together."[11] This reflects the thinking of George-Étienne Cartier: "Some parties ... pretended that it was impossible to carry out Federation, on account of the differences of races and religions. Those who took this view of the question were in error. It was just the reverse. It was precisely on account of the variety of races, local interests, that the Federation system ought to be resorted to, and would be found to work well."[12]

Solidarity

Samuel LaSelva, a professor at the University of British Columbia, writes in a recent book, *The Moral Foundations of Canadian Federalism*, that: "Canadian nationhood presupposes Canadian federalism which in turn rests on a complex form of fraternity that can promote a just society."[13] I think that what LaSelva is talking about is that this institutional structure of federalism is the bearer of a moral principle which I call solidarity. That was the idea of Cartier, who said that our federation had to be founded on "kindred interest and sympathies" between the different communities.

Solidarity, which I define as a sense of the common good and compassion for our fellow citizens, enables us to act together, to join forces and pool our resources. Canadian solidarity is expressed admirably in the principle of mutual assistance among wealthier and less wealthy provinces, through federal government transfers. That principle, which is likely carried further in Canada than in any other federation in the world, means that there are currently seven provinces that receive assistance from what are now the three wealthiest provinces: Ontario, Alberta and British Columbia. In the 1930s, however, Alberta received assistance from the other provinces, including mine. Albertans know that the day might come when they would need Quebecers' help. That's what makes Canadian solidarity so great. Quebecers are currently benefiting from assistance from their fellow citizens in the wealthier provinces, and will one day be able in turn to give special assistance to their fellow citizens in the less wealthy provinces.

That's the real meaning of Canadian solidarity. It's more than tolerance; we not only tolerate others as they are, we want to help them be what they are. I want to help Newfoundlanders to be what they are. I also know that they're not like British Columbians. As a Quebecer and a Canadian, I want them, in their turn, to help me to be part of a majority Francophone society in an English-speaking North America.

The vast majority of Quebecers feel they are Quebecers and Canadians at the same time, but too many of them believe that they have to choose between their identity as Quebecers and their identity as Canadians. Many of them feel more at home in their Quebec environment and are thus inclined to choose their identity as Quebecers. But why do they feel they have to choose between Quebec and Canada? Because they think that other Canadians do not accept their difference. This is a terrible misunderstanding that must be cleared up to guarantee the unity of our country.

In that spirit, the Government of Canada tabled a resolution, which was passed by Parliament, on recognizing Quebec as a distinct society within Canada. In that same spirit, the Government of Canada intends to forge ahead so that the other provinces can, with complete confidence, recognize Quebec's distinctiveness in the Canadian Constitution.

3. Conclusion – flexibility, the road to renewal

Federalism, wrote Paul Gérin-Lajoie in his former capacity as Quebec's Minister of Education, has given human beings a vital tool for coordinating the aspirations of individual communities, making them stronger and giving them broader influence. However, he found a precise definition of federalism to be somewhat elusive. "What makes federalism so difficult to describe," he concluded, "is precisely what makes it so valuable as a political instrument: its flexibility, its versatility, its ability to take any form."[14]

He was right. Canadian federalism is not the same as that found in Switzerland or Belgium, because the contexts are completely different, and the challenges for the populations of South Africa or India are not on the same scale as those facing us in the industrialized countries. Nevertheless, federalism is helping human beings all over the world to live together more harmoniously. That is why I am convinced that federalism is a valuable solution for human societies, a solution that we must preserve for ourselves, our children, and as an example to the world.

But the current Canadian federal system is not only different from its counterparts around the globe. The Canadian federalism of today is very different from that of fifty years ago, and fifty years hence our federation will have undergone a great deal more evolution. That is one of the strengths of federal systems: they are flexible enough to adapt and evolve when faced with new challenges and new contexts.

The flexibility of our federation allows it to respond well to the evolving aspirations of its different component provinces, regions and cultures. This adaptability is part of what Carl Friedrich once called the "federal spirit." He defined that spirit as the ability to compromise and accommodate, which are also elements of what I earlier called solidarity.[15] A renewal of Canada based on this spirit is, as Peter Russell has so aptly put it, "*in keeping with the Canadian political genius and with the forms of political organization which will be the pace-setters in the twenty-first century.*" As Professor Russell has suggested, the alternative – breaking ourselves down into homogeneous nation-states – would be to align ourselves with forces that are receding.[16] I would make one last reference to Cartier's admirable strength of foresight: "Nations were now formed by the agglomeration of communities having kindred interests and sympathies."[17]

It is in this spirit that the federal government is working to renew and modernize the federation. Our government is working with its partners to adapt the federation to the evolving needs of the Canadian population, in line with the moral principles that our system encourages: solidarity and tolerance.

At present, our federal system is undergoing a great deal of change. However, Canadians have shown creativity at many points during the past decades too, constantly renewing their federation according to internal needs and external forces.

The federal system, with its flexibility, can be adapted to face the needs of each successive generation of Canadians. The changes we are making today are part of a continuum, stretching from the early days of Confederation into a future too distant for our imagining. I am convinced that the Canada of the future will inherit certain characteristics from the Canada of today: it will be strong, flexible, dynamic, generous – and united.

This is fortunate, given that the cohabitation of cultures is necessary and, indeed, the only viable possibility, since neither cultural assimilation nor cultural separation is practical or morally acceptable.

The Government of Canada is focussed on the future. Since the Throne Speech in February 1996, we have put forward a plan to reform our federation. We will do so in a way that will strengthen our precious inheritance from the generations who have built this country to date.

NOTES

1 Alexis de Tocqueville, *Democracy in America*, volume I (New York: Alfred A. Knopf, 1987), p. 330.
2 *Parliamentary Debates on the Subject of the Confederation of the British North American Provinces*, Tuesday, February 7, 1865, p. 60.

3 Daniel J. Elazar, *Federalism and the Way to Peace*. Reflections Paper no. 13, presented at Queen's University, 1994, p. 23.

4 Boutros Boutros-Ghali, *An Agenda for Peace* (New York: United Nations, 1992), p. 9.

5 *Ottawa Citizen*, January 18, 1995, p. A2.

6 United Nations Development Program, *Human Development Report 1994* (New York, Oxford University Press, 1994), p. 104, annex table A5.2.

7 Alexis de Tocqueville, *Democracy in America*, volume I (New York: Alfred A. Knopf, 1987), p. 163.

8 Charles Taylor, "Shared and Divergent Values," in Ronald L. Watts and Douglas M. Brown, eds, *Options for a New Canada* (Toronto: University of Toronto Press, 1991), p. 75.

9 Ronald L. Watts, unpublished manuscript, 1996.

10 Peter Russell, "The Constitution, Citizenship and Ethnicity," in Jean Laponce and William Safran, eds., *Ethnicity and Citizenship: The Canadian Case* (London: Frank Cass, 1996), p. 101.

11 Peter Russell, "Can Quebeckers Be a Sovereign People?," *Canada Watch*, 4, 38–9, (November/December 1995): 38.

12 *Parliamentary Debates on the Subject of the Confederation of the British North American Provinces*, February 7, 1865, p. 57.

13 Samuel V. LaSelva, *The Moral Foundations of Canadian Federalism: Paradoxes, Achievements, and Tragedies of Nationhood* (Montreal: McGill-Queen's University Press, 1996), p. xiii.

14 Paul Gérin-Lajoie, "Canadian Federalism and the Future," in Gordon Hawkins, ed., *Concepts of Federalism: Thirty-Fourth Couchiching Conference* (Toronto: Canadian Institute on Public Affairs, 1965), p. 62.

15 Carl J. Friedrich, *Trends of Federalism in Theory and Practice* (New York: Praeger, 1968), p. 39.

16 Peter H. Russell, "Can the Canadians Be a Sovereign People?," *Canadian Journal of Political Science* 24 (December 1991): 708.

17 *Parliamentary Debates on the Subject of the Confederation of the British North American Provinces*, February 7, 1865, p. 60.

Our Two Federations: Contrasting Evolutions and Common Challenges

CLEVELAND, OHIO, DECEMBER 10, 1996

The U.S. and Canada would be unthinkable other than as federations. Federalism has served both our countries well in the past. It is also the way of the future. Indeed, the new global economy brings conflicting pressures, both for larger alliances and for greater regional autonomy. Federalism is a flexible way to reconcile these two pressures – a fact which more and more countries are recognizing. In Europe in particular, but also elsewhere in the world, nation-states are grouping together in quasi-federal arrangements in response to global economic imperatives. We in the United States and Canada are lucky to be enjoying the benefits of a federal system, which many other countries are still striving to achieve.

But federalism is more than an economic advantage, it is an ethic and a moral principle. In a very fundamental way, federalist systems of government are helping human beings all over the world to live together more harmoniously. This is crucial in a world where, according to Professor Daniel Elazar of Temple University in Philadelphia, there are some 3,000 human groups who are conscious of their respective identities. Of the over 180 politically sovereign states now in existence, over 160 are multiethnic in composition. Living side by side, within the same state, with neighbours of different cultural backgrounds, teaches people tolerance and thus makes them better citizens.

The English poet John Donne once said that "no man is an island". His comment applies equally to cultures and peoples. There is no benefit in being isolated and separated from others, trapped behind walls of fear and misunderstanding. Federalism allows us to combine our strengths for projects that will benefit all, but is also sufficiently flexible to facilitate the full expression of regional identities. In short, it allows us the best of both worlds.

Even a cursory glance at the world's federations reveals that no two are the same. Your federation and ours are different. Their evolutions

---

Speech to the Council of State Governments

have been different. But like all countries we face certain common challenges. I will deal first with the past, tracing the contrasting evolution of our two federations. Then I will discuss certain challenges our two federations are now facing. What better forum than the Council of State Governments to have a useful and stimulating discussion on these issues. Thank you for inviting me here today.

A tale of two federations

Those who think constitutions are the first and last word in the development of a federation should be given pause by the experiences of our countries, which have two of the world's oldest constitutions. Although, in their written form, neither has changed a great deal, both our federations have evolved dramatically. They demonstrate that major changes can be brought about without altering a single comma in a constitution. Constitutions evolve – often in fundamental ways – through judicial interpretation, changing conventions, and the exercise, or non-exercise, of powers, rather than solely through formal amendments. The u.s. provides a clear example of this, since it has developed remarkably over time and yet, of more than 9,100 amendments that have been proposed since 1789, a mere 26 have been ratified. In Canada, some of the powers originally intended to give the federal government a strong hand – such as the right of disallowance and the power of reservation, which allowed the federal government to overrule provincial legislation – have fallen into disuse, although they were used extensively in the 19th century. And today, intergovernmental agreements and new collaborative approaches are permitting substantial evolution without requiring amendments to our Constitution.

Federal constitutions are thus not strait-jackets that prevent change – they are instead frameworks which allow change to take place. That is why the u.s. and Canada have been able to evolve in very different directions. The u.s. has become more centralized over time, in spite of a relatively decentralist Constitution. By contrast, Canada's Constitution was centralist at the time of Confederation, but today we have one of the most decentralized of all federations.

The spirit of the u.s. Constitution was decentralist. It gave restricted powers to the national government and placed the residual authority with the states. James Madison, writing as Publius, felt obliged to demonstrate "that no one of the powers transferred to the federal government is unnecessary or improper". By contrast, at the time of Confederation in 1867, the distribution of powers in the Canadian Constitution had a strong centralist bias, including the allocation to the federal government of the major residual authority, phrased as "peace, order and good government."

Canada's Fathers of Confederation wanted to avoid what they saw as a main cause of the American civil war – a weak federal government with an emphasis on state autonomy. They also wanted to ensure national security and pan-Canadian communications and economic development.

However, in spite of its centralist thrust, the Constitution Act of 1867 granted significant powers to the provinces – for example, over language, education and law. Canada's nation-builders believed that they could construct a country with a strong central government, without destroying minority cultures and languages or the particularities of Quebec and other regions. They believed that French and English could live side by side and work together to strengthen our nation. These beliefs are one of the greatest legacies our founders left us.

At the outset, then, Canada's federation was a great deal more centralized than yours. Yet, today, even though there have only been four amendments to the distribution of powers, our federation has become in many respects more decentralized. This is shown by a variety of indicators. For example, in 1991, federal expenditures, after intergovernmental transfers, as a percentage of total government expenditures, were 58.5% in the U.S., as opposed to 40.8% in Canada. In 1961, the comparable proportion for Canada was 49.7%. Furthermore, according to a specialist in comparative federalism, Professor Ron Watts of Queen's University in Ontario, approximately 80% of federal transfers to state and local governments in the U.S. are conditional grants. In Canada, by contrast, no less than 76% are now unconditional. How can we explain this paradox? As I see it, five socio-economic and institutional factors, together, provide at least a partial answer.

First, while the original distribution of authority in the U.S. identified several shared functions, in Canada demarcation of the exclusive responsibilities of each government was emphasized. In the U.S., the federal and concurrent powers are set forth explicitly, but the Constitution left a large unspecified residual power to the states. The courts have tended to interpret what is "implied" in the federal powers as broadly as possible, which, over time, has contributed to increased centralization. By contrast, in Canada, where both provincial and federal powers were explicitly listed in the Constitution, the courts have, since the late 19th century, interpreted certain federal powers narrowly so as to expand provincial powers. Later, the courts' focus on provincial authority over "property and civil rights" effectively transformed that power into a replacement residual clause.

Second, the circumstances of our major minority groups are very different. In your country, minorities are dispersed, and no one group is so concentrated in a single state as to form a majority of that state's population. Therefore, your minorities have tended to look to the federal government to support their interests. In Canada, French-speakers are our most important minority group. They are especially concentrated in Quebec, the second most populous province, where 83% of the population is French-speaking. French-speaking Quebecers have a special relationship with their provincial government, since it is the sole government where the majority of elected representatives are French-speaking. Although the Quebec government has at times supported centralist measures, it has usually acted as a strong advocate of provincial autonomy. There is no equivalent of this situation in the u.s.

Third, in the u.s., the executive and legislature are separated in both orders of government, while in Canada legislative and executive powers are fused in the executive-centred system of parliamentary government. Therefore, in the u.s., divisions between President and Congress have been emphasized. In Canada, the system is defined much more by federal-provincial relations than by the division of powers between the legislative and executive branches of government.

Fourth, while there are 50 u.s. states, Canada has only 10 provinces. This means that the relative clout of each province is considerably greater in relation to the federal government than that of the individual American states. The comparatively smaller number of provinces also contributes to achieving consensus among governments, through such mechanisms as First Ministers' Meetings, and to the building of partnerships between the federal government and the provinces. Then again, it is also easier for the provinces to form strong coalitions in their relationship with the federal government.

Finally, the differing international roles of the u.s. and Canada have had important implications for the domestic status of their federal governments. The superpower rank of the u.s., and its consequent military spending, have focused attention on the central government. Canada, by contrast, is a middle power internationally. Our federal government has therefore not been the focus of a similar level of attention.

The challenges we share in both our countries

Federalism has served our interests well in the past. It has helped us become leaders in terms of economic development and the standard of living our citizens enjoy. It is surely not an accident that four of the world's five richest countries are federations: Canada, the United

States, Germany and Switzerland. Today, we face the question of whether federalism will continue to serve us as well in the 21st century. I am confident that it will. One of the strengths of federal systems is that they are flexible enough to adapt and evolve when faced with new challenges and new contexts.

It is clear that both our federations do face a number of challenges. Today, I will talk about two of the major ones: first, the need to get our fiscal houses in order while maintaining our social policies; and, second, the need to maintain unity while adapting to our increasing cultural pluralism.

The fiscal and social policy challenge

Federalism has been wrongly criticized as promoting duplication and overlap, and thus inflating government spending. This is simply not true. A study released by the OECD in 1985 found that government expenditure as a share of GDP was, on average, some 7% lower in federal as opposed to unitary states. Moreover, today, among the least indebted industrialized countries, you find such federations as Australia and Switzerland. Federalism does not increase the risk of indebtedness, but it does not protect states from it either. However, if a federal state has a debt problem, the flexibility inherent in federalism can help it cope. Both our countries are good examples of this.

The U.S. federal deficit-to-GDP ratio stood at 5.2% in 1986, but in 1998, it will be 1.1%. In Canada, our efforts are also bearing fruit. In 1985–86, Canada's federal deficit-to-GDP ratio was 7.2%, but in 1997–98, that deficit will be only 2% of GDP. On a borrowing requirements basis – the measurement that is used in the U.S. – our budget will be balanced in 1998–99. Canadian short-term interest rates are now about 1.5% lower than those in your country. Our efforts have also, in some cases, directly benefited the provinces. For example, the lower interest rates between January 1995 and June 1996 have provided provincial governments with cumulative savings of about $1.3 billion. Furthermore, the flexibility of our federation has allowed the provinces to find their own ways to address their budget deficits, and seven have now balanced their budgets or are showing a surplus.

Leaders of state and provincial governments in our two countries have expressed concern that budget-cutting at the national level will be off-loading: in the U.S. through what you call unfunded mandates, and in Canada through cuts in transfer payments. You will not have any difficulty in finding provincial premiers who suggest that there has been off-loading. But let me tell you that between 1994–95 and 1998–99, transfer entitlements will fall by 10.5%, while total federal department spending will decline by 21.5%. Furthermore, provinces were notified a year in advance that such cuts were going to be necessary. Making decisions about budget cuts is tough. But I can assure you that, despite the need to make such cuts, Prime Minister Jean Chrétien, Minister of Finance Paul Martin and our government have chosen to cut spending significantly in areas such as transportation in order to preserve our social programs. We are ensuring that cuts, where necessary, are fair to all provinces.

We have also responded to concerns about the use of the federal spending power, which allows the federal government to make payments to governments, institutions and individuals even in areas outside its jurisdiction. The division of responsibilities in federations refers to legislative power, not spending power. A federal spending power within the jurisdictions of member states exists in all federations. In Canada, it has been the basis, for example, of the national health system, a great source of pride for all Canadians. Nevertheless, the provinces have argued that its unilateral use can undermine their ability to set and follow priorities. Therefore we announced this year that the federal spending power will no longer be used to create new shared-cost programs in areas of exclusive provincial jurisdiction without the consent of the majority of provinces. The federal government has taken the unique action of voluntarily limiting its own spending power. This limitation reflects our commitment to moving toward more harmonious and cooperative relations between the federal government and the provinces.

In both countries, we are seeing some redistribution of responsibilities and an attempt to give more flexibility to the states and provinces. In your country, there has been a lively debate on welfare reform, with states taking clearly divergent approaches. At the same time, the public on both sides of the border want assurances that basic standards will be maintained, and that a "race to the bottom," in which states and provinces compete to offer the most stingy policies, will be avoided.

In Canada, we are working with the provinces to clarify the roles of the different levels of government, to find innovative ways to pool our strengths, and to build new partnerships. Two policy areas where we are seeing real progress are job training and child poverty. By 1999, we will have transferred the management of all job training funded through the Employment Insurance program to those provinces interested in taking on this challenge. Meanwhile, the federal government will continue working to ensure the interprovincial labour mobility rights of Canadians are fully respected, and it will continue to provide certain services such as the national labour-market information and exchange system. Last Friday, we announced the first agreement in this area between our government and the province of Alberta. With these new agreements, an important element of flexibility will be injected into a public policy area that is crucial in the new global economy.

Child poverty is a second area where Canadian governments are forging a renewed partnership. Canada and the u.s. are the two industrialized countries with the highest level of child poverty, and I know we are all looking seriously at ways to address this. In the u.s., your new welfare reform law gives states increased flexibility in managing programs for poor families, while encouraging recipients to move from welfare to work. In Canada, a federal-provincial Ministerial Council on Social Policy, jointly established last summer, has agreed to treat benefits for children as a top priority. The ministers are pursuing the idea of folding the existing federal child tax benefit and provincial welfare payments for children into a new joint program.

The challenge of unity and pluralism

Like the u.s., Canada is a very multicultural country. Cultural pluralism will become more and more of a salient issue for both of us. Canada is also bilingual, and both French and English are recognized as official languages. As I mentioned earlier, our most prominent minority is concentrated in a single province, Quebec. This has led to an additional challenge, as it has provided an impetus for a secessionist movement.

It is important that I put the 1995 Quebec referendum on secession into perspective. I am speaking to you as a Quebecer and a Canadian who is very attached to both his identities. I am immensely proud of what Quebecers have achieved together, building a vibrant, flourishing, predominantly French-speaking society in a continent where English dominates. But I am also extremely proud of what Canadians – our wider family – have achieved together, in building a society in which respect for diversity and compassion prevails.

The vast majority of Quebecers feel as I do – they are proud of both identities. What we, as a government, must do, is show Quebecers that they do not have to choose between the two identities that they cherish. We must show them to what extent the Quebec identity and the Canadian identity complement each another.

As a government, we must also demonstrate how well federalism responds to Quebecers' needs, and encourage other Canadians to show how important Quebec is to their sense of being Canadian. We can amply demonstrate the former, and we are working toward recognition of Quebec's uniqueness within the Constitution as a way for Canadians to demonstrate the latter. In the meantime, Parliament passed a resolution in December 1995 recognizing "that Quebec is a distinct society within Canada" by virtue of "its French-speaking majority, unique culture and civil law tradition."

Americans are friends of Canada. The overwhelming majority of Americans support a united Canada. And I know that they want a united Canada not only for economic reasons. You want a united Canada because you don't want Canada setting a bad example for the world, that of division, rather than a positive example, that of unity. I know, for the same reason, that all Canadians – Albertans no less than Quebecers, Nova Scotians no less than Manitobans – must work toward reconciliation. We must do so not just for ourselves and our children, but also for the many other people elsewhere who look to Canada as a source of hope. Many of them can only dream of the advantages we enjoy as part of the Canadian federal system. They want Canada to continue to send the right message, and to show the world a model of harmonious cohabitation.

Let me give you an example which is particularly pertinent, because the country in question has just, in an occasion important for all of us, signed a new Constitution today. That country is South Africa. Unlike Canada, South Africa doesn't have two official languages that are important internationally, but rather 11 official languages. Also unlike Canada, South Africa is not recognized as one of the best countries in the world in which to live. On the country, it has just emerged from the vile experience of apartheid. Through reconciliation and striving for a harmonious cohabitation of cultures, South Africa will gradually regain the strength it needs to take on the human and socio-economic challenges it faces. The only solution for South Africans is unity, not fragmentation. Surely Canada, a country so blessed by fortune, should offer South Africa hope, not an example of break-up.

Conclusion

Our federal systems, which have served us so well in the past, face major challenges on the eve of the 21st century. We can both take inspiration from how the other responds to the challenges we share. Through our trade links and all manner of exchanges, like this meeting today, we can share our ideas, our solutions, and our dreams.

Canada faces a unique challenge – that of secession. Some say that the proof that Canada doesn't work is the existence of a separatist movement in Quebec. I think that, on the contrary, Canada works well. Our federation works, it can be improved, and it will be improved if Quebecers and other Canadians resolutely decide to work together.

And we will choose to stay together, because the forces of unity will prevail. I am confident that our two federal partners in NAFTA – your country and Mexico – will have a united, federal Canada as their partner for many years to come. There is no doubt in my heart and mind that federalism is the way of the future.

Canada: A Fair Federation

Alberta is the home of the pioneer spirit in Canada. That spirit combines the determination to beat the odds and the fortitude to open up new frontiers. But it is balanced by a gentler side. The hardy pioneers who built this province knew that surviving the harsh conditions on the frontier meant helping each other out. It meant sharing and making sure that everyone was treated fairly. This aspect of the pioneer spirit still informs Albertans' actions: 39.6% of Albertans volunteer, a higher percentage than in any other Canadian province.

This January, an article in the Calgary Herald caught my eye. The headline read "Calgarians united by their gentleness." The writer, Peter Menzies, talked about Canadians' commitment to fairness and sharing – a commitment which led thousands of Calgarians to offer their sympathy and cash to the family of Grayson Wolfe. As you will remember, Grayson's parents were facing huge medical bills, which they could not pay. "Instinctively, Calgarians know this is wrong," Mr. Menzies wrote. "In our world, you do not have to go bankrupt to save your baby's life."

This is what our federation is all about. It is about fairness – balancing our belief in individual initiative with a commitment to sharing. Helping one another out in times of need. Supporting one another's endeavours. This sharing makes Canada greater than the sum of its parts.

Indeed, the vast majority of Canadians believe that we have built something special together. Committed to fairness and sharing as personal values, we have built a nation that embodies those same values writ large. This is vital in so vast a country, which, while blessed with tremendous natural and human resources, must nonetheless deal with the challenges which accompany distance, disparity and diversity. It is important that we remain committed to striking the right balance between the self-reliance of individuals – and individual provinces – on the one hand, and the need for sharing and fairness on the other.

Speech to the Calgary Chamber of Commerce

Debates about fairness in Canada are as old as our federation. Perhaps they are inevitable in a country so strongly committed to the ideal of sharing. The National Policy Tariff of 1879, for example, which aimed to develop Canada's manufacturing sector as a whole, to generate the revenues necessary to construct national transportation networks, and to encourage east-west trade, was nevertheless widely viewed in the West as being geared solely to help the manufacturers of Ontario and Quebec. The Crow Rate, popular with Prairie wheat farmers, was nonetheless seen by southern Alberta's beef producers as inhibiting the livestock industry's development.

Then there are some policies that are just plain wrong. Liberal politicians, beginning with my colleague, Natural Resources Minister Anne McLellan, will forever be conscious of the consequences of the National Energy Policy. This is also an example of what can happen if you don't have representation from all regions of the country in government.

These debates continue today. An opinion poll last October found that only 30% of Canadians believe the federal government treats all provinces equally. Polls have shown that Canadians living outside Quebec think that "la belle province" is treated better than the other provinces, while Quebecers think that Ontario is treated best. These are very serious concerns – concerns which, as Minister of Intergovernmental Affairs with special responsibility for national unity, I feel I must address. Interregional jealousy is inherent to federations. But we in Canada are in a unique situation. We are a federation threatened with break-up, and faced with a separatist ideology which promotes suspicion, divisions and envy between citizens. When one group of MPs arrives in Ottawa with the sole mandate of promoting the interests of their own region, this encourages other regions to elect MPs who in turn promote only their interests, and we lose any sense of a national opposition committed to the good of Canada as a whole. It is important that our federal political parties be capable of balancing different regional interests. Otherwise, interregional jealousies will continue to escalate. And it is vital for national unity that our spirit of generosity overcome these jealousies.

Canada should not be seen as a sort of zero-sum game, because, within Canada, we are all winners. If our country dissolved into ten inward-looking republics, Canadians would no longer enjoy the tremendous advantages we share together today. In many provinces, the social safety net would be substantially weakened. Furthermore, internationally, a united Canada is a major plus. Our economy is sufficiently large to afford us membership in the G-7. In major trade discussions, we have the critical size to be invited to the table with the European

Union, Japan and the United States. We constitute the United States' biggest trading partner. Furthermore, Canada plays a key role in the World Trade Organization and other international fora. Together, we enjoy membership in APEC, the Commonwealth and the Francophonie.

Canada is not a zero-sum game. Each province has its own strengths and identity, which together add up to a strong and diverse country. Today, Alberta is a "have" province, but should a time arrive when the global market does not favour your particular strengths, then you know that you can count on the help of other provinces, just as you are helping them now. Indeed, as recently as 1986–87, Alberta received $419 million under the Fiscal Stabilization Program because of a year-over-year decline in its revenues – the second province to benefit from this program, the first being British Columbia. That is what Canada is all about. And this "insurance scheme" aspect of our country also promotes investor confidence. Helping one another helps our economy.

Perhaps our generosity as a country is most evident at times of tragedy, when, like any family, we instinctively band together to help one another out. The Canada-wide efforts in response to the Edmonton tornado of 1987 and, more recently, the horrendous Saguenay floods in Quebec, are good examples.

Canadians' commitment to generosity and fairness is reflected in the fourth Paul Martin budget. In particular, this budget addresses the need for fairness to young Canadians. Intergenerational fairness means sticking to our course of fiscal responsibility, but making targeted, responsible investments in future generations. Thus, following up on the work of the federal-provincial-territorial council on social policy renewal, we announced a federal-provincial partnership to create a new $6 billion Canada Child Tax Benefit by July 1998. We enriched federal assistance for higher education and skills training by $275 million and doubled the annual contribution limit to Registered Education Savings Plans. We have also invested in excess of $2 billion in a youth jobs strategy, to help young Canadians escape the vicious circle of no job, no experience – no experience, no job. To give one more example among many, we agreed with our provincial partners, including your premier, to increase the Canada Pension Plan (CPP) rate in steps to reach 9.9% by 2003, ensuring that it will be sustainable and that no additional burdens will be passed on to Canada's younger generations.

In fact, all four of our budgets have been about ensuring fairness for the Canadians of today – and for tomorrow's Canadians too. Our strict fiscal policy has been accompanied by a commitment to tax fairness. To that end, my colleague Paul Martin established a Technical Committee on Business Taxation. It is considering ways to enhance fairness of the taxation system, to simplify business taxation and thus reduce compliance costs and headaches, and to encourage job creation and economic growth. We are committed to fairness for all categories of Canadians – businesspeople, language minorities, Aboriginal Canadians, young Canadians. But, of course, fairness does not mean uniformity, which is why it is also fair to recognize the specificity of Quebec. After all, if North America were a Francophone continent and Alberta its only majority-Anglophone component we would need to recognize that specificity too.

But my speech today is concerned with fairness between Canada's provinces and regions. I believe that we have a fair federation. That being said, our federation is constantly evolving, and we should always be looking for ways to fine-tune and strengthen it. We must not become blinded by interregional jealousies to everything Canada has to offer.

Interprovincial fairness

How do Canadians think their ideals of sharing and fairness should shape the way our federation works? Well, according to a 1995 Canadian Policy Research Networks' study, only 10% of Canadians believe that government spending on poorer regions should be decreased or eliminated, while 60% believe that Canadians have a right to expect a minimum level of service wherever they live, including 66% of Albertans. Furthermore, an October 1996 CROP & Insight poll revealed that 70 to 80% of Canadians across the country like the fact that the federal system permits Canadians to share wealth between poorer and richer provinces.

Our values of generosity and sharing have been part of our federation from the start. As one of the Fathers of Confederation – George-Étienne Cartier – said, our federation was founded on the "kindred interest and sympathies" of our different communities. And as Queen's University professor Thomas Courchene has argued, the roots of the idea of equalization can be seen at the time of the British North America Act, in, for example, the special grants accorded to Nova Scotia and New Brunswick because of their specific fiscal needs.

A key advance in interregional fairness was proposed in 1937. That year, the Rowell-Sirois Commission recommended the arrangements for federal transfers be formalized in a system of *"national adjustment grants"* to the poorest provinces. In 1957, Canada adopted a formal equalization program along these lines. Although it is hard to imagine against the bustling backdrop of Alberta's economy today, your province was a recipient for the first 8 years of the program. In 1982, the principle of equalization was deemed sufficiently important to be enshrined in section 36 of the Constitution, "to ensure that provincial governments have sufficient revenues to provide reasonably comparable levels of public services at reasonably comparable levels of taxation."

We have achieved a great deal together. However, as I said before, our achievements have always been accompanied by debates about fairness. These debates are, in my opinion, being aggravated and intensified by the lack of a truly national federal opposition party.

Interregional jealousies in the 1990s

Let me transport you for a moment to the House of Commons last fall. We, as a government, were faced with a very strange situation. To caricature it, day after day, the Bloc Québécois stood up to complain that when Calgary-based Canadian Airlines has a problem, everyone stampedes to help. On the other hand, the Bloc alleged, nobody cares about Montreal-based Air Canada because, as usual, Quebec is the victim of the federation. The Bloc wants one airline for two countries, while we want two airlines for one country. Then Reform stood up, saying that if Air Canada were in trouble, we would all rush to help it, because Quebec is the spoiled brat of the federation. But, according to Reform, we were dragging our heels about helping Canadian Airlines because it is a Western-based company, and the West always loses out.

IMAGINE I AM GILLES DUCEPPE ...
Imagine, for a moment, that I am Gilles Duceppe, the Leader of the Bloc Québécois. In *Ensemble le défi, ça nous réussit* , the working document of the Bloc's 1997 Congress, I will tell you that over the past three decades, the federal government has taken many decisions which have had negative repercussions on the Quebec economy. That the Borden line favoured the development of oil refineries in Ontario, at the expense of Quebec. That the federal government's decision to cease obliging foreign air carriers to service Montreal's Mirabel airport in order to gain access to Toronto's Pearson airport made the former lose its position as a major international gateway. That the 1965 Automobile Pact with the United States ensured Canada's car manufacturing industry was concentrated in Ontario, at the expense of Quebec. And that the federal government went out of its way to favour rail transport in the West, while allowing Quebec's sector to dwindle.

Still as Gilles Duceppe, I look at the Chrétien government's record and tell you that the proposed Canadian Securities Commission will undermine Montreal's role as a financial centre. That Coast Guard fees will have negative repercussions on the competitiveness of Quebec's ports. That AECL's decision to move 26 positions from Montreal to Mississauga will undermine the former's position as a centre of nuclear expertise.

It's difficult to pretend to be Gilles Duceppe. Being the leader of the Bloc Québécois requires a very active imagination. So now I'll go back to being Stéphane Dion.

The Borden line was established, as you doubtless know, to create a domestic oil industry by establishing a market for Western Canadian crude oil. Did it negatively impact Quebec's petrochemical industry? Far from it. While all points west of the Ottawa Valley were required to purchase Canadian crude at higher than international prices, Quebec and points east were able to continue importing cheaper foreign crude. This actually gave them a competitive advantage. Montreal oil refineries were closed down in the 1970s and 1980s, it is true, but so were refineries elsewhere – as a result of economic factors stemming from the oil crisis, not because of the Borden line.

Did the federal government's 1986 decision on foreign airlines hurt Mirabel airport? Well, what we do know for sure is that its previous, coercive position was driving interested carriers away from not only Montreal, but from Canada as a whole. The best way to attract international air carriers to a particular airport is for government and local leaders to demonstrate that servicing it is both attractive and potentially profitable.

The Auto Pact does not stipulate where companies should locate their production facilities. Rather, it provides a framework to encourage production within Canada. Did the federal government negotiate a pact to favour Ontario? No. But the federal government cannot control U.S. economic geography nor the locational decisions of the private sector, and the plain fact is that Detroit, the U.S. "motor city", is located close to the southern Ontario border. Furthermore, whereas Quebec now has a flourishing auto parts industry – not to mention General Motors' factory in Ste-Thérèse – without the Pact, Canada's auto industry would have been much smaller.

Has the federal government favoured Western rail transport at the expense of Quebec? Historically, the federal government has invested billions of dollars to build transportation infrastructure of various sorts throughout Canada. This has been very important for expanding the Canadian economy – and has historically benefited Quebec manufacturers, for example. Today, it is no longer possible to invest billions in new transportation infrastructure, and the emphasis has shifted to restructuring and modernization. Privatization has placed CN and CP on a level playing field, and CN is positioning itself for a future of long-term growth as a strong, Montreal-based transportation company.

The Canadian Securities Commission is a voluntary one and Quebec will therefore not be penalized for choosing not to participate. Rather, Quebec-based companies wishing to raise capital elsewhere in Canada would benefit from the single window a national securities commission could provide. Moreover, a national securities commission would work with its provincial counterparts to improve coordination and promote harmonization of securities regulations. The argument that it would remove a large part of Montreal's remaining financial sector is simply not true.

Will Coast Guard cost-recovery fees hurt Quebec ports? Well, according to an in-depth economic impact study commissioned by the federal government, the average impact over the next two fiscal years would be minimal – a mere 0.09% of the value of commodities shipped. Furthermore, the Minister of Fisheries and Oceans will be working closely with industry stakeholders to establish principles to guide regional fee structures and service levels. Additionally, the introduction of ice-breaking fees was deferred until 1998/99, lessening the impact on regions such as Quebec which are dependent on this service. And it should be remembered that the whole point of cost recovery fees is to decrease the burden on Canada's taxpayers, while continuing to ensure the safe and efficient operation of Canada's waterways.

Moving 26 AECL positions from Montreal to Mississauga is part of an overall internal restructuring geared to making Canada the world leader in the nuclear reactor field. Will this undermine Quebec's nuclear industry? Not at all. In fact, Quebec industry benefits to the tune of some $100–150 million from each CANDU reactor sale abroad. Therefore, it is in Quebec's interests that AECL operate as competitively as possible.

IMAGINE I AM PRESTON MANNING ...

Now that I have briefly dealt with Mr. Duceppe's complaints, let's imagine that I'm Preston Manning. I will tell you that Alberta and British Columbia are carrying the seven poorer provinces, through programs like equalization and the Canada Health and Social Transfer. That the federal Liberals do not care about or understand Western issues. That when times are bad, the British Columbia and Alberta economies are left to fend for themselves, but when times are good, they are exploited for the benefit of Eastern and Central Canada. That the federal government's regional development programs also exploit the West. Mind you, I should mention that Reform's ability to make political capital out of interregional jealousies has been blunted by the realization that, as Preston Manning told a Vancouver audience, "the real test of Reform's progress is whether we break through in Ontario and to what extent."

Sadly, this did not stop Reform's Monte Solberg suggesting that federal aid to flood victims in Quebec's Saguenay region was politically motivated. With a particularly unfortunate choice of words, Mr. Solberg alleged that "the floodgates opened when it was time to provide aid in Quebec," but that there had been little help for the victims of flooding in his riding. For the record, federal financial assistance to disaster victims is based on a fixed formula.

Are equalization payments fair – are Alberta and British Columbia "carrying" the poorer provinces, as Preston Manning said recently in Winnipeg? Equalization payments are calculated on the basis of a formula that is set out in legislation. Basically, the amount a province could raise at national average tax rates is compared with a representative standard (based on the capacities of Quebec, Ontario, Manitoba, Saskatchewan and British Columbia). If a province's total revenue-raising ability falls short of this standard, its per capita revenues are raised to the standard level through federal equalization payments.

Taken out of context, the figures involved might seem unfair. For example, in 1996–97, Newfoundlanders are estimated to have received, on average, $2,520 per person in major cash and tax federal transfers, compared with $1,469, on average, for every Quebecer and $816, on average, for every Albertan. But put these figures in context: Alberta tops Canada's GDP-per-capita tables with a predicted $33,353 for 1997, while Newfoundland will produce only half as much ($17,785). Let me stress that again: Alberta's GDP is twice that of Newfoundland, yet Newfoundlanders will receive only $1,704 per capita more in federal transfers.

Would it be fair to Newfoundlanders, Quebecers, and other beneficiaries if these payments did not exist? I don't think so and, as I indicated earlier, nor do the large majority of Canadians.

Let's look at the Canada Health and Social Transfer, which replaced the Canada Assistance Plan and Established Programs Financing with a single envelope. Is it fair? Well, in restructuring it, we took note of suggestions from the Alberta government and others about how to make it more equitable. As a result, each province's allocation of funding will be gradually adjusted to more closely reflect the provincial distribution of population. For example, we have set financial year 2002–03 as the benchmark for halving per capita disparities.

Has our government ignored the interests of Alberta, British Columbia and their Prairie neighbours? You will remember that, during the Mulroney years, Mr. Manning campaigned with the slogan "The West wants in." I haven't heard him use that line in quite some time, because with Prime Minister Jean Chrétien's government, the West is in. I can assure you all that Natural Resources Minister Anne McLellan and

Senate Leader Joyce Fairbairn are very strong voices in our Cabinet, as are David Anderson, Lloyd Axworthy and Ralph Goodale.

The initiatives taken by both levels of government to change the oil sands tax regime have helped current investors and contributed to Shell's recent announcement that it will be investing $1 billion in a new oil sands project. I should mention that a 1995 study conducted by the Institute for Research on Public Policy showed that, in terms of federal tax breaks, Alberta is the biggest winner in relative terms, benefitting from almost 16% of total tax breaks while its economy accounts for under 11% of GDP. At the international level, we have pushed forcefully for reductions in agricultural subsidies during the Uruguay Round of Multilateral Trade Negotiations, and now under the auspices of the World Trade Organization. And our government is putting the combined strength and solidarity of all Canadians behind your bid for Expo 2005. Your city, in turn, will make an excellent showcase for all of Canada.

The issue of equitable immigration settlement funding was of particular importance for British Columbia. Last month, we announced extra funding for certain provinces to reflect the number of immigrants they are welcoming. British Columbia will receive an additional $22.4 million this year, Alberta $2.9 million and Manitoba $730,000. In responding to the announcement, B.C. Premier Glen Clark observed: "We've had grievances with the federal government ... The Prime Minister listened. He listened to us and we worked hard and we resolved several historic problems." This is an excellent example of our step-by-step approach to resolving regional grievances and was, as Premier Clark observed, "a victory for British Columbia and a victory for Canada."

The West has benefited from many development measures, such as, historically, grain transportation subsidies, funds for branch-line subsidies, and funds for hopper car purchases. And, as I mentioned earlier, the first two provinces to receive funding under the Fiscal Stabilization Program were B.C. and Alberta. The federal government has also provided substantial amounts of cash for "one-offs", including $200 million for the Calgary Olympics, $27.8 million for the Fraser River Action Plan and funding to the B.C. government for this year's APEC infrastructure.

Other regional grievances

Of course, other regions have their grievances too – I will mention one or two briefly. The Atlantic provinces sometimes argue that federal industrial policy favours Central Canada. Yet the Atlantic region has benefited from the frigate program, assistance to the fishery sector, and the important support provided by the Atlantic Canada Opportunities Agency to the region's industries. Certain Atlantic provinces have raised a concern about the current formula used in the equalization transfer program, which means that "have-not" provinces see their equalization benefits decline as natural resource revenues increase. Yet the equalization transfer can be, and has been, adapted to provide flexibility when a "have-not" province depends heavily upon a natural resource revenue that is cyclical or temporary in nature. And, of course, it should not be forgotten that equalization payments are there to provide transitional funding to ensure reasonably comparable levels of services regardless of the level of income flowing from the local economy into the provincial treasury, not to provide a permanent source of revenue.

Meanwhile, Ontario shared British Columbia's complaint about immigration settlement funding, but will receive some $35.3 million in additional funding this year. And, of course, there are also intra-regional grievances – need I mention the rivalry between your city and the provincial capital?

We should look for fairness in the big picture. In that picture, no Canadian province can say it is getting a raw deal. Canada should not be seen as a sort of cheque book to be divided out among provinces. Canada is a family of provinces, territories and people, which has equity as its underpinning principle. As Premier Klein has said, "our goal must be a strong Alberta, in a strong and united Canada."

Your former – and greatly admired – provincial treasurer, Jim Dinning, has earned kudos across Canada for helping your premier put Alberta's fiscal house in order. Mr. Dinning eloquently summed up the fairness issue when he said: "Albertans believe in the principle of equity. Clearly those who have sometimes are going to be asked to pay more than those who have not ... I don't believe this government is a believer in cheque book federalism." Reflecting on Alberta's experience in the 1920s, 1930s and 1940s, Mr. Dinning concluded that Albertans "are in fact net beneficiaries of being a partner in this country."

Conclusion

In fact, Canadians from coast to coast to coast are net beneficiaries of being partners in our country. Canada is a fair federation. It responds to the varying needs of its citizens and component regions, but it does so in a way that ensures all are treated in a just manner. The big picture is a fair picture, one in which we can all take pride. Of course, we must keep working to ensure that this fairness is maintained, and that legitimate grievances are addressed. The recent Paul Martin budget took major steps to address the concerns of young Canadians. And our government will continue its step-by-step approach to addressing other fairness issues, and to building a better future for us all.

I am confident that, in spite of the challenges we face, our federation will enter the 21st century strong and united. Why? Well, one reason is my faith in the generosity of Canadians. As I've already said, Albertans are very generous Canadians and will contribute a lot to the movement for national reconciliation. Canadians do not pass by on the other side of the road. Our generosity and fair-mindedness will win out against interregional jealousies, and against those who seek to manipulate these jealousies for short-term political gain. For the sake of our country, it must do so.

SECTION 2

A Changing Federation

Federalism: A System in Evolution

OTTAWA, APRIL 25, 1996

Alexis de Tocqueville was a fervent defender of the federal system, which he saw as one of the combinations most favourable to the prosperity and freedom of man. Accordingly, he said, "I envy the lots of those nations which have been able to adopt it."

Well, that act of foresight is testimony to de Tocqueville's reputation as a prophet of democracy. Four of the five wealthiest countries, in terms of per capita GDP, are federations. Canada is one of those countries. And yet, here at home, we rarely hear people saying good things about our federal system. It is accused of being cumbersome, inefficient and impossible to reform. Nevertheless, my academic research and my new experience within the Government lead me to conclude that a great deal of the criticism of Canadian federalism is based more on myth than reality.

I would therefore like to take advantage of the forum I have been given here today to try to make an accurate diagnosis of how our federation works. At a time when the unity of Canada is threatened, I believe it is essential that we be able to pinpoint the positive elements of our federal system, as well as the areas where improvements must still be made to serve Canadians better and bolster their confidence in their system of government.

As senior managers in the federal public service, you are directly concerned by these matters. You administer government programs; you must continually do more with less. You know better than anyone what works and what doesn't. You are an indispensable asset for the Government in its efforts to renew our federation. For that reason, I am very grateful to APEX for having invited me to talk about how the federation works.

Speech to the Association of Professional Executives of the Public Service of Canada (APEX)

The advantages of federalism for Canada

I won't be revealing any state secrets if I tell you that Canada's performance in economic and social terms is among the best in the world.

- Year after year, the UN ranks Canada number one in terms of quality of life.
- Canadians' life expectancy is among the highest in the world, and Canada is number one in terms of the school attendance rate.
- Canada is one of the top five OECD countries in terms of per capita income and per capita GDP.
- Between 1960 and 1990, Canada was number two among the G-7 countries in terms of economic growth, and number one in terms of job creation.
- Canada leads the G-7 countries and is in second place in the OECD (behind Sweden) in terms of the lowest *long-term unemployment* rate, meaning unemployment lasting longer than 12 months.

Canada's excellent performance is not just an accident. Our federal system has something to do with it. I believe that federalism has helped Canada to prosper first and foremost because it is a flexible and dynamic system that has struck the right balance between two fundamental principles: solidarity and diversity.

Under the principle of solidarity, the government works for the common good of all citizens and all regions, especially those less fortunate. And the principle of diversity leads to the autonomy of local powers, citizens and institutions.

Canada has attained a level of democracy, freedom, fairness and prosperity that is almost unequalled in the world, in large part because we Canadians have been intelligent enough to develop a way of practicing federalism that well reflects the ideals of solidarity and respect for diversity.

First of all, we have put in place a network of social programs and a system of equalization payments so that all citizens can have a comparable level of well-being. We have even entrenched that principle of equalization in section 36 of the Constitution Act, 1982. That commitment to social solidarity is unparalleled in the world.

Second, the constitutional division of powers, which gives the provinces exclusive jurisdiction over such key areas as health, education, natural resources and welfare, illustrates our commitment to extensive local autonomy. Indeed, in terms of both sectoral powers and taxing and spending powers, Canada's provinces are in many ways stronger than the American states, the German Länder or even the Swiss cantons.

When I talk about the types of advantages that federalism gives Canada, I am not talking only to Quebecers who might be tempted by the sirens of secession. I am also talking to those who feel that our country is over-governed and who dream of a unitary Canada.

Centralizing powers to a national government is not the solution. Imagine for a moment the bureaucratic monster we would have to put in place if we had only one ministry of education to administer every school in the country, from St. John's to Victoria.

The importance of debunking myths

Over the past decade, those who believe in Canadian federalism, including myself, have not always made the necessary effort to explain the advantages of our system to Canadians. By leaving the field open to our opponents, we have let a number of myths and falsehoods about our federation take root in public opinion.

I'd like to take a few minutes to take a closer look at some of the main criticisms made about our federation.

Is Canada really over-bureaucratized and over-governed?

If our system of government were truly cumbersome and inefficient, our public spending, our tax burden and the size of our public sector, including all levels of government, would be higher than in other comparable countries, particularly *unitary* countries. And yet that is not the case.

Our public spending is not particularly high when compared with the average among OECD countries. In 1993, for example, total government spending in Canada represented 49.7% of Canada's GDP. This ratio is almost identical in Canada and Germany (49.7% vs 49.4%), and it is higher than Canada's in a number of unitary OECD countries, such as France (54.8%), the Netherlands (55.8%), Italy (56.2%), Norway (57.1%) and Sweden (71.8%).

The size of Canada's public sector is not unusually high, either, when compared with the average among OECD countries. In the early 1990s, public sector employees had 20.6% of the jobs in Canada. That proportion is only slightly higher than that of the United Kingdom (19.4%), and lower than that of France (22.6%), Denmark (30.5%), Sweden (31.9%) and Norway (32%). Need I remind you that all those countries have a unitary structure?

Finally, the tax burden is lighter in Canada than in many OECD countries. In 1993, total revenues collected by the various levels of government represented 42% of Canada's GDP. That ratio was *higher than in Canada* in 11 of the 19 OECD countries for which data are available.

International comparisons highlight the fact that unitary states are not more effective and efficient than federal systems. For one thing, the characteristic centralization of unitary states makes it necessary to set up an extremely cumbersome bureaucracy within the national government. For another thing, unitary states cannot function either without creating different levels of government administration. Unitary states also have regional and local authorities, the difference being, however, that those authorities have much less autonomy in relation to the central government than do Canada's provinces.

Are jurisdictional duplication and overlap really costing Canadian taxpayers billions of dollars?

Despite international comparisons that are actually to Canada's advantage, many Canadians remain convinced that the federal and provincial governments are duplicating activities in a host of areas. After all, we do have federal and provincial departments of health, the environment, agriculture, natural resources, fisheries and transport.

A number of studies have shown that there is indeed a great deal of jurisdictional overlap between Ottawa and the provinces. For example, Germain Julien and Marcel Proulx, researchers at Quebec's École nationale d'administration publique, have estimated that 60% of federal programs overlap those of the Government of Quebec. A 1991 study by Canada's Treasury Board Secretariat concluded that 66% of federal programs at least partially overlap those of the provinces.

And yet, all the studies on overlap and duplication, including the notorious Le Hir studies by the Government of Quebec, concluded that in the vast majority of cases, federal and provincial activities are complementary rather than redundant. For example, the Government could not withdraw from activities such as management of national parks or correctional services without considerably affecting service to the public.

It is also important to note that overlap is not the exclusive bane of the Canadian federation, or even of federal systems in general. It is an issue that concerns unitary states as well.

I'd like to share an example that was recently brought to my attention. Much has been said lately about duplication of employment assistance measures. The Official Opposition and the Government of Quebec often talk about blunders caused by the approximately one hundred federal and provincial measures currently implemented in Quebec. Incidentally, employment insurance reform is expected to reduce the number of federal measures from 35 to 5.

Well, according to a recent edition of the French magazine *L'Express*, there are currently some 2,300 different employment assistance measures in France. That plethora of programs is due to the fact that municipalities, departments, regions and the central government all implement their own measures, without paying much heed to what the others are doing already. And to think that some people would have us believe that we're the only ones who have problems with overlap!

> *Is Canadian federalism truly an adversarial system*
> *where everything is subject to endless squabbling*
> *between Ottawa and the provinces?*

Although disagreements between the federal government and the provinces often get a lot of press, it should not be concluded that our federation is plagued by disagreement and conflict. Many issues are resolved every day, often at your level, without attracting any media attention.

The most recent Inventory of Federal-Provincial Programs and Activities, which came out last year, contains no fewer than 457 *bilateral and multilateral programs or agreements between Ottawa and the provinces*. That means that the federal government and the provinces are managing to get along and co-ordinate their activities in a host of areas.

With your support, our government has taken various measures to promote a renewed partnership with the provinces:

– the Efficiency of the Federation Initiative;
– the Canada Health and Social Transfer;
– the National Infrastructure Program;
– "Team Canada's" trade missions;
– the Employment Insurance Reform, particularly Part II of the bill on active employment assistance measures;
– withdrawal from certain areas of provincial jurisdiction, including labour-market training, social housing, mining, forestry and recreation; and finally
– limitation of federal spending power in areas of exclusive provincial jurisdiction.

> *Is Canadian federalism really a gridlocked system*
> *that cannot be reformed?*

The experience of recent decades shows that the small number of constitutional changes has not prevented the federation from evolving considerably on all fronts.

Let's take the example of the Program Review headed by my colleague Marcel Massé. That exercise has already yielded impressive results, making it possible to rebalance responsibilities among the federal government, the provinces and the private sector. Unfortunately, those achievements have too often gone unsung.

The Program Review will allow the Government to save some $19.2 billion by 1998–99 and cut more than 45,000 positions from the federal public service, a reduction of almost 20%.

Our federal system has not evolved so substantially through greater centralization of decision-making in Ottawa. The trend is clearly toward greater decentralization. A variety of indicators confirm that:

– The number of federal employees in relation to the country's labour force has dropped by almost half since the early 1950s.
– In 1950, the federal government collected $3.30 for every dollar of revenue collected by the provinces; in 1993, it collected only $1.20.
– In addition, for every dollar spent by the provinces on goods and services, the federal government spent $2.46 in 1960, and only $0.67 in 1993, a drop of 76% in 33 years.

We have thus seen a gradual and remarkable redistribution of the federal government's taxing and spending power to the provincial governments over the past four decades.

As you can see, my assessment of how our federation works is largely positive. Our federal system has allowed us to take on challenges in the past, and I am convinced that it is also the best system to help us take on the challenges that will unfold in the coming years.

Why federalism will help us take on the challenges facing us at the dawn of the 21st century

The strengths of our federal system, namely its flexibility, its dynamism, its solidarity and its ability to respect diversity, have served us well so far and will continue to do so more than ever in the coming years, if we give them the chance.

Throughout the world, we see countries and supranational organizations such as the European Union trying to strike a balance between solidarity and autonomy. In that regard, Canadian federalism has a lot to teach the rest of the world in terms of how to balance those principles, and it will help us to take on the new global challenges for which that balance is more essential than ever.

Because of economic globalization, more and more decisions with major repercussions on Canadians' lives are being made at the international level. Belonging to the G-7, NAFTA, the Commonwealth, the Francophonie, the Organization of American States and the Asia Pacific Economic Cooperation Council is a considerable asset for Canadians in defending their interests internationally. Without the federal union, we would lose a number of those assets.

Furthermore, trade liberalization at the international level favours specialization of regional economies. The Canadian federation's characteristic respect for diversity and regional autonomy will also serve us well in that regard.

In social terms, a number of relatively new phenomena are helping to transform the challenges facing Canada. An aging population, growing numbers of single-parent families, diminished job security and a growing proportion of citizens who depend on income security programs are issues that concern all Canadians and are making us rethink our social protection system.

Once again, the core principles of our federation – solidarity and local autonomy – will prove to be invaluable advantages. On the one hand, the extensive autonomy the provinces have with regard to social policy will help them find innovative solutions tailored to their specific needs. On the other hand, Canadian solidarity will ensure that all citizens, no matter what region of the country they live in, will have access to a comparable level of services.

In addition, federalism fosters emulation among the provinces and the dissemination of productive experiences. Those are key elements for putting in place effective public services.

Canadian society is increasingly bilingual and multicultural:

– Between 1981 and 1991, the number of people who said they had a mother tongue other than English or French rose by 22%, while Canada's population increased by only 13% over the same period.
– In addition, the number of people who can speak French has never been as high: according to 1991 census data, 32% of Canadians, or almost 9 million people, are able to express themselves in French.
– In Quebec in particular, the French language has continued to flourish. 93.5 per cent of Quebec residents say they can speak French fluently; that is the highest rate of francisation since the beginning of Confederation.

Those indicators reflect our federation's respect for diversity. That principle will enable us to continue to affirm Canadian society's linguistic duality and multicultural nature. By respecting diversity, we will be able to make the Canadian federation evolve in a way that makes

Canadians in all parts of the country feel more at home and better recognized.

What will we have to do to improve our federal system?

I am convinced that the federal system will be able to deliver the goods if we continue to rely on those things that make it strong: solidarity and diversity. In practical terms, we will have to focus our efforts on three tasks.

First, we must continue our efforts to *make our federation more efficient*.

We can better clarify the roles and responsibilities of the federal government and the provinces, especially in areas of shared jurisdiction such as the environment and agriculture. That clarification will yield both greater accountability and greater efficiency.

In trying to minimize unnecessary overlap, our challenge also lies in effectively managing overlap that is inevitable. We must ensure first that the activities of the different levels of government complement one another well, and second that there is productive co-operation between the different governments.

Second, we have to try to *make our federation work more harmoniously*.

Because the federal government and the provinces share areas of activity, good co-operation is essential. In areas where overlap is inevitable, unilateral action is not desirable. In most cases, it can create conflict, duplication and contradictions between federal and provincial policies.

For effective co-ordination of federal and provincial efforts, *we must work in partnership*. That's true for us as elected representatives and it's also true for you as public servants. By working together with the provinces, we will succeed in serving the public better, making our federation work more harmoniously and, ultimately, strengthening national unity.

For that reason, I feel it is essential that, before they are implemented, all new federal policies and programs take into account the federal-provincial dimension and the need for a more harmonious federation. Decisions that might affect provincial governments' operations should ideally be made together with the provinces. I can only encourage you to make co-operation with the provinces one of your main criteria for excellence as senior managers in the federal public service.

Third, and finally, to come back to my first point, we have to *debunk the far too many myths* circulating about our federation and how it works. As federal public servants, you have a key role to play in giving back our fellow citizens confidence in their institutions.

You have the responsibility, which you share with the members of the Government, to explain well to Canadians what the Government of Canada is doing. As public servants, your responsibility is to clearly explain the programs, services and activities you manage and to set the record straight about them if need be.

To be able to make an accurate judgement about their system of government and their institutions, Canadians have to have balanced information. Too often in the past decade, they have been given only one side of the story.

Our federation certainly has its problems, as do all countries; in addition, its unity is threatened. It is thus high time to underscore the federation's tremendous achievements in terms of democratic and individual rights, freedom, social solidarity, economic prosperity and respect for diversity.

Canada has considerable assets to maintain its privileged place among the nations of the world. Our federal system is undeniably one of those assets. Let's make sure we know how to put them to good use and make them work better.

Let's make an accurate diagnosis of our federation, so that we can prescribe the right course of treatment for it.

History and Prospects of the
Canadian Social Union

OTTAWA, NOVEMBER 18, 1996

The defenders of Canadian unity in Quebec and elsewhere have been accused, sometimes correctly, of reducing the case for Canada to a merely economic argument. While there is indeed a powerful economic argument for Canadian unity, it is true that this is not the whole story. There is far more to Canada than trade balances and interest rates, and the other arguments must also find their voice. Today, over a year after the trauma of the last referendum, I would like to focus on another of the most important arguments for Canadian unity, namely the strength of the Canadian social union.

One of Mr. Bouchard's arguments during last year's referendum campaign was that Canada had abandoned its traditions of promoting social justice and generosity towards those in need. According to Mr. Bouchard, there was a "cold wind from English Canada" – from Alberta, from Queen's Park, from Ottawa – that was leading to a crueller, harsher Canada, and that only in an independent Quebec could generous social programs be maintained. Today, as Lucien Bouchard has become Premier Bouchard, and has discovered that he too must balance the desire to preserve the social safety net against the need to be responsible with public finances, we may question the validity of his argument. Getting our economic house in order does not contradict the goal of preserving our social contract. In fact, the one is a prerequisite to the other.

Now that the federal government, under the leadership of Prime Minister Jean Chrétien and Finance Minister Paul Martin, has made tremendous progress towards putting Canada's economy back on a sound basis, the Government, in cooperation with the provincial governments, will increasingly focus on the renewal of Canada's social union. The social union talks with the provinces, led on the federal side by my colleagues Pierre Pettigrew and David Dingwall, will lead to a reshaping of Canada's social programs as we enter the 21st century.

Speech to the Canadian Club of Ottawa

This will not be simply an exercise in cost-cutting or division of powers between governments, but in focussing all government programs, federal or provincial, on a common objective: providing a better quality of public service that meets the genuine needs of people. And the principles and values that will guide this process will be the same principles that have guided Canada over the past decades in creating one of the most generous systems of social benefits in the world.

Today, I would like to talk about the values and principles that have guided Canadians in creating our social union, and to discuss the history of the development of our social union from Confederation to today. For only with a clear understanding of what our common convictions are and of where we have come from will we be able to create a renewed social union that builds on the strengths of the past in responding to the challenges of the future.

The values of Canada's social union: Solidarity and subsidiarity

What then are the core values that have guided Canadians and their governments in the creation of Canada's generous social system? I believe that if we examine the history of Canada's social development, we can identify two key principles at work, and a constant search for balance between them. These are the principle of solidarity and the principle of subsidiarity. I have talked elsewhere about these two principles of solidarity and subsidiarity, but as I think they are particularly relevant to the social union aspect of the Canadian federation, I would like to expand a little on where these principles of solidarity and subsidiarity come from and what they mean.

The use of this terminology is fairly new, borrowing from recent debates within the European Community. But it is fair to say that the development of the Canadian social union is one of the best examples of the search for balance between the principles of solidarity and subsidiarity to be found in the world. Indeed, like Molière's *Bourgeois Gentilhomme* who spoke prose all his life without even knowing it, Canada has been practising solidarity and subsidiarity ever since Confederation without knowing it.

Solidarity is a word most associated historically with the labour movement. One thinks of the union hymn "Solidarity Forever" or the struggle of the Solidarity trade union in Poland. To be in solidarity with one's fellow citizens means to have compassion, especially for the less fortunate, and to provide aid to those in need. But it is more than merely a sense of pity or charity, it is a sense of mutual responsibility. Being in solidarity means sharing a sense of common belonging and common good. Canadian solidarity means that all citizens in all regions

of Canada feel part of a greater whole. To borrow another phrase from
the trade union movement, when we are in solidarity with others, "an
injury to one is an injury to all."

We saw the spirit of Canadian solidarity at work in the aftermath of
the Saguenay floods earlier this year. The outpouring of voluntary,
spontaneous support from ordinary citizens from within Quebec and
also from all parts of Canada for the victims of the flood was marvellous evidence that Canadians from coast to coast feel that we are part
of a common whole, that we share a sense of solidarity.

Governments, when they act to support citizens and regions which
need help, give formal expression to this sense of solidarity among
citizens. But solidarity, the belief in mutual responsibility and support
for the less fortunate, does not mean that we must create a nanny
state, where central government provides for all human needs. Indeed, the best way of helping others can often be to let them help
themselves.

This is why solidarity must be balanced by respect for the principle
of subsidiarity. Subsidiarity is a less familiar term which comes originally from Catholic social teaching of the 1930s, but which is now
used broadly in discussions of governance in Europe and elsewhere. It
means essentially that the State must respect the legitimate autonomy
of individuals, families, communities, and more local levels of government and help them in fulfilling their own responsibilities, rather than
taking them over. To quote from its classic definition by Pius XI, "It is
a fundamental principle of social philosophy ... that one should not
withdraw from individuals and commit to the community what they
can accomplish by their own enterprise and industry. So, too, it is an
injustice ... to transfer to the larger and higher collectivity the functions
which can be provided for by lesser and subordinate bodies."

This principle of subsidiarity has become a key concept in the formation of the European Community. The Maastricht Treaty on European
Union of 1991 states that: "the Community shall take action, in accordance with the principle of subsidiarity, only if and insofar as the objective of the proposed action cannot be sufficiently achieved by the
Member States and can therefore, by reason of the scale or effects of
the proposed action, be better achieved by the Community." Today, as
the European Community moves from being a mere free trade area to a
fuller economic, social, and political union that unites sovereign countries within federal institutions, Europeans are debating today precisely
the question that we have faced over the last century, as Canadians
worked to create a strong national identity in the context of a federation with strong provinces: how to reconcile a spirit of solidarity with
respect for subsidiarity.

In Canada, our federal system is the primary means we have used to reconcile solidarity with subsidiarity. Federalism allows us to share in a common citizenship with common national goals and objectives, but also means that we respect the autonomy and diversity of the constituent units of the federation, namely the provinces and territories.

The history of the Canadian social union

Canadian federalism has been a dynamic system. It has evolved considerably over the years, at times more centralized, at other times more decentralized, at times emphasizing solidarity, at other times subsidiarity. There has been no status quo in Canadian federalism, no constant, but rather ceaseless change.

Nowhere is this more true than in the development and evolution of our Canadian social union. Let me briefly explain how our social union has evolved over the years as Canadians have moved to act in solidarity while respecting subsidiarity.

Canada in 1867 did not have an extensive system of social programs. Governments concerned themselves primarily with essential public infrastructure such as railroads and postal services. Under the British North America Act of 1867, education was an exclusively provincial jurisdiction, which was especially important for Quebec in order to preserve its distinctive linguistic and religious identity. But in the main, the provision of health, education, and social assistance was not a state matter, but was left to private individuals, communities, charities, and religious bodies, with the provinces playing an overseeing role. As the Canadian economy grew and expanded, this system seemed to work fairly well. The subsidiarity not only of provinces, but of the local community, was fully respected, while a spirit of solidarity moved the citizens of a rich and growing nation to give generous charitable support for the locally run network of social services.

But with the Depression of the 1930s, the economic and social crisis led many to call for government to take on some of these social functions to help those most in need. The first and most pressing demand was for some form of unemployment insurance to help those dislocated by the upheavals of the Depression. In 1935, the Conservative government of R.B. Bennett tried to respond to the economic crisis with a sweeping Employment and Social Insurance Act. But several provinces objected, and the Act was found to be beyond federal powers by the courts in 1937. So from the beginning, accommodation between solidarity and subsidiarity had to be found in building Canada's social programs. The King government negotiated with the provinces and, with the unanimous consent of the provinces, amended the Constitution in

1940 to allow a federal role in Unemployment Insurance and introduced a new Unemployment Insurance Act in 1941.

Other social initiatives followed a pattern of cooperation between
federal and provincial governments and emulation among provinces to
gradually create the network of programs Canadians enjoy today. For
example, Saskatchewan introduced Hospital Insurance in 1947. It was
followed by British Columbia and Alberta in 1949. Then in 1957, the
federal government offered to share costs with provinces that introduced similar programs, and by 1959, citizens in every province en-
joyed emergency Hospital Insurance – a great example of the flexibility
of the federal system in balancing solidarity and subsidiarity, contributing to the common good of all Canadians. Similarly, with the later introduction of universal Medicare, Saskatchewan led the way in 1961,
with other provinces joining in a jointly funded federal-provincial program over the next ten years.

The Canada Pension Plan is another example of successful emulation
and cooperation. Ontario introduced its Pension Benefits Act in 1963,
regulating and requiring mandatory contributions to private plans. The
federal government called for a national government-run pension program in 1965. Quebec expressed a desire to have a separate, but comparable, program, and thus by 1967 a national Canada Pension Plan
and a parallel Quebec Pension Plan were put in place.

This is the story of social policy in Canada: creativity and innovation
at the provincial level, which leads to cooperation on a national basis,
a skilful balance of the two principles of solidarity and subsidiarity. It is
to this same flexibility and creativity that we must appeal today as governments begin to think about how to reorient Canada's social programs for the 21st century.

Quebec and the development of the social union

Movement towards a comprehensive review of social programs on
both an interprovincial and federal-provincial basis is now underway.
The interprovincial Ministerial Council on Social Policy report this
spring had some interesting suggestions on social policy. The federal-
provincial forum being chaired by Pierre Pettigrew and Stockwell Day,
Alberta's Minister of Family and Social Services, will provide the opportunity to discuss these and other suggestions to improve our social
union.

Unfortunately, the Province of Quebec has chosen not to be a full
participant in these efforts. At the Jasper meeting of the premiers, Premier Bouchard tried to justify this non-participation on the basis of
Quebec's traditional constitutional positions, saying that "it's a histori-

cal stand of Quebec premiers not to accept any intrusion from the federal government, or from the provinces, into Quebec's jurisdictions, namely into social programs."

But an examination of the historical record shows a more nuanced picture. It is true that all Quebec provincial governments, of whatever partisan stripe, have insisted on the maintenance of provincial autonomy and protection of the constitutional jurisdiction of the provinces in social policy. But there is also a history of pragmatism and cooperation working within the constitutional framework between Ottawa and Quebec City on social policy going back to the 1930s in order to ensure the best quality of service to citizens.

For example, Premier Duplessis accepted the necessity of a federal system of Unemployment Insurance in 1937 due to the length and depth of the Depression, stating that this would not infringe on provincial jurisdiction. Adélard Godbout consented to the constitutional amendment for Unemployment Insurance in 1940, and was open to an increased federal role in social policy during the war years. In 1959, Premier Paul Sauvé stated that Quebec had no constitutional objections to a federal system of hospital insurance. The Lesage government stated its preference in the social sphere for Quebec-run programs with compensation instead of cost-shared programs, and was able to arrange with the Pearson government for federal compensation to run separate pension and student loan programs compatible with the objectives of the national programs. These are all positive examples of pragmatic, cooperative federalism at work to create programs that expressed a pan-Canadian sense of solidarity while fully respecting the principle of subsidiarity by safeguarding provincial jurisdiction.

Nor have past Quebec governments been unwilling to praise the benefits of the federal system in building our social programs. At the 1946 Dominion-provincial conference, the Duplessis government stated that: [translation] "The federal system likely offers advantages in the area of social legislation that do not exist in countries with only one government. Indeed, the co-existence of several governments which are all autonomous in their own respective fields, because it creates points of comparison, is likely to create beneficial emulation, for the greater good of citizens." In 1970, Robert Bourassa said that while Quebec claimed "a primary responsibility" in social policy, it also recognized "the key role of the federal government in ensuring an acceptable standard of living for all Canadians. Administration of social policy programs would be mixed, however, depending on whether the type of program defined by each province is more suited to centralized administration, or, on the contrary, calls for decentralized management" [translation]. Mr. Bourassa maintained this belief in a constructive cooperation on social policy between the federal and provincial levels all his life – a life which ended far too soon, only a few weeks ago.

Now whatever one thinks of Premiers Duplessis and Bourassa, everybody will admit that they were vigilant in preserving the traditional constitutional rights of Quebec. Yet these two statements capture precisely the spirit of dynamic federalism in reconciling solidarity with subsidiarity that I have been discussing. I hope that Premier Bouchard has the courage and vision to act in the tradition of Duplessis, Godbout, Sauvé, Lesage, and Bourassa – a tradition of preserving subsidiarity and provincial autonomy while acting in solidarity with other Canadians to build a stronger social union.

It seems to me that, whenever the Government of Quebec has made tangible, constructive proposals that make sense in terms of public service quality within the specific context of Quebec, the federation has been able to make the necessary arrangements. With good will on all sides, we will succeed again during the negotiations currently underway.

Canada's federalism as an advantage in creating our social union

Canada has created a strong social union, with national measures to ensure comparable services for all citizens, but a strong respect for provincial autonomy and flexibility in administration. The nature of our federal system means that many of these programs have come together in a way that can seem to be ad hoc or piecemeal over a number of years. There have been few examples of one government imposing a radical new innovation in social policy all at once. Rather, things start small in one or two provinces and then spread across the country, often with a greater or lesser degree of federal encouragement or cooperation. But this pragmatic, step-by-step approach to building our social union seems to have served us well.

Compared with unitary states such as the United Kingdom or France, Canada has a social union which is efficient and flexible. But compared with some other federations, notably the United States, which has perhaps too many legal and legislative checks on national social policy measures, we have been able to achieve a strong sense of solidarity through our national social programs and collective action. There are few people here, I believe, who would trade Canada's health care system for the centralized National Health Service of Great Britain or the non-existent universal medical protection of the United States.

Canada's position is comparable to only a few other nations, such as Germany, which shares with Canada the distinction of being a federation with strong, autonomous units – the Länder – but which has nonetheless succeeded in building a generous social safety net and a strong sense of national solidarity. Like Canada, Germany has legal and constitutional provisions to ensure local administration and flexibility in the delivery of programs and revenue equalization programs to ensure that poorer regions can offer the same standard of social services as richer regions. If anything, Canada is more decentralized than Germany when it comes to national standards and program design for social policy. But what the parallels between Canada and Germany illustrate is that the federal system is an asset in building our social union. I doubt that either a centralized, unitary state or a series of ten isolated and egotistical republics would have been able to create the kinds of social programs that we enjoy as Canadians.

The Canadian style of federalism will always seem inefficient and cumbersome to centralists who wish the federal government could create national social policies by decree, or will seem aggressive and domineering to radical decentralists who believe that everything should be left to the provinces alone or the private sector. But the Canadian search for the balance between solidarity and subsidiarity is in fact an enviable record, and has given us a system that we can be proud to compare with any other in the world.

The situation today: Reforming the social union

Our successes in the past are no guarantee that Canadians will continue to enjoy the same quality of social services in the future. Federal and provincial governments face new challenges – the fiscal challenge of controlling debt, the demographic challenge of an aging population and a growing Aboriginal population, the challenges of competing in a global economy – which will all affect the future of our social union.

The biggest challenge that this government faced when it came to power was the spiralling federal debt and deficit. The three Martin budgets have moved us a long way towards fiscal order, and guarantee that the federal government will continue to be able to act as the supporter and guardian of Canada's social union. The social programs Canada enjoys, many of which were created by the work of Paul Martin, Sr., will be preserved for future generations by the work of Paul Martin, Jr. The cuts that were made were difficult, but they were done without endangering the most vulnerable in our society, and with the federal government leading by example in cutting its own programs more deeply than its transfers to the provinces.

But there has been more to the record of the first three years than deficit reduction. Since coming to power, the Liberal government has made some important steps to the restructuring of Canada's social programs for the next century. The existing system of Established Programs Financing was reformed into the Canada Health and Social Transfer, which increases the flexibility of the provinces in program delivery and guarantees a permanent cash floor for federal transfers in support of health, post-secondary education, and social assistance. However, the federal commitment to mobility rights for all Canadians and to the five principles of the Canada Health Act remains undiminished. The Employment Insurance reforms initiated by Minister Axworthy reorganized the complex array of federal employment development programs into a few basic measures and reduced overlap in services with the provinces. It is these reforms that paved the way for the current federal-provincial negotiations on labour-market measures.

Over the past year, the Government has taken further steps to modernize the social union. The Prime Minister committed the Government to withdrawing from labour-market training and to negotiating increased provincial control over labour-market development with those provinces that wish to exercise these powers. Minister Young released the details of the federal negotiating position on labour force in May to widespread praise from provinces, business, and labour, and negotiations are now ongoing with several provinces, including Quebec. This is a field of government action in which all provinces have a legitimate interest because of its close relationship with the provincial field of education. The proposals tabled by Minister Young, and currently under negotiation by Minister Pettigrew, will respond to the needs of all provinces in a supple and flexible fashion, including the particular needs of Quebec.

More broadly, the Government committed itself in the Throne Speech to discussing with the provinces the values, principles, and objectives underlying our social union. Since then, the provinces have released the Ministerial Council report as a basis for future discussions, and at the First Ministers' Meeting, the federal and provincial governments, excluding Quebec, agreed to further talks on modernizing our social union. Federal ministers Pettigrew and Dingwall are now actively engaged in consultation with their provincial colleagues, and the first meeting of federal and provincial ministers on the future of the social union will be held next week.

The social union of tomorrow

What will social policy look like as Canada enters the 21st century? How will the provinces and the federal government come together to reconcile solidarity and subsidiarity in light of the new challenges Canada faces?

Without wanting to anticipate the results of the work of Ministers Pettigrew and Dingwall and their provincial colleagues, it is fair to say that there is an emerging consensus on some of the priorities and directions for the future of the Canadian social union.

There is widespread agreement that the federal and provincial governments must cooperate to preserve the social safety net that Canada has built during the post-war years, especially our Medicare system, which is a source of pride to the vast majority of Canadians. But the future of the Canadian social union will not be just preserving the fundamentals of our existing system, but will also require a creative response to new problems and new priorities.

One of the greatest challenges facing Canada today is the problem of child poverty. Canada introduced Old Age Pensions, the Guaranteed Income Supplement, and the Canada and Quebec Pension Plans to address the terrible poverty that many of our seniors had faced. Over time, the rate of poverty among seniors in Canada has dropped dramatically. We can be proud of this, and we will continue to help seniors and to reduce the level of poverty among those citizens who have done so much to build this country.

Tragically, however, while we have been making progress against poverty among seniors, poverty among children has been increasing in recent decades. Younger workers have faced higher unemployment rates and lower real wages in the 1980s and 1990s, making conditions more difficult for their children. We have seen higher levels of family breakdown and a rise in the number of single-parent families. Aboriginal communities, still among the poorest in Canada, have a much younger average age than the rest of the Canadian population. All of these trends have contributed to an unacceptable rate of child poverty in Canada, and increasingly we hear calls for concerted action at both the federal and provincial level to address child poverty. For this reason, it is an important priority of both provincial and federal governments in the upcoming discussions on improving our social union.

There is already a foundation to address child poverty, in the federal Child Tax Benefit system. This tax measure redistributes $5 billion annually to assist families with children. There has been considerable discussion of the idea championed by Premier Romanow of Saskatchewan, among others, of building on this foundation to improve the Child Tax Benefit system through greater federal-provincial cooperation and combination of resources to help poorer families with children.

Whether a joint federal-provincial response to child poverty takes the form of an integrated Child Tax Benefit or some other combination of measures, this idea points towards another trend in the evolution of the Canadian social union: the two levels of government working cooperatively, but focussing on those tasks that each level of government is best equipped to perform. In many ways, the provinces are best positioned to provide most frontline services and have extensive infrastructures to provide health, educational, and social services directly to citizens. Therefore, it may make sense to enter into arrangements for the provincial governments to provide some of the other frontline services previously administered by Ottawa, for example in the area of job training. On the other hand, through Revenue Canada and Human Resources Development, the federal government has the system and infrastructure required to provide income support directly to people, and it is relatively easy for the federal government to administer certain forms of provincial income support programs to reduce administrative costs.

I expect that in dealing with child poverty and the other challenges facing the federation, we will see more of this common-sense specialization in areas of expertise, based on the principle of providing the best possible service to the public.

Conclusion: The social union and a united Canada

I have talked today about the past, present, and future of our common Canadian social union, and relatively little about the Constitution or the recognition of Quebec's distinctiveness, or other topics related to unity. But that I have discussed social policy rather than change in the Constitution does not mean that I have been avoiding the importance of national unity. A strong social union is crucial for the preservation of the Canadian political union.

If we continue in the directions that the federal government and many provincial governments have proposed, we have every reason to be hopeful for the strength and vitality of Canada's social union for tomorrow. We will face our economic and demographic challenges. We will address the scourge of child poverty. And we will do it together. We will act with a strong sense of Canadian solidarity, looking out for the common good of all citizens, especially the least fortunate, while respecting the autonomy of the provinces and communities in a spirit of subsidiarity.

This is a great collective project. Quebecers must be a full part of it. With their culture and their sensitivity, they must help one another and other Canadians, their fellow citizens, to make our social union even stronger. It is not true that Quebec would be better positioned to address these social challenges alone. There are many areas where constructive cooperation is possible without diminishing Quebec's autonomy. On the other hand, an independent Quebec, burdened by debt, cut off from the spirit of Canadian solidarity, would face extreme difficulty in preserving its social safety net. The cuts to social spending that Quebec and other provinces have faced would be minuscule compared to the social crisis that would be faced in the event of an attempted secession. If Premier Bouchard really stands for the interests and the well-being of the people of Quebec, he will join with his provincial counterparts, and with the noble tradition of many Quebec governments, in offering constructive solutions for the social challenges we face together as Canadians.

A great country is not just a country where the social and economic status quo are comfortable, or where staying together is a better alternative than breaking apart. A truly great country is a country where all of its citizens can share common goals and a vision for an even brighter future. And building a stronger Canadian social union, a union which enhances the solidarity of our citizens while respecting the subsidiarity of provinces and communities, is one of the great collective goals we can share as Canadians. So let us work together for a stronger social union, knowing that in doing so we not only enhance social justice and help those most in need among us, but make all of Canada a stronger, better, and more united country.

Amendment of Section 93 (Education) of the Constitution Act, 1867

Mr. Speaker, I have the honour to inform the House that later today, I will be giving notice to bring this constitutional amendment resolution before the House and to refer it to a Special Joint Committee which will be asked to report back to Parliament.

One week ago, on April 15, 1997, the Quebec National Assembly voted unanimously in favour of a resolution for a constitutional amendment that would end the application to Quebec of subsections (1) to (4) of section 93 (education) of the Constitution Act, 1867.

On receiving such a proposed amendment, Members and Senators must ask themselves three fundamental questions. First: what amending formula is applicable to this particular case? Second: is the proposed amendment a good thing for the citizens affected by it? And third: does this amendment enjoy a reasonable degree of support from the citizens affected by it? I will give the Government's answers to each of these three questions in the case of the amendment we have received from the Quebec National Assembly.

1. Amending formula

In the opinion of the federal government, section 93 can be amended pursuant to section 43 of the Constitution Act, 1982. Section 43 deals with the provisions applicable to one or more, but not all, provinces. The amendment can be made with the approval of the House of Commons and "chaque province concernée" in the French version, or "each province to which the amendment applies" in the English version, which is more specific here. This means that the amendment will affect only Quebec, but will not change the constitutional provisions applicable to the other provinces.

Before the constitutional amendment of 1982, it would have been impossible to amend section 93 unless the traditional means provided by the Constitution Act, 1867 had been used. It would have been necessary to ask the Westminster Parliament to ratify the amendment.

The constitutional amendment passed by the National Assembly clearly falls within the class of bilateral amendments provided for in section 43 of the Constitution Act, 1982. The legal opinions we have received are quite definite on that point. And that is what I told my counterpart Jacques Brassard, Quebec's Minister of Intergovernmental Affairs, at our first meeting on this matter on February 7 this year.

Since this is a bilateral amendment, it must be debated by each of the two Parliaments. But these debates should not be simultaneous, in order to avoid possible confusion. For each of the four bilateral amendments made to date, the debate was held first in the province's legislative assembly, since the initiative came from the province. And again on this occasion, since the initiative came from the province, and in view of the fact that it concerns one of its areas of jurisdiction – education – it was necessary for the debate to take place first in the National Assembly. That debate has just ended with a unanimous vote in favour of the proposed amendment.

The federal Parliament can now play its part. Since the Constitution requires its assent, it must make its own decision as to the value of the proposed amendment. Indeed, it is its duty to do so, since it represents the citizens affected by the amendment, as does the provincial assembly. The Parliament of Canada is also the Parliament of Quebecers. Federal institutions are also the institutions of Quebecers.

2. *The value of the constitutional amendment*

The federal government believes that the proposed constitutional amendment is a good thing, and I will now explain why. The origins of section 93 of the Constitution Act, 1867 predate Confederation. This section was included in the Canadian Constitution to grant education to the provinces and to reassure religious minorities as to their rights at the time when the single Province of Canada was about to be divided to create the provinces of Quebec and Ontario. The purpose of the section was to protect the Catholic and Protestant religious minorities. Those guarantees were then extended to other Canadian provinces.

Until the Quiet Revolution, Catholic and Protestant Quebecers were apparently satisfied with this system based on 19th century political and social values. However, following the report of the provincial Commission of Inquiry on Education in 1966, there were many discussions in Quebec on the appropriateness of a system with denominational foundations. Like most other Western societies, Quebec society was now secular.

On the Francophone side, the present organization of school boards makes it more difficult to integrate newcomers into Francophone society, as provided by provincial legislation. The Anglophone community long regarded the Protestant school boards as an institution vital to its development. However, these school boards have never encompassed Catholic Anglophones. On the other hand, they have accepted a growing number of children whose language of instruction is French. As a result, there is a danger that, in the medium term, the Anglophone community may lose control of boards that are an increasingly inadequate reflection of their social reality and that, in any case, cannot respond to the needs of their Catholic populations.

That is why many voices, both Francophone and Anglophone, Catholic as well as Protestant, have been heard over the last twenty years advocating a system based on language rather than religion. A consensus on the need to reorganize school organization along these lines has existed in Quebec for some time.

However, for various reasons, all previous attempts have failed, including the proposal by Quebec's Minister of Education, Ms. Pauline Marois, last June. The Government of Quebec then contemplated a constitutional amendment to allow secularization of school organization.

This amendment raises the issue of religious rights, but also, indirectly, the issue of linguistic rights, in view of the historically close links between Protestant school boards and the Anglophone community.

Let us look first at the religious issue. The contemplated amendment will end application of subsections (1) to (4) of section 93 of the Constitution Act, 1867 to Quebec, and will accordingly eliminate these religious guarantees.

Although Quebecers approve of secularization of school organization, many are attached to religious instruction. Quebec's Minister of Education, Ms. Pauline Marois, has already indicated that schools that so wish may retain their denominational orientation. Furthermore, the right to religious instruction is still guaranteed by section 41 of the Quebec Charter of Human Rights and Freedoms.

Let us now consider the language issue. The proposed amendment would not weaken the constitutional rights of the Anglophone minority. The Act which amended the Canadian Constitution in 1982 guaranteed minority language educational rights for the first time, in section 23 of the Canadian Charter of Rights and Freedoms.

While it is true that the National Assembly does not recognize the Constitution Act, 1982, the resolution it is sending us is preceded by a "whereas" clause which "reaffirms the established rights of the English-speaking community of Quebec." Indeed, the Charter was drafted at the time bearing in mind Quebec's policies on the language of education. And the Government of Quebec does not contest its applicability. The resolution I am tabling today is preceded by a "whereas" clause which reaffirms that the Canadian Charter of Rights and Freedoms applies everywhere in Canada.

Section 23 of the Charter provides strong constitutional guarantees to the minority language community. Section 93 guarantees only the existence of denominational administrative structures in Montreal and Quebec City, and the right of dissent in the rest of the province, but it does not protect language rights. Furthermore, the control and management of linguistic school organization are in fact guaranteed by the case law flowing from section 23 of the Charter and not from section 93.

In the *Mahe* judgement (1990), the Supreme Court ruled that section 23 "confers a right which places positive obligations on the government to alter or develop major institutional structures." Since that time, other judgements have confirmed the interpretation of the *Mahe* decision.

It is true that the scope of the right to instruction in the minority language provided in section 23 varies according to the number of students involved. In the case law, however, the bar for granting the minority the right to establish and control an administrative structure such as a school board, or simply to participate in it, has not been set very high. Although there were only 242 Francophone children attending a school in Edmonton at the time of the *Mahé* decision (1990), the Supreme Court ruled that this created a right for the minority to manage and control its schools through a system for linguistic minority representation within the school boards.

It is, in a way, thanks to the constitutional amendments of 1982 that the Government of Quebec can proceed as it is intending to do today. It is precisely because the right to instruction in the language of the minority and the concomitant right to administer structures are protected by the Constitution Act, 1982 that it is possible for the Quebec government to propose that denominational rights no longer apply within the province.

3. *Support for the proposed amendment*

It is certainly preferable that a proposed constitutional amendment garner the support of the population in question, including minorities if they are affected.

Not that minorities are always right. (By that logic, we would still be under the sway of aristocrats!). But Members of Parliament are duty bound to be guided by a favourable bias towards minorities. This principle applies to constitutional matters in particular, for constitutional democracies exist to protect individual rights as well as minority rights. At least, that is the Liberal government's vision of Canada.

In the matter before us, the Government of Canada notes the unanimous vote in the National Assembly and the existence of a reasonably broad consensus, which includes members of all components of Quebec society.

Some Catholics are opposed to the amendment but their bishops do not object to it. Some groups from the Anglophone community would have liked the National Assembly to take this opportunity to strengthen the linguistic minority's constitutional rights. This is, to be sure, a noble objective. The Government of Canada would welcome with open arms any province that wanted to strengthen the rights of its linguistic minority and become an example to the other provinces. We did not demand of the province of New Brunswick that the other provinces adhere to official bilingualism before agreeing to New Brunswick's request to entrench the equal status of its own two linguistic communities in the Constitution in 1993. Our passion for equality must never be synonymous with the lowest common denominator.

However, the fact that a constitutional amendment does not strengthen a minority is not a sufficient reason to object to it. The important thing is that the amendment not infringe on this minority's rights and that it garner a reasonable level of support in the minority community.

The broader the consensus, the easier it will be to implement the constitutional amendment under the right conditions. The Government of Canada believes that the Parliamentary Committee it intends to form could provide an opportunity to broaden the consensus. The important issues raised by the amendment will be studied within a parliamentary framework, in accordance with the democratic culture that Quebecers share with other Canadians. A variety of experts, groups and citizens could thus be given the opportunity to express their points of view and to listen to the responses of their Members of Parliament.

In order to match speed with due parliamentary procedure, this will be a Joint Committee, enabling MPs and Senators to do their work simultaneously.

Conclusion

The Government is of the view that the proposed constitutional amendment we have received from the National Assembly falls within the class of bilateral amendments provided for in Section 43 of the

Constitution Act, 1982. The Government believes that this amendment should be passed expeditiously, in accordance with parliamentary procedure, for it will have positive consequences for Quebec society, including both of its linguistic communities.

Quebec society has succeeded in reaching a consensus on a constitutional issue which touches upon the vital issues of schooling, language and religion. This demonstrates the remarkable nature of Quebec society and the extent to which it contributes, in its way, to Canada's greatness.

Amendment of Term 17 of the Terms of Union of Newfoundland with Canada (Newfoundland Schools)

A Section 43 amendment

Mr. Speaker, today I have the pleasure of introducing a resolution to authorize a bilateral amendment to Term 17 of Newfoundland's Terms of Union with Canada.

Newfoundland's Terms of Union form part of the Constitution of Canada. Section 43 of the Constitution Act, 1982 provides for an amendment to the Constitution of Canada in relation to any provision that applies to one or more, but not all, provinces. Such an amendment may be made by proclamation issued by the Governor General under the Great Seal of Canada, where so authorized by resolutions of the Senate and House of Commons and of the legislative assembly of each province to which the amendment applies.

On September 5, 1997, the Newfoundland House of Assembly unanimously adopted a resolution authorizing certain amendments to Term 17 of its Terms of Union, which will only apply to Newfoundland. The amendment will have no legal application or effect on education or denominational minorities in other provinces. In keeping with established practice, the Speaker of the Newfoundland House of Assembly conveyed to the Clerk of the Privy Council a certified copy of the resolution, which was received on September 8, 1997.

Our role and responsibility as parliamentarians is to consider the proposed amendment and to decide whether to approve it. As I have already indicated on several occasions, Mr. Speaker, the Government of Canada supports the proposed amendment, which will allow Newfoundland to proceed with major reforms to its education system.

Following many years of rancorous and divisive debate in Newfoundland over the role of the churches and religion in education, it is the Government's view that the proposed amendment strikes a workable balance. In Newfoundland, the proposed amendment appears to

---

Speech in the House of Commons

enjoy a high level of consensus, including a reasonable degree of support from affected minorities. The Government bases its assessment in part on the House of Assembly's unanimous endorsement of the amendment resolution, and on the results of the provincial referendum in which 73% of voters approved a proposal to reform the education system.

Nevertheless, the Government of Canada is of the view that any attempt to alter entrenched minority rights should be marked by processes that are fair and thorough. To this end, the Government is striking a special joint committee to examine Newfoundland's resolution to amend Term 17. It is our belief that the hearings will help to enhance public input and understanding of the proposed amendment.

Moreover, the committee's work will aid Parliament in making its independent assessment on the facts of the case and on the merits and appropriateness of the proposed amendment.

The proposed amendment to Term 17

Mr. Speaker, as you and our colleagues will recall, this is the second time in less than two years that Parliament has been asked to consider an amendment to Term 17 of Newfoundland's Terms of Union. While this situation may seem unusual, the Constitution does not set any limits on how often legislatures may seek constitutional amendments. It is up to Parliament and the provincial legislature to which the amendment applies to determine the appropriateness of each proposed constitutional change.

To understand fully the circumstances which have given rise to this second amendment proposal it is necessary to briefly review the provisions of Term 17. It is also helpful to reexamine the extensive efforts that have been made over the past seven years to reform the education system in Newfoundland.

In lieu of section 93 of the Constitution Act, 1867, constitutional authority for education in Newfoundland was set out in Term 17 of the province's 1949 Terms of Union with Canada. Term 17 granted six denominations the right to operate their own publicly-funded schools. In 1987, Term 17 was amended to extend denominational school rights to the Pentecostal Assemblies. These seven denominations operated four separate schools systems: the Integrated School System (Anglican, Presbyterian, Salvation Army and United Church), the Pentecostal Schools System, the Roman Catholic School System and the Seventh Day Adventist Schools System.

In 1990, the Government of Newfoundland and Labrador appointed Dr. Len Williams, a former teacher, principal and president of the provincial teachers' association, and current university professor, to chair a Royal Commission on educational reform. The Commission was asked "to obtain an impartial assessment of the existing education system and to seek an appropriate vision for change."

The 1992 Report of the Williams' Royal Commission recommended the reorganization of the education system in Newfoundland and Labrador to permit government to administer the system in a more efficient manner. The Commission proposed the creation of a single "interdenominational" school system encompassing the four separate denominational systems in operation at the time.

Initially, the Government of Newfoundland sought to achieve this change through non-constitutional negotiations with denominational leaders. When nearly three years of discussions failed to achieve an agreement, the Government of Newfoundland sought educational reform through a constitutional amendment to Term 17 of its Terms of Union.

But the amendment that Newfoundland sought, and which was authorized by this House and proclaimed by the Governor General on April 21, 1997, represented a compromise. The amendment would not have eliminated all single denominational schools. The amendment was designed to provide the Newfoundland House of Assembly with additional powers to organize and administer public education through a system of "interdenominational" schools, while retaining the rights of Roman Catholics and Pentecostals to "unidenominational" schools under certain conditions. These conditions were to be set out in provincial legislation that was equally applicable to all schools, either unidenominational or interdenominational.

However, the attempt to legislatively implement the new Term 17 under a revised Schools Act was successfully challenged in the Newfoundland Supreme Court. On July 8, 1997, Mr. Justice Leo Barry granted representatives of the Roman Catholic and Pentecostal churches a temporary injunction halting the entire educational reform process. In Justice Barry's view, the new Schools Act favoured interdenominational over uni-denominational schools. Therefore, he found that a trial judge would likely find that the legislation was contrary to the amended Term 17, which required that interdenominational and unidenominational (i.e., Roman Catholic and Pentecostal) schools be given equal treatment.

As even Mr. Justice Barry acknowledged and anticipated, the injunction resulted in a "significant disruption" for teachers, principals and students who had been reassigned to different schools on the basis of the new schools legislation. It also resulted in the reopening of some schools and the re-hiring of some teachers who had been laid off following certain school closures and redesignation. For the Government of Newfoundland, and citizens who thought the divisive education debate was behind them, the injunction raised many questions and a great deal of uncertainty about the future structure of the school system.

The Government of Newfoundland filed an appeal, but did not pursue the matter. Instead, on July 31, 1997, Premier Tobin announced in a province-wide telecast that he would hold a referendum on September 2 to secure a mandate to amend Term 17 once again. Premier Tobin explained that for five years the provincial government, school boards, the teachers' association, the churches, parents and students, "have all been engaged in what seems to be a never ending debate about how to reconcile the need for reform of our education system with the rights of the denominations in the education system."

While not referring specifically to the injunction blocking educational reform, Premier Tobin argued that: "During the last five years, we've seen every attempt to reconcile these two ideas ... education reform and denominational rights end in more confusion and more conflict."

Consequently, Premier Tobin decided to go to the people once again to seek a mandate for an amendment to Term 17. The purpose of that amendment, which we are asked to consider, is to create a single, publicly funded and administered school system. The brief text of this Term 17 amendment, which only contains three clauses, is plain and clear and states that:

(1) In lieu of section ninety-three of the Constitution Act, 1867, this section shall apply in respect of the Province of Newfoundland.
(2) In and for the Province of Newfoundland, the Legislature shall have exclusive authority to make laws in relation to education, but shall provide for courses in religion that are not specific to a religious denomination.
(3) Religious observances shall be permitted in a school where requested by parents.

Support for the proposed amendment

The proposed amendment, which constitutes a major restructuring of Newfoundland's education system, is supported by a substantial majority of the province's population and enjoys a fair degree of support from affected minorities.

In addition, the House of Assembly gave the resolution unanimous approval on September 5.

In considering this amendment, the Government has sought to ensure that its process is thorough and gives due respect to affected minorities. You will recall, Mr. Speaker, that the issue of minority rights was not central to the Government's consideration of the previous Term 17 amendment. The old Term 17 granted certain rights to seven denominations representing 95% of the population. However, following the amendment to Term 17, the Integrated Group (Anglican, Presbyterian, Salvation Army and United Church) became one majority class of persons comprising 52% of the population. The Roman Catholics became a sizable minority of 37%. The Pentecostals are a minority of 7%.

Given this amendment's impact on minority rights, a mere 50+1 referendum majority would not have been sufficient or adequate in measuring the degree of consensus among affected Roman Catholics and Pentecostals. But the referendum did not result in a narrow majority: it was an overwhelming majority of 73%, which provided evidence of minority support. The proposal carried in 47 of Newfoundland's 48 electoral districts.

Voter turn-out was 53%, but given the high probability that opponents of the education reform proposal were most likely to vote, the results send a clear message that there is substantial support for this amendment.

Analysis indicates that in heavily Roman Catholic areas, the proposal was supported by a majority. The St. George's Bay region, which is 74% Roman Catholic, voted 59% Yes. The Avalon Peninsula, which is 48.5% Roman Catholic, voted 72% Yes. Coincidentally, the Burin Peninsula is also 48.5% Roman Catholic and it also voted 72% Yes. Approximately 75% of all Roman Catholics in Newfoundland and Labrador reside in these three regions.

It is difficult to assess accurately the exact degree to which members of the smaller Pentecostal community supported the proposed amendment. However, in the four electoral districts where Pentecostals are most heavily concentrated, the resolution carried with majorities of 57% to 64%.

Moreover, on September 5, the four members of the Pentecostal faith who sit in the Newfoundland House of Assembly, and represent districts with significant Pentecostal populations, joined their colleagues in unanimously supporting the resolution to amend Term 17.

Indeed, in assessing the proposed amendment, Parliamentarians should accord due respect to the fact that all of the members of the House of Assembly voted in favour of the resolution to amend Term 17. This included all Catholic and Pentecostal members who had campaigned for the No side and voted No in the provincial referendum.

The overwhelming support the amendment received in the referendum and the House of Assembly represents a clear consensus that appears to include a reasonable measure of support from the affected minorities. Parliament should interpret this as a clear signal that the population of Newfoundland and Labrador wants to proceed expeditiously to reform its education system in a manner that is fair to all.

The merits of the proposed amendment

In the midst of the confusion that resulted following the injunction halting the implementation of the 1997 Term 17 amendment and after years of debate over educational reform and the role of the churches, Newfoundlanders want to move on. And the results of the referendum and the unanimous vote of the House of Assembly indicate that they feel the proposed amendment strikes a fair and workable balance that allows reform to proceed.

The proposed Term 17 clearly states that education is a matter of exclusive provincial jurisdiction. However, the amendment will not take religion out of the schools. The new Term 17 contains a mandatory provision that guarantees that "courses in religion" must be taught and "religious observances" must be "permitted in schools where requested by parents."

Correspondingly, the Term will not require children to attend religious observances or classes if their parents object. This interpretation is supported by the legal opinions of two eminent lawyers, well-known constitutional expert Mr. Ian Binnie, and former federal Justice Minister, the Honourable John Crosbie.

The Government acknowledges that the Newfoundland and Labrador Roman Catholic bishops and the leadership of the Pentecostal church have concerns about the new amendment. However, we feel the Government of Newfoundland is demonstrating a spirit of openness with regard to a continued role, albeit non-constitutional, for the churches.

In anticipation of the Term 17 amendment's adoption, the Newfoundland Department of Education has begun setting up a consultative process for developing the new religious education curriculum. Although there is no requirement to do so, the Department of Education has indicated that this process will seek representations from the province's various denominations.

Conclusion

In the future, should another province come forward with a proposed change to its terms of union or to section 93, it will be up to Parliament to make its own assessment on the facts of that case and on the merits and appropriateness of the proposed amendment. Parliament will also wish to carefully assess whether the amendment enjoys a reasonable degree of support from the citizens affected by it.

In the case before the House, the Government of Newfoundland and Labrador has, under section 43, properly authorized an amendment to Term 17 that will only apply to that province.

The Government of Canada believes that the amendment is appropriate. We believe it enjoys adequate support from affected citizens, including minorities. And we believe that it merits Parliament's support and ultimate approval.

However, the joint committee and individual parliamentarians will have to make their own assessment of this amendment, which will allow Newfoundland to carry out necessary and long-sought educational reforms.

The Decentralized Nature of
the Canadian Federation

OTTAWA, MARCH 25, 1998

"We tend to forget that in reality Canada is highly decentralized."

Jacques Parizeau[1]

In another life, when I was a political science professor at the Université de Montréal, I conducted various studies on federal public administration. I remember discovering, along with my colleague Jacques Bourgault, a professor at the Université du Québec à Montréal, that the University of Ottawa had become the main breeding ground of deputy ministers. More of our senior public servants have graduated from your university than from any other. So you can imagine how nervous I am to be here today, facing so many future servants of the nation.

And I'm all the more nervous because my topic today is, precisely, the federal government, and more broadly, the federation as a whole. In effect, I essentially have two things to say to you today.

First of all, our federation is decentralized. That is very clear when you compare it with the other major federations. And that's a good thing, by the way. Such a large and diversified country as Canada could not function other than under a very advanced federative form. It is a good thing that we have strong provinces, and I am a great admirer of "the provincial state", if I may use such an expression. Each province can try out solutions that are specific to its own culture and its own context, and through healthy emulation, learn from the others. At the same time, however, the provinces cannot behave as ten inward-looking republics, and there are broader responsibilities that are the purview of a federal government. That's why it's also a good thing that we have a federal government that is strong in its areas of jurisdiction, and consistent, sustained relations between the two orders of government.

Second, the federal government and the provinces have greatly improved the federation in the past two years. The objective of these reforms has been to clarify the roles of and strengthen cooperation

---

Speech at the University of Ottawa

between the two orders of government. This federation serves us well and compares favourably with other federations in many respects, but it is far from perfect. It will always be changing. Prime Minister Jean Chrétien is determined to continue improving our federation, step by step, in a spirit of cooperation.

Why do I want to talk about these two things today? Once again, I have two reasons. For one thing, it so happens that there is a government in my province that is proposing secession, alleging, among other things, that the Canadian federation is too centralized. For example, in a press conference on December 10, 1997, Premier Lucien Bouchard expressed fears about the provinces being reduced to [translation] "a sort of sterile entity that would not even be a large municipality". His Finance Minister, Mr. Bernard Landry, said on February 24, 1998, that he was witnessing the [translation] "spectacle of a once confederate and then federal state that is moving toward a unitary state." The way the separatist leaders describe the Canadian federation is, in my opinion, completely surreal. I'd like to explain why.

For another thing, I believe that we have to be fair to our federation, and not talk about it only when there are problems. Tensions and conflicts between orders of government are normal. That exists in all federations. It is also normal, I suppose, that these conflicts get more headlines than do the agreements that are regularly reached by governments. But allow me, as Canada's Minister of Intergovernmental Affairs, to say here today that this federation works, and it's getting better.

1. A decentralized federation

The statement by Bernard Landry that I mentioned a moment ago to the effect that the Canada of 1867 had been conceived as a very decentralized confederation, where the provinces retained most of the major public responsibilities, is a very widespread myth. I believe this confusion stems in large part from the word "confederation" itself, which evokes an association of sovereign states. In fact, in our case, confederation signified the act of federating. And the people who designed that federation meant it to be centralized. John A. Macdonald, as you know, would even have preferred a legislative union. It was the delegates from Canada East (Quebec) and the Maritime provinces who, very fortunately, pressed for the federal choice.

This compromise among the Fathers of Confederation put in place a system that was designed to be centralized, in which the federal government was to keep the provinces in check through its right to disallow their laws. The federal government inherited the main fields of taxation and most of the public responsibilities then deemed important, including those of an economic nature. Since it effected two-thirds of public spending, it dominated the provinces, two-thirds of whose funding depended on federal subsidies. (*The Rowell-Sirois Report*, vol. 1 [Toronto, McClelland and Stewart, 1963], p. 188).

Today's Canada no longer bears any resemblance to that centralism. The Judicial Committee of the Privy Council and later the Supreme Court of Canada have interpreted the Constitution in a way that respects the autonomy of the provinces. The power of disallowance and the power of reservation are no longer used. The emergence and development of the welfare state have considerably expanded provincial jurisdictions relating to education, health and social affairs. In 1960, federal spending was twice that of the provinces and municipalities combined; today, it is lower overall.

So, the Canadian federation is decentralized compared with what it was in the past. But is it decentralized when compared with other federations today? Experts on comparative federalism say that it is. Professor Edmond Orban of the Université de Montréal concluded in his study for the Bélanger-Campeau Commission that [translation] "the [Canadian] provinces enjoy relatively greater autonomy and, in the case of the larger provinces, relatively greater opportunities than do the [German] Länder and, in particular, the Swiss cantons."

I can illustrate this comparison between federations with an example especially dear to the heart of Mr. Bernard Landry: the Canada Prenatal Nutrition Program. On February 24, he exclaimed: [translation] "Just imagine, in this era of the principle of subsidiarity, the era of building large-scale economic agreements, the era in which Canada is boasting of its membership in the G-7 (...), it is infiltrating prenatal care." When you describe it like that, it conjures up mental images of federal bureaucrats wandering the streets handing out pints of milk! But what's the real story?

The Canada Prenatal Nutrition Program is designed to protect the health of babies of mothers deemed at risk. It was established in 1992 – by the Conservatives, then, so you can see how nonpartisan I am. The program is implemented in a province only if the federal government signs a memorandum of understanding with the government of that province. The agreement can be cancelled at any time at the request of either party. And guess which province was the first to sign such an agreement: that's right, Quebec. Federal funding is used on the basis of priorities and programs established by the Government of Quebec.

Now, where did the idea for this program come from? From a similar initiative by the United States federal government: the Special Supplemental Food Program for Women, Infants and Children. That's United States as in federation, as in G-7 country.

In fact, on a recent fact-finding mission to Europe, I was struck by how much control Canadian provinces exercise in the health care field in comparison with their counterparts in other federations.

In Belgium, for example, the federal government is entirely responsible for setting policy in the health sector. In Germany, health is an area of shared jurisdiction, but the Länder cannot legislate in this field if the federal government has already done so. In Austria, the federal government remains constitutionally responsible for both legislation and implementation of most health care measures. In Switzerland, federal legislation sets very detailed standards that must be respected by each canton.

Here at home, health care falls largely under provincial jurisdiction. The federal government acts essentially through its spending power, which is based on a clear constitutional foundation, as the courts have confirmed. Incidentally, all major federations have a federal spending power. With regard to health care, our federal government ties its financial assistance to the provinces' adherence to just five standards, which are in fact moral principles popular throughout the country: universality, accessibility, comprehensiveness, portability, and public administration. The objective is to protect our health care system from a process of Americanization that would make it less accessible for everyone.

In making this comparison with other federations, I do not wish to suggest that we toe the line of other federations and give the federal government certain provincial responsibilities for health. Nor do I claim that everything is perfect in our federal-provincial relations with respect to health policy. I am merely saying that the current arrangement is in no way a centralizing straitjacket; quite the opposite is true.

The way in which our provinces and the federal government work together certainly has something to do with Canada's being ranked fourth for the health of its population and second for the quality of its medical practices (British *Economist* Intelligence Unit, 1997). At the same time, however, Canadians see that our health care system is under tremendous pressure at this time, even though we are one of the countries that earmark the greatest part of their collective wealth for health care. More than ever, our governments face the challenge of coming up with ways to work together while respecting their jurisdictions.

Let me take another example from the headlines that places our federation in a comparative perspective: the Millennium Scholarships. The federal government has decided to establish a private foundation and provide it with initial funding of $2.5 billion over ten years, to give scholarships to low- and middle-income students. The federal government is committed to consulting the provincial governments to ensure that the foundation avoids duplication, uses existing provincial needs assessment mechanisms, and has the power to contract with the provincial authorities to select recipients. Moreover, Canada's Council of Ministers of Education will play a key role in determining the foundation's directors.

The Government of Quebec is understandably concerned about the risk of duplication. Indeed, that province has developed a very complete scholarships program since it exercised its right to opt out with financial compensation in this field in 1964. So the governments need to talk and find a solution to help each other help students.

But while the Government of Quebec's concerns are understandable, it is completely unjustified for Quebec's Finance Minister to see the establishment of this foundation as the hallmark [translation] "of a unitary state that pays no heed to federal structures". For what can be said of other federations? In the United States, 75% of public financial assistance to students comes from the federal government (United States College Board). In Germany, it's 65% (Ulrich Teichler, in Higher Education in Federal Systems, Douglas Brown, Pierre Cazalis and Gilles Jasmin, eds.). In Australia and Austria, legislative authority for postsecondary education lies with the federal government. In Switzerland, federal legislation to assist universities is very complete and detailed. In Canada, education is an area of exclusive provincial jurisdiction under the Constitution. The federal government does not legislate with respect to education. Nevertheless, financial assistance to give Canadians better access to provincial educational institutions has long been a field in which both orders of government are active. That joint action is more necessary than ever in today's knowledge economy, where the competitiveness of our work force is the key to maintaining our quality of life.

I could give even further examples of the decentralized nature of our federation. But I will merely add here that all federations have a federal spending power, but only in our federation is there a right to opt out with financial compensation. I might also refer you to research by Professor Watts of Queen's University, which indicates that the Canadian provinces are unquestionably less dependent on conditional transfers from the federal government than are the components of other comparable federations, and that our federal government clearly attaches the fewest conditions to its intergovernmental transfers. Canada is not the champion of decentralization in everything, but the fact is that, in the very real world of federations, there is doubtless nothing more autonomous than a Canadian province.

2. *Our federation after two years of change*

It is in the nature of our federation to be continually evolving. The status quo does not exist. Governments must simply ensure that this change takes place with respect for the constitutional jurisdiction of all and with the objective of a better quality of service to benefit citizens. In my opinion, the federal government hasn't done too badly in working with the provinces since the Liberal government was elected in October 1993, especially since the Throne Speech of February 27, 1996. Why don't you be the judge:

Limiting the federal spending power. The unilateral use of the federal spending power can undermine the provinces' ability to set priorities. Therefore, in the 1996 Speech from the Throne, the Government of Canada stated that it will no longer use its spending power to create new shared-cost programs in areas of exclusive provincial jurisdiction without the consent of the majority of provinces. Moreover, any new shared-cost program in an area of exclusive provincial jurisdiction will be designed so that provinces that exercise their right to opt out are compensated, provided they establish equivalent or comparable programs. The Government of Canada is the only federal government that has voluntarily placed limits on the use of its spending power in this way, and the only one with such an arrangement for opting out with compensation. Although this commitment is not entrenched in the Constitution, it goes further than the Meech Lake Accord, which did not require the agreement of a majority of the provinces.

Passage of the Act respecting constitutional amendments (C-110). The Government tabled Bill C-110 on regional vetoes. No constitutional amendment can be tabled in Parliament and passed without the consent of each of the following regions: Atlantic Canada, Quebec, Ontario, the Prairies, and British Columbia.

Adoption of the distinct society resolution. The Government tabled a resolution in the House of Commons recognizing Quebec as a distinct society in Canada that includes a French-speaking majority, a unique culture and a civil law tradition. In the resolution, which was adopted on December 11, 1995, the House and the Government committed themselves to be guided by this reality.

Reduced conditionality of the main federal transfer to the provinces. The replacement of the Canada Assistance Plan (CAP) and Established Programs Financing (EPF) with the Canada Health and Social Transfer in 1995 has given the provinces greater flexibility. The provinces must continue to respect the five national health care standards and the non-imposition of residency requirements for social assistance. In other respects, they choose to utilize funding in accordance with their own priorities on health care, post-secondary education and social assistance.

Clarification of roles in various fields. To eliminate unnecessary duplication, the federal government has largely withdrawn from the sectors of mining and forest development, recreation and tourism. The Canadian Tourism Commission is building on its partnerships with the provinces and businesses. The federal government is also negotiating the transfer of the administration of social housing to the provinces; five agreements have been signed to date.

The new job training agreements. The federal government has now signed job training agreements with nine provinces and both territories. The agreements allow the provincial or territorial governments either to assume full responsibility for training measures funded through the Employment Insurance account or to develop a new co-management partnership with the federal government. Unemployed Canadians and those seeking to upgrade their skills will have "one stop shopping" for their training needs, thus fostering the additional objective of making services more responsive to citizens' needs.

The National Child Benefit System. At their request, the federal government developed this major initiative jointly with the provincial governments. The federal government will increase the value of child tax credits, allowing provinces to redirect resources toward new programs to assist low-income families and promote entry into the workforce. At a recent meeting of ministers responsible for social services, a number of provinces presented their planned reinvestment initiatives. In the last budget, the federal government committed to a second contribution of $850 million to the System during the present mandate.

Environmental harmonization. On January 29, 1998, the governments of Canada and all the provinces but Quebec signed an agreement to improve cooperation between governments so as to guarantee better environmental quality and the implementation of subsidiary agreements on establishing national standards, inspection and environmental assessment. The initiative includes a "one-stop shopping" approach, under which each order of government will look after the activities it is best positioned to handle, in an effort to eliminate overlap and achieve better results in this field.

Harmonizing federal laws with the new Quebec Civil Code. To capitalize on the bijural character of our country, the Government of Canada has decided to harmonize its laws with the new Quebec Civil Code adopted on January 1, 1994. A bill will be tabled in the House of Commons by June 1998.

Agreement on internal trade liberalization. The Agreement on Internal Trade, which came into effect on July 1, 1995, is designed to reduce barriers to interprovincial trade and improve trade among the provinces. Ministers responsible for internal trade met in Ottawa on February 20 and, with the exception of British Columbia and Yukon, signed an agreement on provisions for expanding the government procurement chapter to the MASH sector (municipalities, municipal bodies, school commissions and boards, higher education bodies, government-funded health services or social services).

Infrastructure Program. The infrastructure program is a good example of the Government of Canada's willingness to work in partnership with the provinces and municipalities to address the expectations and needs of Canadians. Because this program was such a resounding success in our first term, it has now been renewed. By March 31, 1999, $8 billion will have been spent under this program.

The Team Canada formula. Team Canada was created in 1994 as a unique partnership in which the Government of Canada, the provinces, the territories and municipalities pool their resources to work together with businesses and help more Canadians succeed on world markets. The "Team Canada" formula and the trade missions that apply the principles of that formula remain a core component of our job strategy.

The Canada Pension Plan. Population aging is a phenomenon Canada intends to be better prepared for than other industrialized countries. The Government of Canada and eight provinces have reached agreement on changes to guarantee the viability of the Canada Pension Plan (CPP), so that the Plan does not lack funding and contribution rates never reach 14.2%, as they would if nothing were done. Legislation has been passed to establish the contribution rate increases, implement a new investment policy, and make minor changes to benefits.

The constitutional amendment for Quebec school boards. This constitutional amendment will enable the Government of Quebec to modernize its education system and establish linguistic school boards. Thanks to the Constitution Act, 1982, this amendment could be effected bilaterally.

The constitutional amendment for Newfoundland school boards. The amendment to Term 17 of the Newfoundland Terms of Union will make it possible to secularize Newfoundland's school board system, a request made by the provincial government following a province-wide referendum on September 2, 1997.

Social policy reform. The Government of Canada is committed to working with the provinces to develop a more concerted approach to social policy reform. In June 1996, the governments set up the Ministerial Council on Social Policy Renewal, a forum in which they can discuss the best ways to modernize and assure the viability of Canada's social programs. The Government and all the provinces except Quebec also agreed at the last First Ministers' Meeting to begin negotiations on an eventual framework agreement on the social union based on respect for the constitutional jurisdictions of each order of government and cooperation between federal and provincial partners with respect to planning and managing the Canadian social union.

Support for the Calgary Declaration. The Calgary Declaration of September 14, 1997, which was made by the nine premiers who believe in a united Canada, sets out fundamental values that can unite Canadians. It recognizes the equality of citizens, the equality of status of the provinces, Canada's diversity as expressed by its Aboriginal populations, its two official languages and its multicultural character, as well as the unique character of Quebec society. Public consultations on the declaration have been conducted in every province except Quebec. It has now been adopted in every provincial legislature except British Columbia, Ontario and Nova Scotia.

Conclusion

I have just listed 17 changes achieved or underway, many of which have been initiated in the past two years. I believe that this is an impressive list of achievements. But the question is whether it is a list of disparate, unrelated elements, or whether some consistency can be found in the whole. In my opinion, the latter is true. There is an inherent logic in the improvements that have been made to our federation in the past two years. That logic is no better expressed than in the seventh principle of the Calgary Declaration: "Canada is a federal system where federal, provincial, and territorial governments work in partnership while respecting each other's jurisdictions. Canadians want their governments to work cooperatively and with flexibility to ensure the efficiency and effectiveness of the federation. Canadians want their governments to work together particularly in the delivery of their social programs. Provinces and territories renew their commitment to work in partnership with the Government of Canada to best serve the needs of Canadians."

This is the key: what the most recent constitutional platform of the Quebec Liberal Party calls "an inevitable relation of interdependence" between governments, while respecting their jurisdictions. (*Recognition and Interdependence*, p. 44). We are no longer in the 19th century, when the financial weight of the public sector as a whole was marginal in the economy. It now accounts for almost half of the economy, so that government jurisdictions meet in almost all activity sectors. The success of modern federalism lies in interdependence and clearly defined roles.

And that, after all, is what Canadians want, including Quebecers. The majority of them do not want much more centralization or much more decentralization; they want better cooperation between their governments, if the polls are anything to go by. (CROP/Insight, October 1996; CROP, March 1997; EKOS, November 1997) That said, there will always be conflicts between governments. But the consequences are not always negative. Federations draw their energy from a sort of ongoing tension. It sometimes makes life difficult for politicians and bureaucrats, but citizens benefit from it. The reason the smart money is on the federative form of government is that it is easier to find solutions when disagreements are out in the open, among constitutional partners, than in the rarefied atmosphere of huge centralized bureaucracies that weigh down unitary countries.

So we need to seek cooperation and put in place effective conflict resolution mechanisms. Above all, we need to be fair to our federation and appreciate it for what it is: a decentralized federation that works well. Canada is not a perpetual constitutional dispute, it is a principle of caring, one of the greatest that humanity has invented. It is thanks to the federative form that Canada has developed, that different populations, speaking different languages and not always sharing the same cultural references, have been able to unite around common objectives and attain one of the best qualities of life. We must remain together and improve further this decentralized and generous federation that is our common achievement.

NOTE

1 From a speech delivered at the University of Edinburgh, reported in the *Globe and Mail* on December 9, 1997.

Zero Deficit: Our Common Objective

SAINTE-THÉRÈSE, MAY 20, 1998

My topic today is public finances. Yes, you heard correctly, I didn't say: my topic today is the Constitution. Don't get too excited, though: both topics can be pretty dry. But not so long ago, when I was teaching public finances at university, my students found that I was able to make it interesting. Let's see if I have the same success with an audience of businesspeople, who know a thing or two about this very subject.

I am not only the Constitution minister. In fact, as Intergovernmental Affairs Minister, I assist my Government colleagues in everything that affects how the federation works, including fiscal federalism. I have also been given the mandate by Prime Minister Jean Chrétien to advise the Government on Canadian unity. And on that very point, I feel that the link between public finances and Canadian unity has not been highlighted enough.

After explaining how I see that link, I'll look at one specific aspect in greater detail, namely the less agreeable aspect of the cost of political uncertainty. But first, let me set the stage by reviewing the state of Canada's public finances.

I hope that after this presentation it will be clear that a zero deficit, or at least getting our public finances in better shape, is the common objective of all Canadians, and that we will have a better chance of achieving that goal if we resolutely decide to stay together.

Putting public finances in order

We Canadians want both freedom and comfort; we want to ally individual initiative and social solidarity, to combine the best of the United States and Europe. But we are not in Europe, we are in North America, neighbours of a giant that is fiercely competitive in cultural, economic, fiscal and monetary terms. In that context, and in light of our ambitions in terms of both quality of life and social justice, we need to

---

Speech at La chambre de commerce de Thérèse-De Blainville

manage our public finances very prudently. Without that discipline, we will not have the means of our ambitions, and poverty and social distress will continue to plague us.

We have been lacking in budgetary discipline in our recent history, and we have paid the price. We have had to undergo a difficult process of putting our financial house in order. While it is still too early to proclaim victory, the progress we have made so far is impressive.

In 1993–1994, the combined deficit of the federal and provincial governments, as calculated by the Department of Finance, was C$62 billion, or 8.6% of our gross domestic product (GDP). The OECD pegged our deficit as the 7th highest of 22 industrialized countries. That was the situation just a few years ago. In comparison, in 1998, Canada is the only country to have balanced its budget, again according to OECD projections. We can see that we have made progress.

Cutting the deficit was done by both orders of government. The federal government's deficit has been eliminated, while five provinces have succeeded in balancing their budget or achieving a surplus, three have only a small deficit, Ontario is proceeding with tax cuts, and Quebec is continuing on its path to a zero deficit. In 1993–1994, all ten provinces were in the red.

Canadians have had to make sacrifices to achieve that result. Our greatest achievement is that we have done so while maintaining the essential components of our social programs, containing inflation, kick-starting jobs and growth, and keeping the tax burden on the economy below the average for OECD countries. Winning the fight against the deficit has helped to lower interest rates, a key condition for growth.

Between 1994 and 1997, Canada's GDP grew by 2.9% a year on average, the strongest performance of the G-7 and putting us in 14th place of the 29 OECD countries. Average annual employment growth was 1.8%, the best performance (on a par with the United States) of the G-7 countries and in 9th place among OECD countries. The unemployment rate dropped from 11.4% in September 1993 to 8.4% in April 1998, the lowest it has been in Canada since August 1990. Some 543,000 jobs have been created since the beginning of 1997. On the whole, this is a remarkable performance for a country that, during the same period, eliminated one of the worst deficits in the industrialized countries. Now that our finances are in order, the prospects are very encouraging: the OECD forecasts that we will have the strongest economic growth of G-7 countries for 1998 and 1999.

This financial house cleaning has put Canada in the best position to face the major economic and social challenges of the new century. And those challenges are urgent, be it creating jobs, alleviating poverty, improving our health system, or becoming more competitive. The last

Martin budget reflects that concern to step up our efforts in these sectors, but without going on a spending frenzy.

What we need to do now is stay disciplined. Tax cuts and new spending measures must be effectively targeted. We mustn't forget that the Canadian public sector as a whole is $806 billion in debt, $583 billion for the federal government and $223 billion for the provinces. Our total public debt is equal to 97% of our GDP for the 1997–1998 fiscal year. That's one of the highest total debt to GDP ratios among the OECD countries, behind only Italy, Belgium and Greece.

This year, 29 cents out of every tax dollar you send to Ottawa will go to servicing the debt. For every dollar you send to Quebec City, 18 cents will go for debt servicing. If we don't bring the debt under control, those ratios will remain too high and will hamper for too long our flexibility for program financing and reducing the tax burden for Canadians.

The budget surpluses some provinces and the federal government are showing are too valuable to squander on short-term priorities. The economic upheaval in Asia reminds us that an economic slowdown is always possible; natural disasters, which seem to be more frequent nowadays, are very costly; and the Auditor General is calling on us to plan our finances more effectively in connection with the aging population. We will need healthy public finances to deal with all these long-term phenomena, and with many others besides. And more than ever, we will need a united Canada.

Public finances and Canadian unity

I am convinced that Quebecers' opinion of the Canadian economy influences their opinion on Canadian unity. It's not the only factor that influences their judgment, but it's certainly a factor.

The difficult post-Meech Lake constitutional debates coincided with an economic recession that hit eastern North America in the early 1990s. Many Quebecers began to doubt not only their own place within Canada, but Canada itself. With unemployment skyrocketing, public finances increasingly awash in red ink and the *Wall Street Journal* calling us a candidate for the Third World, many Quebecers concluded that Canada was an economic basket case. "Canada doesn't work any more," it was often said.

"Studies" were evoked showing that the federation was costing us "billions of dollars" in unnecessary duplication between the orders of government. Those notorious studies were trumped-up, to be sure, but many of our fellow citizens swallowed them hook, line and sinker. "Show us the studies," Jacques Parizeau challenged Daniel Johnson in the 1994 election campaign TV debate. But once he was in power, Mr. Parizeau found only a pile of documents that proved absolutely nothing.

Now that our economic and financial recovery has won us the admiration of other countries, which describe it as a sort of miracle ("the maple leaf miracle", according to *Business Week*, or the "top dog" of the G-7, according to the *Financial Times*), Quebecers, and other Canadians as well, are regaining confidence in Canada.

Things must be looked at in the proper perspective: Canada was not "bankrupt" in the early 1990s, but it was starting down a very slippery slope. Like many other countries, we were the ones that had got ourselves in trouble, and we were the ones that had to get ourselves out of it. We have been able to regain our discipline and capitalize on the enviable assets our union gives us.

Do you know of many countries that have as much potential as Canada? Look at our openness to the world, with our two official languages that are international languages, our multicultural population that gives us a foothold on every continent, and our geographic position between Europe, the United States and Asia. As businesspeople, you know how much belonging to Canada opens doors for you.

But did you know that the World Economic Forum now ranks Canada fourth (out of 53 countries) for our competitiveness, or that the World Banks ranks us third (out of 92 countries) for the abundance of our natural resources, or that the Institute for Management Development ranks us second out of 46 countries for the quality of our human resources and sixth for the quality of our infrastructure?

An independent Quebec would not have the same potential. Oh sure, it would be "viable". But we Quebecers, like other Canadians, have great ambitions for our quality of life. We too aspire to nothing less than the best of Europe and the United States. To make that aspiration a reality and beat back unemployment and poverty, we must depend on the potential of the resources and talents that Canada comprises.

All of Canada belongs to us, and to all Canadians. We have put enough into it: it is ours. We need to accept help from other Canadians and continue to offer them ours. They couldn't do without us, either, without losing a great deal. For example, while the financial recovery of recent years is the achievement of all Canadians, its three main architects are three Quebecers: Jean Chrétien, Paul Martin and Marcel Massé.

It is not taking anything away from the Quebec genius, the Quebec culture, the Quebec identity, to state that we would not do as well without a united Canada. I would say the same thing for all of

Canada's provinces, including the wealthiest ones. Professor Roger Gibbins, the head of the Canada West Foundation, recently published a study showing how much Alberta would be negatively influenced by Quebec's separation. The fact is, we would all lose out.

Mr. Lucien Bouchard, as is his right, has a different opinion. He says that Canadian federalism is hurting the Quebec economy. How, exactly? In recent years, he has given three answers, which are difficult to reconcile with one another.

First of all, during the 1993 federal election campaign, it was the theory that Canada was on the edge of "bankruptcy." Quebecers had to get off the Canadian train before it derailed. "If they [Canadians outside Quebec] intend to go bankrupt, too bad for them. But we're going to save our skin," he said on August 14, 1993.

And then came the first U-turn. In the 1995 referendum, it was putting public finances in order that became the target of Mr. Bouchard's criticisms. A Yes vote, he explained, was protection against the "cold wind" of cuts blowing in from English Canada.

Once he became Premier, Mr. Bouchard could no longer denounce cuts, since he now had to make them himself. So he had to make another U-turn: first it was a bankrupt country, then it was a cold wind, and now it's a zero deficit. Mr. Bouchard has taken to reiterating that achieving a zero deficit would be the signal for the Government of Quebec that Quebec can become sovereign, the proof that we need sovereignty. The following is just one in a series of this type of declaration, this one reported in *Le Droit* on December 20, 1996: [translation] "I am convinced that if we achieve the zero deficit objective and call a referendum, we'll win it."

So, according to Mr. Bouchard, it seems that we no longer need sovereignty to avoid cuts; we need to make cuts to achieve sovereignty. And we'll achieve this demanding objective of a zero deficit in a country that should logically have gone bankrupt. Mr. Bouchard really is the master of the U-turn. But there's no logic to his reasoning. If the federation really is hurting us, if it really is unfair and ineffective, then we ought to get out as soon as we can, so as to be in a better position of achieving a zero deficit. That's what Mr. Bouchard would be saying if his arguments were logically coherent. But he knows that almost no one would follow him. So that's why he's relying on Canada today, to convince us to leave it tomorrow. Quite a contradiction.

In the meantime, Mr. Bouchard is fed-bashing every chance he gets. When things go wrong, it's the feds' fault. When they go well, it's in spite of the feds. His main accusation is offloading: the federal government has offloaded its deficit onto the provinces. In all fairness, it must be admitted that the other premiers are making the same point, more

or less forcefully. Allow me to summarize the federal government's response to these reproaches:

– The first Martin budget concentrated the cuts in direct federal spending, and even increased transfers to the provinces. But at the same
  time, Mr. Martin let the provinces know of the cuts to transfers they
  could expect in the coming years. He gave them the time to adjust
  and guaranteed them a predictable base of funding. The Government
  of Quebec, for its part, was not only notified of the cuts to federal
  transfers in advance, but went so far as to exaggerate their size in its
  budget estimates. The first Landry budget referred to federal transfers $1.7 billion higher over the fiscal years 1995–1996 to 1997–
  1998 than those forecast in the Campeau budget, just before the referendum.
– Another measure that helped the provinces was folding the major
  federal transfers for health, social assistance and postsecondary education into a single envelope. This gave the provinces additional budgetary flexibility.
– The federal government took care not to make equalization subject
  to the planned cuts, which greatly helped the less wealthy provinces,
  including Quebec, which currently receives 47% of equalization payments, or $4 billion for the 1998–1999 fiscal year.
– On the whole, from 1993–1994 to 1998–1999, cuts to transfers to
  the provinces (7.4%) will have been less than cuts to direct program
  spending by the federal government (10.8%). The largest cuts were
  made in the areas of defence (30.2%), international assistance
  (20.0%), and transport (60.9%). The federal public service cut
  51,000 positions and had a wage freeze for six years, from 1991 to
  1997.
– Incidentally, the provinces' finances have benefited from the lower
  interest rates that are the result of getting federal finances in order.
  The Government of Quebec alone has saved a total of $1.05 billion
  in the past three fiscal years, according to Finance Department estimates released in the last Martin budget.
– And now that its financial situation is improving, the federal government is giving priority to helping out the provinces, which will directly receive 38% of the new spending initiatives (that is, additional
  spending or rescinded cuts) set out in the last Martin budget.
– The federal plan for cuts has been fair to all the provinces, taking
  into account their respective wealth. For example, the Quebec government will continue to receive, every year, about 30% of the main
  federal transfers to the provinces. If Quebec had only received the
  equivalent of its portion of the population in federal transfers, those

transfers would have been $1.8 billion dollars less in 1998–1999. Those transfers total $10.4 billion for the 1998–1999 fiscal year, more than those to any other province. They represent some $3,360 per Quebec household ($1,400 a person). That's 14% more than the Canadian average of $2,950 per household.

– Some provinces have cut their own transfers harder and faster than the federal government. For example, the cuts to federal transfers between fiscal years 1993–1994 and 1998–1999 represent 3.0% of the Quebec government's total program expenditures (representing a reduction of $1.1 billion in discretionary expenditures of $35.4 billion), while the latter is asking its municipalities, within a much shorter time, to absorb cuts representing around 5.8% of their program spending (a percentage taken from a press release published by the Quebec Minister of Municipal Affairs on October 20, 1997).

That's the federal government's take on the recent history of our fiscal federalism. It's not all there is to say about this topic, I grant you. The provinces are saying, for example, that the feds are cooking the books by including the increased value of tax points, rather than cash transfers only. They are forgetting that it was they who suggested this type of accounting, back in 1977. (*Federal-Provincial Financial Arrangements: The Provincial Proposal*, Meeting of Ministers of Finance and Provincial Treasurers, December 6–7, 1976)

These are issues I'd like to look at with you in greater detail if I had the time. For now, however, I'll merely point out that such difficulties between governments inevitably crop up in a period of deficit reduction. Similar difficulties occurred between Australia's states and Canberra, to use the example of another federation that has put its financial house in order, and no one down under felt the way to solve those difficulties was to break up the country.

I would add that the Government of Canada cannot have been as hard on the provinces as is claimed, since five of them managed to balance their budget before Ottawa did. Only the two largest provinces are still forecasting substantial deficits in their budgets. But the Government of Ontario has chosen to cut taxes by $4.6 billion and defer reaching a zero deficit. And what about the Government of Quebec? Why is its financial house cleaning lagging behind that of the other provinces?

The referendum mortgage

I've just reproached Mr. Bouchard with blaming everything on the federal government, which is a convenient way to explain away all of

Quebec's difficulties. I won't now do the opposite and say that the sole source of all our problems is the political uncertainty generated by secessionist ambitions. I'm not denying that the reason Quebec currently has one of the worst economic and financial records in Canada is due in large part to structural causes. Indeed, according to the most recent data, Quebec is the province:

- whose residents, in general, have the largest individual tax burden, and the largest total tax burden, after Saskatchewan;
- which has the highest deficit to GPP ratio, after Ontario;
- which has the highest debt to GPP ratio, after three Atlantic provinces;
- which spends the greatest portion of its revenues on debt servicing, after Nova Scotia;
- which pays the highest interest on its borrowing: since the beginning of 1997, it has had to pay around 50 basis points more than the federal government on 30-year Canadian dollar bonds; even Newfoundland (at around 40 points higher than the federal government) pays less;
- which has the highest unemployment rate, after the Atlantic provinces (April 1998);
- whose per capita income is the fifth lowest of all the provinces – 13% below the Canadian average;
- which has the third worst rating in terms of its share of Canadian investments (18.7%) in comparison with its demographic weight (24.7%);
- which has had, together with Newfoundland, Nova Scotia and British Columbia, a rate of economic growth lower than the Canadian average during each of the past three years;
- whose poverty rate, or more specifically, low-income rate, is the highest of all the provinces: 21.6% versus the Canadian average of 17.6%.

While I admit that there are other causes of the Quebec economy's poor performance, such as the aging of a portion of the industrial infrastructure and the westward movement of economic activity, I believe that political uncertainty is clearly a substantial hindrance. I don't see how political uncertainty could have negative effects everywhere else it exists in the world, but not Quebec.

Quebecers can see that cost for themselves: eight out of ten (83%) believe that political uncertainty is hurting the economy (EKOS, April 1998).

"Montreal is the only major city in Canada and the United States that has to deal with political uncertainty, which has a substantial impact on its competitiveness," noted a committee of business leaders led by Brian Levitt, in October 1996.

"The temporary lifting of the referendum mortgage has also helped push Canadian short-term interest rates below the U.S. rates," wrote France's Ministry of the Economy in a document published during a visit to France by Mr. Bouchard in September 1997.

Mr. Bouchard's efforts this week in the United States are designed to calm concerns about his plan for independence and have earned him some diplomatic encouragement. Nevertheless, comments by U.S. business leaders show just how persistent those concerns are.

For example, the president of a U.S. venture-capital firm, Palmer Partners' John A. Shane, was quoted as saying: "I would say the only thing that has put a slight chill on that [interesting investment prospects], I think in the last two decades, has been the separatist actions." Mr. Shane added that it would be helpful if Premier Bouchard announced he would put aside plans for a new sovereignty referendum.

Mr. Ken Rossano, chairman of the New England-Canada Business Council, stated: "Business likes predictability. There is no guarantee of the stability of your investment 5 or 10 years down the road with this kind of project." A Brooklyn-based investment banker, Andre Danesh, also indicated: "There is a lot of fear among U.S. investors [...]. If and when Quebec separates, what happens next? It is a drawback that no one knows."

Premier Bouchard himself has admitted that political uncertainty brings economic costs. He stated on the program *Le Point* on March 21, 1996: [translation] "I'm not denying that there may be foreign investors who are saying, let's just wait until things are settled in Montreal and Quebec." He admitted on February 20, 1997, that "our creditors are giving us funny looks because they don't have that much confidence."

And yet Mr. Bouchard is contradicted by his Finance Minister, Mr. Bernard Landry, who said on April 7, directing his comments at Mr. Jean Charest, admittedly: [translation] "Those who begin their political career in Quebec by saying that the economy is not doing well because there are referenda are making hugely erroneous statements that are not supported by any figures. In fact, the figures say just the opposite." To back up that assertion, Mr. Landry quoted Statistics Canada data announcing a good year for investments in Quebec in 1998. But that good news cannot alter the fact that Quebec's share of Canadian investments is only 18.7%, compared with 22.3% in 1990.

Standard and Poor's recently revoked its negative warning about the Government of Quebec's credit rating. Mr. Landry took the credit for that on behalf of his government, but without saying that one of the positive factors mentioned by Standard and Poor's is, and I quote, "moderating support for the sovereignty option mitigates potential economic and political uncertainty."

This isn't the first time that a rating agency has expressed concern about the political uncertainty we are inflicting on ourselves. For example, in December 1997, Standard and Poor's noted that political uncertainty was a serious drag on Montreal's economy. In July 1996, Standard and Poor's downgraded Quebec's rating, again citing political uncertainty. Moody's has also noted recently (November 1997, May 1997) not only that Quebec's rating would have to be revised in the eventuality of fundamental changes in its political status within Canada, but also that the impact of the uncertainty about Quebec's status extends to the other provinces and the federal government as well.

Political uncertainty is undeniably harmful for the economy. Throughout the world, the very prospect of secession entails a host of uncertainties, a political and social upheaval. No sociological law can protect us against this universal rule.

And let's not forget the tremendous waste of energy entailed by these "neverendums." Let's not forget how the PQ government has twice, in 1980 and again in 1995, used our tax dollars in an attempt to buy, at a very high price, the votes of public sector employees. Having placed itself in an impossible financial situation, it then had to backtrack after the referendum by confronting its former allies, the labour leaders, which aggravated social tensions in Quebec.

Some separatists admit that political uncertainty does hurt our economy, but add that the way to disperse those negative effects is to vote Yes. After a Yes victory, they say, there would no longer be political uncertainty, because Quebecers would have made their choice. I don't know how they can say that with a straight face. It is obvious that it is not uncertainty per se that is worrying economic agents in particular, but the consequences of a post-Yes period; you don't have to think about those consequences too long to realize that they would plunge us into a whole new sea of uncertainties, be they fiscal, monetary, commercial or others. After all, if economic agents looked favourably or even neutrally on secession, political uncertainty obviously wouldn't hurt us. The economic agents would tell themselves they have the choice between the current situation and an equivalent or improved situation after a Yes vote.

So let's be a little more specific. Rather than political uncertainty, let's talk about the possibility of secession, and admit that this possibility is hurting our economy. Without it, there would be less unemployment, less poverty, more investment, and the fight against the deficit would be further advanced and less painful.

Mr. Parizeau knew full well in 1995 that a Yes victory entailed enormous economic risks. He wanted to use $17 billion of our savings in a vain attempt to calm the markets. Naturally, he didn't breathe a word about that "Plan 'O'."

And to think that Mr. Bouchard is now claiming that it is the Calgary Declaration that is dangerous for Quebecers. He would be funny, if he weren't gambling with their money.

Conclusion

It is true that Quebec's economy has structural weaknesses. But it also has enviable strengths, as evidenced by the successful reorientation of the manufacturing industries toward high technology. You won't find the MP for Saint-Laurent with any misgivings about the Quebec economy! The Government of Canada is proud to be a major partner. In a way, that Quebec's economy has managed to accomplish so much, in spite of political uncertainty, shows just how resilient it really is.

As an integral part of the Canadian economy as a whole, it has extraordinary potential. Think of the synergy we could create if we freed it from the threat of secession. To do that, we need a premier and a government in Quebec City that believe in Canada. A premier and a government that believe in Quebec's destiny within a united Canada. A premier and a government determined to draw fully on Quebec's genius and Canadian solidarity.

It appears that the vast majority of Quebecers do not want another referendum. And they're absolutely right.

My Praxis of Federalism

I'm sure you will remember that in the 1970s, every professor, to be popular with a certain category of student, not only had to be a Marxist, but also had to have a "praxis," that is, to put his or her ideas into practice through active involvement in a revolutionary party.

And so, in memory of my student days, and in front of a number of my former professors who are present here today (but who weren't particularly Marxist!), I've entitled this speech My Praxis of Federalism.

I couldn't have found a better audience to explore this topic with. Having been a member of your Advisory Council for two years, and having run up an intellectual debt with a number of you, I know how much you have both thought about and practised Canadian federalism in various roles. Each of you has an interesting praxis you could talk about.

A few years ago, my father, Léon Dion, told me the following story. Having expressed his disagreement with an initiative by Jean Chrétien, who was then a minister, the latter replied, in the words of George Bernard Shaw: "Those who cannot do, teach!" My father, who held teaching in the highest esteem, answered back: "Those who cannot teach, do!"

I was reminded of that story when I was sworn in as Minister on January 25, 1996, and saw both of them talking together, in a very friendly fashion I must say, in the Governor General's drawing room. I wondered then whether I would succeed in putting into practice what I had taught about Canadian federalism.

In other words, I wondered whether I would be able to prove *Minister* Jean Chrétien wrong, by proving that "Those who teach can also do!" Especially since I would also be proving *Prime Minister* Jean Chrétien right, for having put an academic with no direct political experience in charge of federal-provincial relations, at a time of great uncertainty in Canadian history.

Speech to the Institute of Intergovernmental Relations, Queen's University

Federal-provincial relations and the Canadian unity debate

So, what did I have to say as an academic about Canadian federalism? First of all, that nothing in this federation justifies secession; that the arguments in favour of secession are either weak or just plain wrong; and that it is an outrageous strategy to tell Quebecers, "The sovereignists are pretty much right today, Canada is unacceptable, but give us the chance to reform it from stem to stern and we'll be able to make it acceptable tomorrow."

Second, that changing the federation must be guided by improving service to the public, and not by a list of traditional demands. Do you think the Quiet Revolution was achieved through traditional demands?

I defended those ideas at a time of genuine constitutional obsession. Without major constitutional change, it was said, Canada could not respond to the aspirations of Quebecers or Western Canadians, or succeed in getting out of its financial crisis. "Allaire-ism" proposed to inflate the Quebec government with new responsibilities. This was not intended to improve public policy, but to give "gains" to Quebec federalists, because of course, shrinking the federal role was a "gain."

I believed that you don't save a country by relying on such a logic of internal separatism – especially not when the country is already, in many ways, a decentralized federation in comparison with others in the world. Transfers of power cannot allay separatism if they are made for that purpose alone. Every new transfer would lead Quebecers to withdraw ever further into their territory, to define themselves by an exclusive "us," to see other Canadians increasingly only from afar, and to reject the Canadian government and common Canadian institutions as a threat to their nation, a foreign body.

And given the lack of support for a special status for one of Canada's provinces – a phenomenon that can also be seen in other comparable federations, such as the u.s., Switzerland, Belgium and Germany – the same concessions would have to be offered to the other provinces, to avoid regional jealousies. This spiral of concessions could lead to a sort of balkanization. And yet if the federal government refused to grant the other provinces the same powers as Quebec, it might give rise to a powerful backlash, from Western Canada and other regions as well, which would inevitably be interpreted as a rejection of Quebecers. A federation is living on borrowed time when its only logic for change is to reward separatist blackmail.

I maintained that it was identity, rather than the division of powers, that is at the source of our unity problem. Francophone Quebecers want the assurance that their language and culture can flourish with the support of other Canadians. They want to feel that their language and culture are seen by other Canadians as an important asset, rather than a burden. They want the assurance that they can be both Quebecers and Canadians, and that they don't have to choose between Quebec and Canada.

When I met with people in my riding and elsewhere in Quebec, my conviction was strengthened that the most fundamental issue is related to identity, rather than the division of powers. When I ask those who call for more powers for Quebec to specify which ones they want, they are quite often unable to come up with an answer.

I told myself that if the defenders of Canadian federalism don't explain to these citizens just how much Canada is a principle of sharing, rather than endless constitutional bickering, no rejigging of powers can win them over to supporting Canadian unity in a lasting way.

Especially not a rejigging ill-conceived in terms of quality of service to the public, which would create new inconveniences for these citizens. Because then the separatist leaders would have a field day showing them how, even with the best will in the world, Canada doesn't work.

This is what we must succeed in doing: showing that Canada is a principle of caring, a country where Quebecers have the opportunity to express their culture and their identity, both for themselves and to better help other Canadians, while accepting their help in turn. In other words, everyone needs to realize just how much this Canadian sharing is taking place each and every day, not just during ice storms.

Canada is not an emergency cord to be pulled only one week every 15 years, just before a referendum vote. There are universal values tied to the Canadian ideal; we must be able to express them and show how much Quebec society is a part of this ideal. And at the same time as we express those values, and highlight the reasons to be strongly attached to Canada, we also show that breaking that ideal, to which so many people are so deeply attached, breaking Canadian unity, would be a very sensitive operation. It would be one for which many precautions would have to be taken: a mutually agreed on, rather than unilateral, procedure; clarity, rather than confusion; legality, rather than anarchy.

So there's no contradiction between the so-called Plans A and B; rather, they are part of the same process of clarifying what Canada is all about.

Putting federal-provincial relations into principles

And where does improving the federation fit into all this? Well, if we succeed in making this federation more harmonious and more efficient, the improvement in governments' ability to work together will enhance Canadians' image of their country – just as putting public finances in order and revitalizing the economy increased their confidence in Canada.

You know as well as I do that, apart from all of us here today, the machinery of federal-provincial relations is of interest to few people in this country; similar disinterest can be seen in other federations as well. With the possible – but by no means certain – exception of the job training agreements, it would be presumptuous to say that the changes we have made to this federation in the past two years have had an immediate positive effect on public opinion.

In fact, things work in the very opposite way: a series of failed negotiations with the provinces would definitely have sapped support for Canadian unity. If the federal-provincial negotiations on the pension plan, environmental harmonization, extending the infrastructure program, liberalizing internal trade, the constitutional amendments affecting certain school boards or the national child benefit had all failed, or had generated the same divisions as the agreement on hepatitis c, there is no doubt that Canadian unity would be weaker today.

It is very frustrating for all governments to see how many success stories go almost unnoticed, while a few failures get all the headlines. It's like the Calgary Declaration, which proceeded apace without any fuss, and yet a snag in even one province would have produced a great hue and cry.

The question that specialists like yourselves need to answer is whether the changes we have made in the past two and a half years, as well as those we are currently working on with the provinces, will have long-term benefits in terms of the effectiveness of the federation. Will we have better social policies, better health policies, better environmental policies, a more dynamic internal market, a better trained workforce? Will all these pragmatic changes enable us to draw the greatest potential from the federal and provincial governments and to improve the synergy between the two orders of government?

In the latest volume of the *State of the Federation,* some of you have judged the trend that is emerging in the Canadian federation in a rather positive light. The editor of this work, Harvey Lazar, sees a promising new balance arising, marked by greater cooperation among governments. Similarly, Robert Howse sees "a new way of doing federalism" which strengthens the feeling of coexistence.

I hope that these academics are right, and I share their optimism. The main reason for my optimism is that, while working pragmatically one step at a time, on a case-by-case basis, we have always been guided by solid principles of action, which we must always strive to respect more fully. Those principles are as follows:

The Constitution must be respected. We must do away with the all-too-convenient excuse that a given governmental initiative responds to a need that is too urgent to be stymied by issues of "jurisdiction."

Infringement of jurisdiction creates confusion which damages the quality of public policy.

Close cooperation must be established where it is needed. And it must be done often, because government jurisdictions touch on each other in almost all sectors. I used to say that my responsibilities required me to support my colleagues in almost every area but the military. But ever since the ice storm that hit three provinces, I now have to give a hand to the Minister of National Defence as well. There are few policies that the Government can accomplish alone without the active cooperation of the provinces. It's all very well for the federal government to negotiate wonderful international agreements on the environment, but they'll get absolutely nowhere without the provinces' cooperation. And everyone knows that a national home care policy is just not going to happen without the agreement of the provinces. The federal government simply does not have the capacity to act alone in this sector, nor in the vast majority of social policies. That is why the new Ministerial Council on Social Policy Renewal is an excellent innovation. Through the Council and its task forces, governments are coordinating their activities more effectively on issues such as child poverty and programs for youth and persons with disabilities.

Governments' ability to act must be preserved. We mustn't let our quest for cooperation leave us with a federation where no government can do anything without asking the permission of the ten others, not to mention the territorial governments and First Nations representatives. Autonomous spheres of activity are important in our federation; they must not be needlessly whittled away so that we fall into what the Europeans call the "joint decision trap." For example, the Environmental Harmonization Accord signed on January 29, 1998, commits the federal and provincial governments to work together to harmonize their standards and regulations, while preserving the ultimate right of each if a consensus is not possible, to make its own laws. This means that citizens and businesses will normally face a single set of standards, for example on toxic emissions, and will only have to deal with one inspector. Another example is the agreement concluded on February 20, 1998, by industry ministers, which will further liberalize government contracting. This agreement has been approved by all ministers but British Columbia's. Rather than waiting for unanimity, which is not yet forthcoming, the ministers wisely decided to proceed with the agreement, hoping that B.C. would join later.

The federation must be flexible. In striving for joint action, we must also take into account the diversity of the country. The provinces have their own specific characteristics and sometimes adopt differing policies. So, for example, the job training agreements allow the provinces to choose between a co-management formula with the federal government or greater autonomy. In the same way, federal funding for the new child benefit comes with budgetary flexibility that allows the provinces to use the funding in accordance with their own child and family poverty policies. The objective here is to reconcile joint action with the provinces' capacity to innovate and establish a healthy emulation among themselves. This would not be possible if the federal government tied its assistance to painstakingly detailed national standards. This federal flexibility is even more necessary in this period of economic globalization, where each province must be able to choose its strategies in facing its own expanding external market.

The federation must be fair. Canada will have succeeded in bringing down the $62 billion deficit of all its governments in less than five years. It is extraordinary that this feat has been accomplished without creating more friction between the federal government and the provinces or more jealousy among the provinces. Nevertheless, occasions for conflict will not diminish now that the surpluses around the corner are attracting envious glances. The Premier of this province is particularly active on that front at the moment. The federal government is aware of the difficulties the provinces are having after all these years of cuts: 38% of the new spending initiatives (that is, additional spending or rescinded cuts) set out in the last Martin budget will go directly to the provinces.

We must exchange information. Unilateralism and upstaging must be avoided. Governments must be notified in advance of any new initiatives that could have a significant effect on their activities. Exchanging information also allows governments to compare their performance, assess their respective initiatives and establish among themselves the healthy emulation I mentioned earlier.

The public must be aware of the respective contributions of the different governments. That's right, the famous visibility. While it would be very bad if visibility were the main motivation driving our actions, citizens have the right to know what their governments are there for. They must be able to assess the performance of each one; it's a question of transparency. And governments will agree more readily to work together if they have the assurance that credit for their initiatives will not be claimed by others. I can assure you that my job as Intergovernmental Affairs Minister would be much easier if I could guarantee my Cabinet colleagues that cooperation with the provinces will not make the Government of Canada invisible to Canadians. My provincial counterparts say the same thing about their colleagues. For example, if the new National Child Benefit Agreement was negotiated successfully, it was in part due to its guarantee that each government will clearly receive credit for its own actions and, at the same time, be held accountable for them to citizens.

Conclusion

These are the main principles guiding us. One question we must answer is whether to formalize them in frameworks or within new structures such as the Ministerial Council on Social Policy Renewal. What is important, however, is that these principles be respected in a way that increases cooperation between governments and makes it possible to manage conflicts better. Because those conflicts will always, always be with us. We've got to stop seeing every single conflict as proof that the country doesn't work.

Incidentally, those conflicts don't always have negative consequences. One of the advantages of the federative form of government is that solutions can be found more easily when disagreements take place out in the open, among constitutional partners, rather than in the ivory towers of huge centralized bureaucracies that weigh down unitary countries.

The principles I have set out constitute our praxis of federal-provincial relations. A praxis which, nevertheless, is not at all revolutionary. There won't be any "now or never" ratifications of huge package deals that will solve everything. Instead, we'll see an approach, à la Jean Chrétien, step by step, solid and determined.

Social Union: Canadians Helping Canadians

TORONTO, DECEMBER 10, 1998

Social union may be a new expression, but the Canadian social union definitely exists. We are not in the process of creating the social union, but of improving it. After describing just what the social union is and the nature of the social union negotiations by our governments, I'll look at the links between these negotiations and our federal system on the one hand and our problem of national unity on the other.

Indeed, two fears have been clearly expressed recently in connection with the negotiations, particularly in Ontario. You may share those fears yourselves. Let us see if I can alleviate them.

Many people are afraid that the quality of our social programs and our health system will be sacrificed, 1) to buy peace with the provinces, or 2) to accommodate the separatists. I can assure you that this will not happen. Those fears are unfounded. Prime Minister Jean Chrétien and his government have but a single objective: to find a decision-making framework that is most likely to produce better social and health policies for all Canadians, wherever they live in Canada. And by focussing exclusively on the quality of services to Canadians, we will improve our federation and strengthen the unity of our country.

A women's association such as yours is the perfect venue to talk about the social union currently being negotiated in Canada. A number of studies show that women tend to have more pronounced social concerns than men do. This is because women are more intelligent, of course ... but mostly, because they are the ones who bear the brunt of the shortcomings in our social and health policies.

1. What is the social union?

The social union is Canadians helping Canadians; one of the best principles of caring ever invented by human beings. It encompasses the

---

Speech to the Women's Canadian Club of Toronto

aspects of caring most essential to Canadians: health, social protection, equality of opportunity.

Wherever we live in Canada, we want to have access to high-quality health care services for all, regardless of personal income; we want to receive the help we need if we lose our job or become unable to work because of a disability; we want our young people to pursue their studies under good conditions; and we want pension plans and seniors' benefits that enable us to preserve our quality of life in our old age. These programs and services make up what we call the social union.

All industrialized societies launched new social programs after the end of the Second World War, but few have been as successful as we have. According to a 1997 study by the British Economist Intelligence Unit, for example, Canada ranked fourth in the world in terms of the health of its population, and second in terms of its medical practices. According to the World Economic Forum, Canada ranks first among 53 countries in terms of post-secondary enrolment. More generally, our government practices seem to be of high quality when compared with other countries. A study on government quality recently released by an American research centre, the National Bureau of Economic Research, ranked Canada fifth among 150 countries.

Nevertheless, according to a recent UN report, governments in Canada are not doing enough for our most disadvantaged citizens. And you know of our country's troubling child poverty problem. Our social union has serious shortcomings, and there is much that needs to be done. The time has come to review how we do things, now that governments have put their public finances in better order and hope to be able to reinvest in health and social services.

And this brings us to the federal-provincial negotiations now under way. At the express invitation of the Prime Minister of Canada and the Premier of Saskatchewan, the country's first ministers and territorial leaders agreed last December 12 to try to improve the Canadian social union. They assigned this mandate to their ministers. The negotiations are being co-chaired by my colleague Anne McLellan, chair of the federal Cabinet Committee on Social Union, and Bernie Wiens, Saskatchewan's Intergovernmental Affairs Minister.

The objective of these negotiations is for governments to improve the Canadian social union together. We need to find the most appropriate decision-making framework for helping governments to help Canadians.

2. The social union and federal-provincial relations

To improve our social union, we need to build on the strengths of our federation. Neither the federal government nor the provincial governments can succeed on their own. Governments must work together more effectively while respecting their constitutional powers and jurisdictions. That is why we have a federation.

By the way, let's ask ourselves: why do we have a federation? My answer: to pursue common objectives within the diversity of experiences.

Unitary countries set common objectives for themselves, but they cannot draw on the rich diversity of experiences to the same extent as federations. Ten egoistic republics north of the United States might try out many different things, but they would not have anywhere near the same capacity to pursue common objectives and help one another as our federation has.

We have strong provinces that are capable of trying out their own solutions. And we have a strong federal government that can help extend the most valuable provincial experiences to all Canadians. In this way, we Canadians have successfully developed a health system that is infinitely more humane than that of the United States. And in this way, more recently, the National Child Benefit was developed, a new federal-provincial initiative to reverse the upward trend in child poverty.

To make our social union even better, we need to enhance our capacity to identify common objectives and try out different solutions. We need to assess the merits of these different solutions more effectively, and to compare them with one another more systematically through healthy emulation.

It is only natural that the provinces are concerned in particular with the diversity of their experiences, that is, with their own autonomy, while keeping in mind the need to have common objectives within Canada.

Conversely, it is only natural that the federal government, as the government elected by all Canadians, be concerned in particular with common objectives, while keeping in mind the country's diversity.

This natural difference of perspective between the two orders of government can create friction between them, especially in a context of budgetary austerity. These tensions make for headaches for politicians and bureaucrats, good copy for journalists, and ultimately, through synergy, better services for citizens.

I am telling you all of this because this is precisely what is happening with the current negotiations on the social union.

The first ministers gave their ministers a mandate to negotiate on December 12, 1997. The provinces presented a joint position on June 18, 1998. The federal government released its own proposal one month later, on July 16. The Premier of Quebec joined the discussions on August 7.

Since that time, we have been discussing the two proposals together: the one by the provinces and the one by the federal government. Both proposals are being examined. I won't disguise the fact that the provinces are pushing for a greater capacity to try out their own solutions, and it is legitimate for them to do so. For its part, the federal government will not sign anything that does not consolidate the common objectives we already have, such as those set out in the *Canada Health Act*, and we also want to expand our capacity to have other objectives, including equal opportunity and mobility of all Canadians throughout the country. The federal government also insists that government action throughout the country must be more transparent and more accountable to the public.

The purpose of the negotiations is not to conclude an unwieldy compromise between the two perspectives, but rather to draw on the best of each, so that we can enhance our capacity both to have common objectives and to try out different solutions. It would be easy to weaken one order of government, to the advantage of the other. But it requires much more imagination to strengthen both orders of government in their legitimate roles, and in particular, to enhance their capacity for joint action.

We need to have imagination, but we also need to have faith in this country. This brings me to my final topic: the link between these social union negotiations and Canadian unity.

3. *Social union and Canadian unity*

A federation obliges governments of different political stripes to work together. It is almost impossible, for example, to have 13 Liberal governments – federal, provincial and territorial – in Canada all at the same time. Coexistence of governments with different party allegiances is inevitable. This requires both judgment and open-mindedness, on the part of governments and citizens alike.

For example, let's look at the current political situation in your province. There are many people in Ontario who reproach the current Conservative government for lacking a social conscience. It is not my role to comment on whether or not that reproach is justified, at least not as the Minister of Intergovernmental Affairs, who must work with that government. But those men and women who do believe that reproach is justified may well be inclined to hope that the current social union negotiations will strengthen the role of the federal government and weaken the Ontario government. In aiming to improve a social union, however, we need to take a more long-term approach. You can't rule out the possibility that a very conservative government may one day take power in Ottawa, at the same time as a government very open to social policies is in power at Queen's Park. Many people would then be very happy to count on a provincial government with sufficient jurisdictional clout to counterbalance the neo-conservatism in Ottawa.

This is why the negotiations under way to improve our social union must be above partisanship. It becomes more difficult, however, when one of the governments sitting at the table has the official objective, as set out in the first article of its political platform, not of improving the federation, but of breaking it up.

That government has just been re-elected by Quebecers. As a result, the other governments have a constitutional responsibility to work with it, provided that those efforts are to improve Canada. Prime Minister Jean Chrétien made a public commitment to do so on the same night that Mr. Bouchard's government was re-elected.

Improving Canada means seeking better policies for Canadians. It doesn't mean giving in to the so-called "politics of booty."

This expression, the search for booty, which dates back to former Quebec Premier Maurice Duplessis, was dusted off and brandished in their own way by the separatist leaders in the Quebec election campaign. Former Premier Jacques Parizeau summed it up perfectly in a speech about the social union negotiations:

[Translation]
"We can't lose. In that sense, there's no contradiction between an intelligent strategy to get something out of Ottawa, or pulling off a hold-up in Ottawa, as the case may be, and preparing for a referendum on sovereignty." (Speech in Trois-Rivières, November 26, 1998)

Let me sum up this separatist-style politics of booty in another way. It consists of demanding something from the federal government: more power, more money. If the federal government says no, then you return to Quebecers and you tell them: You see how unyielding and unfair this federation is to you, we've got to get out! If the federal government says yes, the message to Quebecers becomes: You see the bargaining power you get by electing separatists, so imagine the power you'd have if you voted Yes in a referendum; we'd go get you that wonderful partnership we've promised you.

So how does one thwart this logic of booty? Quite simply, by refusing to play the game. By stating very clearly that one has no intention of giving in to this kind of blackmail. By placing the improvement of services for citizens above all other considerations, while respecting the constitutional jurisdictions and powers of each level of government. And by never losing sight of the fact that it is through developing better health policies, better social, economic and environmental policies, that we will strengthen the desire of Quebecers and other Canadians to stay together.

We won't improve this social union by trying to accommodate the separatists or those who might be tempted to vote for them. We will improve it by enhancing our capacity to pursue common objectives within the diversity of experiences. The results of our efforts will benefit Canadians and thereby strengthen Canadian unity. This is the link between the social union and the unity of our country.

There was a lot of talk about booty during the Quebec election campaign. But that campaign is now over. Together, we have a country to improve, and it is with that perspective that the Government of Canada is determined, I repeat, to work with the Government of Quebec as it does with every elected government in the country.

But "can you promise us that the social union negotiations have nothing to do with Quebec" some Ontarian columnists ask me. I'm afraid I can't make such a promise, because it is obvious that these negotiations have everything to do with Quebec, just as they have everything to do with Ontario and the other regions of Canada.

Just because an idea comes from Quebec doesn't mean that it should automatically be considered as booty politics or separatist blackmail. Quebec society is a hotbed of very interesting ideas about social policy. The other provinces will better realize this as we improve the exchange of information, the assessment of results and accountability to the public, which are all objectives of the current negotiations.

It is certain that Quebecers, because of the unique nature of their society, will always exert a certain pressure within the federation for provincial autonomy. In doing so, they provide a useful counterbalance to other forces in the country which, if left unchecked, would move us toward a uniformity likely to erode the provinces' capacity to innovate in trying out their own solutions.

But there also exists in Quebec a tradition of openness to other Canadians, a desire for joint action to achieve shared objectives. Too often, unfortunately, this desire has been smothered by the logic of booty and separatist blackmail.

An improved social union will never be a step toward separation. It will give Quebecers the opportunity to try out their own social and health policies, with the help of all Canadians, by pursuing common objectives with them.

Conclusion

The social union is neither social disunion nor social uniformity. It is all of the social and health policies by which Canadians help each other in the diversity of their experiences.

The negotiations under way to improve our social union are progressing well. It would be unfortunate, however, if this round were to fail, but that would not make Canada unacceptable to Quebecers, any more than to other Canadians. Canada is already more than acceptable. It is infinitely preferable to the secessionist gambit, and is seen as such by the vast majority of Quebecers.

But Canada must always be improved, be it through a new social union framework or through other means. And together, without ulterior motives, without separatist blackmail, without taking dogmatic positions in favour of the provinces or the federal government, by resisting prefabricated slogans that close minds and by remaining steadfast in our efforts to help all of our fellow Canadians, men and women alike, we will make our country better able to take on the daunting and exhilarating challenges of the coming century.

SECTION 3

Canadian Identity and the Quebec Society

The Canada We Share

Our country is in danger. After the cliffhanger result of the October 30, 1995, referendum, the prospect of break-up has never been so real or so close.

I know that many Canadians are simply tired of this issue. I know that there is a feeling of resignation among many Canadians, a sense that the secession of Quebec may be inevitable. This is understandable after years of seemingly endless constitutional disputes – the so called "neverendum." Many people are thinking "What is the use of trying again?"

I know that British Columbians often feel very alienated from this debate, which seems so far removed from their direct concerns. This province of British Columbia has been especially generous toward the rest of Canada financially, and often does not receive any thanks for it.

I know that you have tried patiently to work to reconcile Quebec with Canada, for example by some of you or your children going to French immersion schools. Now many sincerely wonder if that was a practical way to build a bilingual society, or just a noble illusion.

I know that British Columbians feel far removed from Ottawa, and feel that your specific problems – whether in the fishery, or Asia Pacific trade, or in receiving a fair share of federal spending – are not well understood.

I know all this. But what is the solution? For British Columbians or others to give up on Canada? To let our country fall apart? A split between Quebec and Canada without any assurance that the other nine provinces would stay together?

I am not resigned to accepting that outcome. I feel that we have a duty to try again. This is why I accepted the responsibility of joining Jean Chrétien's cabinet on January 25, 1996 as Minister of Intergovernmental Affairs.

Speech to the Liberal Party of Canada (B.C.)

The Value of Canada

I am proud to be part of Jean Chrétien's Team Canada along with David Anderson, Hedy Fry, Raymond Chan, and the other caucus members, because we all want to keep our country together. Our party, the Liberal Party of Canada, is now the sole national party with Members of Parliament from each province, where Francophones and Anglophones can work together.

In the past, as much as Liberals may have disagreed with the Conservatives and the NDP, at least we knew that we shared a common belief in Canada. Today, with the regionalist parties of the Bloc and Reform, this is not the case. We need many leaders, not just Liberals, who will speak up again for our common Canadian values. I know that all of you are Canadians before you are partisans, and that you will want this country to return to a healthy national political culture.

Why is being Canadian so valuable?

Each of us has our own answers, but I will tell you mine. It is not because our flag is the most attractive, although it is very popular and well recognized internationally. It is not because of the grandeur of our scenery and the immensity of our territory, as impressive as it may be. And it is not simply because of our enviable standard of living, although the United Nations consistently rates us the best in the world.

No, the reason I consider myself so fortunate to be Canadian is not because of what is distinctive and particular to this country, but because of our achievement of universal human ideals. Canada is the greatest example of what the world must become in terms of tolerance, openness, and capacity for harmony between different communities.

As the Prime Minister said in his speech to the House this Wednesday: "we have seen that when the world looks to Canada, what they see is the future. Or rather the best hope for the future of the world. Together, let's build that model of hope and confidence. That model for all mankind."

Unfortunately, we Canadians are not often aware of what we represent as a model for all mankind. Let me give you a recent example of this collective self-deprecation. When wrangling at the United Nations threatened a reduction of the U.N. military assistance necessary to keep civil order in Haiti, it was Canada that offered to compensate by sending 750 soldiers at our own expense outside of the U.N. forces.

In other countries like France or Britain, such a generous action would have been a cause of national pride and would have dominated the news. In Canada, this has not been the case – we simply take it for granted that Canada always has and always will do more than its share in every United Nations peacekeeping effort. This is an example of Canada's incredible openness to the world.

Or consider your own achievements here in British Columbia. We all know the troubled and war-torn history of the encounter between Asian and European civilization, and that these cultures often fail to understand each other. Rudyard Kipling said: "East is East, and West is West, and never the twain shall meet." Where else on earth but this city, Vancouver, and this province, British Columbia, is there such a wonderful chance to prove Rudyard Kipling wrong, that Asian cultures and European cultures can work together harmoniously and create an even richer society? It is much more because of this great human achievement than because of our Rocky Mountains that I want to leave British Columbia to my daughter as part of her country.

There are many reasons to explain why Canada has achieved this degree of tolerance and such an openness to different cultures. But there is one that I want to point out, because it has been a powerful help, and that is our linguistic duality.

The institutional and legislative arrangements this reality has required, starting with the Quebec Act of 1774, have made Canada more open to diversity in all its forms. In turn, our diversity has helped us to evolve and grow and has made us more open to the challenges of the modern world and global citizenship.

Canada is a unique human achievement. Not just as British Columbians or Quebecers, not just as the holders of milk quotas or investors in savings bonds, but as human beings, we have no right to impose upon the world the end of this Canadian dream. Canada is considered the world over to be a model of generosity and openness. Let us live up to our reputation and send the rest of the world a positive signal of reconciliation.

We, whether Francophones or Anglophones, Aboriginals or new Canadians, Easterners or Westerners, will favour solidarity and reconciliation over division and break-up. It is within ourselves and the history of what we have always been able to do that we must find the way to reconciliation.

As we have seen from our history, finding reconciliation always requires some compromises. British Columbia was promised a railroad within ten years when it joined Confederation. When the railroad was late, many people in B.C. wanted to separate. Can you imagine how different history might have been for British Columbia if the earliest settlers had not been willing to compromise by waiting a few extra years?

We will find the courage to compromise. The problem in British Columbia, as it is elsewhere in Canada, is that those who speak loudest are not necessarily those who are open to others. I urge all of you, people of good will who are tolerant and open, to speak out as loudly and clearly as the voices of anger.

Politicians especially must act as Canadians first and be prepared to take risks on behalf of Canada. We need leadership – a new form of leadership which is able to act but is not afraid to listen and consult. I am here to suggest some directions for our future, and I am also here to listen to your ideas as to how they may be adapted and implemented.

In the Speech from the Throne last Tuesday, there was a signal both of federal leadership and a commitment to consultation that will include all Canadians in all parts of the country by all useful means.

There are two goals from the Throne Speech that I especially want to emphasize here today. First, an intelligent rebalancing of the federation and clarification of the roles of all levels of government. And second, the recognition of Quebec's distinctiveness within Canada. Those two goals give us the opportunity to greatly improve the capacity of the federation to better serve its citizens. Also, they will allow us to eliminate dangerous misunderstandings, prejudices, and false beliefs.

Rebalancing the federation

Let's start with the first goal: rebalancing powers within the federation.

Speaking of false beliefs, there is a myth of a centralized federation which is well entrenched in Quebec and also in many parts of the West. In fact, the Canadian federation is very decentralized, one of the most decentralized in the world. And the trend in recent decades is towards even more decentralization. For example, federal program spending was one and a half times provincial and municipal spending during the 1950s. It was only three quarters in 1990, and will fall to two thirds in 1996.

Another false belief is that the decentralized nature of Canada is a weakness – in fact, it is one of our strengths. It is no coincidence that four of the world's five richest countries are federations: Canada, the U.S., Germany, and Switzerland. It is our diversity as a country that allows us to have different ways to be Canadian and to celebrate Canada.

The problem with our federation is not that it is too centralized, but that it is too adversarial – there are too many disputes between federal and provincial governments. We need a more harmonious federation. We need to find better ways of achieving our common goals and ideals than, for example, imposing rules on the provinces through the use of conditional federal spending. Hence, we must find more cooperative ways to protect our shared Canadian values.

This is exactly what the Government is suggesting in the Throne Speech. The federal government has committed itself to no longer using its spending powers to create new cost-shared programs in areas of exclusive provincial jurisdiction without the consent of a majority of the provinces. We will offer compensation to provinces that decide to opt out as long as they establish equivalent or comparable initiatives.

This is the first time in our history that any federal government has unilaterally agreed to this long-standing provincial request outside of formal constitutional negotiations. Regarding existing shared-cost programs, the federal government is open to establishing new, non-coercive ways of maintaining and securing national standards.

As well as problems of spending, there are also long-standing issues of overlap and duplication. The federal government will withdraw entirely from sectors that are more appropriately the responsibility of the provinces or others such as labour-market training, forestry, mining, and recreation. We are open to negotiations to clarify roles in such areas as environmental management, social housing, food inspection, freshwater fisheries and tourism.

Once we have clarified these roles and responsibilities, the federal government will be better positioned to act in those areas that are more properly federal jurisdictions. The federal government will continue to play a key role in promoting Canada's economic union, and we will take measures to promote labour mobility and interprovincial free trade.

We would like to build common national institutions, with the support of the provinces, to secure our economic union, such as a single Canadian securities commission and a national revenue collection agency. The First Ministers' Meeting this spring will be an important opportunity to consider ways to clarify the roles of governments, and to better promote our social and economic union.

As you see, the Throne Speech indicates clearly that the federal government is showing leadership in rebalancing the federation, but that we are open to the needs and suggestions of the provinces and others. We will also, of course, ask for the ideas of ordinary Canadians as to how their governments can provide better service.

Recognition of Quebec

A second key step in national reconciliation will be a formal recognition of Quebec's distinctiveness – the famous distinct society clause.

I know that this idea is not especially popular in this province, but you may be aware that in Quebec too I am also saying things that are not very popular about the likely consequences of secession. But I must tell you the truth, and the truth as I see it is that a recognition of Quebec's distinctiveness would only help Canada.

Perhaps the words "distinct society" have been tainted by years of angry constitutional debate. If this is simply a problem with words, if "distinct" is seen as implying "superiority" in English as some say, then let's change the words. I am not concerned with semantics, I am concerned with the substance. If somebody can suggest to me a better term or better legal language, I am open to their ideas.

What then is the substance of a distinct society clause?

The distinct society clause would be an interpretative clause, similar to section 27 of the Charter which recognizes multiculturalism. What it offers is a guarantee that in the grey areas of the Constitution, those areas where the rules require interpretation, the Supreme Court will take into account Quebec's distinctiveness in such areas as language, culture, and civil law.

This will be a useful clarification, but it will not change the distribution of powers within the Constitution in the least. It is not a request for special status or special privileges.

All Canadian provinces are obviously distinct from one another. But with its difference in language, Quebec is different in a fundamental way which requires specific attention.

Other multilingual democracies like Switzerland and Belgium have these kinds of arrangements. They give the minority language community the ability to feel secure and to make a more positive contribution to the country.

It is obvious that language is central in shaping a whole society. Just compare the interprovincial mobility of Francophone Quebecers with that of other Canadians and you will see this. Imagine having to move with your family to Jonquiere, a 99% French speaking community. Imagine what this would mean for your children's education, for meeting new friends, and adapting to the community. It would certainly be more demanding than moving to Lethbridge.

Or imagine how British Columbians would feel if every other province had a French majority, in a world where the language of the United States was French, and French was the international language of business and media, and B.C. was the only English-speaking community in North America. Wouldn't a simple recognition of B.C.'s English-speaking identity be the least people would want?

I know that it was not intended as such outside Quebec, but many Quebecers interpreted the rejection of Meech Lake as a rejection of Quebec's culture and identity.

In fact, recognition of Quebec's distinctiveness would be a great example of the Canadian values of openness and toleration that we all cherish. It will give Quebecers the confidence to make a full contribution to our federation.

This is why I want people to embrace Quebec society in their hearts. This is much more important than writing it on a piece of paper. Even if it was possible to impose a distinct society clause against the objections of B.C. and Alberta, it would be worthless, because Quebecers, British Columbians, and Albertans would not feel reconciled in their hearts, whatever the Constitution might say.

Finally, what remains as an argument against the distinct society concept? There is only one, and it is a weak one, but I hear it very often. Many people tell me: "Well you know, Stéphane, I accept the distinct society personally, but it will never fly in my province, so you are wasting your time trying to defend it." This is precisely the attitude of resignation and despair that I will never accept.

Conclusion

We must never give in to fear or resignation. If we do, we are only defeating ourselves. We can make the changes necessary to rebalance the federation, and make Canada more acceptable to all Canadians. We can celebrate and embrace our differences, including recognition of Quebec's distinctiveness.

We must come together in hope and confidence to achieve these goals, and that is the only way we can save Canada, and our Canadian ideal which is a model for all mankind.

Fears About "Distinct Society" Status Are Unfounded

THE *CALGARY HERALD*, JULY 18, 1996

I wish to address Peter Menzies' comments in his column ("Unity Minister Sings Familiar Refrain," July 11, 1996) that in proposing a constitutional recognition of Quebec's distinctiveness I am promoting a concept which is both unoriginal and unpopular (at least in Western Canada). Unoriginal and unpopular as the idea may be, I still think it is a good one. I will support any good suggestion or valid argument, even if it has been made before.

One of the main reasons I entered politics was to challenge myths and false ideas. In Quebec, I argue against many myths: that Canada is a centralized and repressive federation; that Quebec has never received its fair share in the Canadian federation; that secession would be easy and could be done unilaterally by the Quebec government. My positions are criticized as unoriginal and unpopular by many Quebecers, but I will continue to state them because I think they are true. You should expect me to show the same frankness when I am dealing with myths about Quebec.

In a country that has spent 30 years debating every semicolon and comma of our Constitution, it would be hard to discover something truly new to say. And while the case for Quebec's distinctiveness has indeed been made in the past, it has been poorly understood, in part because there has been more focus on questions of personality and political tactics than the actual substance of the clause.

I hope that this can be the beginning of a new, more substantive debate about this and other unity issues. The sole concrete argument Menzies advanced against recognizing Quebec's distinctiveness is the prospect that "distinct-society status will ... divide [Canada] into legal categories based on language, as Albertans fear." In other words, there is a fear that the constitutional recognition of Quebec's distinctive character will lead to some form of special status, implying additional legal powers for the province of Quebec.

Guest column in the Calgary Herald

These fears are unfounded. Many legal experts have testified that recognition of Quebec's distinctiveness would not change the division of powers between governments, nor would it detract from the authority of the federal or any provincial government.

What then would distinct-society recognition do? At the legal level, its effects would be modest: it would require the courts to interpret constitutional and Charter cases in light of Quebec's unique linguistic and cultural situation in an Anglophone North America. This would not be a radical change in our constitutional jurisprudence. As former chief justice of the Supreme Court of Canada Brian Dickson, a Saskatchewan native, said recently in Winnipeg:

In fact, the courts are already interpreting the Charter of Rights and the Constitution in a manner that takes into account Quebec's distinctive role in promoting its Francophone character. As a practical matter, therefore, entrenching formal recognition of Quebec's distinctive character in the Constitution would not involve a significant departure from the existing practice in our courts. As the former head of Canada's highest court, Dickson should know what he is talking about!

Why entrench distinct society recognition if it would not involve a change in the balance of power, or even a major change in judicial interpretation? For two reasons. Legally, it would turn a matter of constitutional convention and practice into a permanent guarantee that could not be undermined by some future court.

Second, and more importantly, beyond legalities and from a human point of view, it would be a way for all Canadians to express solidarity with Quebecers in their effort to preserve a vibrant and dynamic Francophone society in North America. It would show that all Canadians embrace their majority Francophone province as a fundamental characteristic of Canada.

I know that most Canadians admire and encourage the effort to preserve the French fact in Quebec and elsewhere in Canada. That is why there is strong support, even in the West, for bilingualism in federal institutions. That is why French-immersion schools have been vastly popular in Calgary. Bilingualism is a competitive advantage for Canada. It gives us two windows on the world for trade and culture.

Many American education reformers see the lack of second language education as a key weakness of the American system.

New Brunswick has found its bilingual workforce has become an advantage for them in attracting companies from Europe and the United States.

These efforts are appreciated by Quebecers, despite the dismissal of bilingualism and other measures to support the French language as insignificant by some separatist politicians. Recognizing Quebec's distinctive character would enhance and build upon these other ways of recognizing our linguistic duality, and demonstrate to Quebecers that English-speaking Canadians support them in preserving the only majority French-speaking society in North America. In my view, this would go a long way to reducing the linguistic and cultural insecurity that is the root of the separatist appeal in Quebec.

If you disagree with my interpretation, if you think there are substantive dangers posed by constitutional recognition of Quebec's distinctiveness, then I would be happy to debate them. But is it too much to ask, with the future of our country potentially at stake over a failure to agree on two words, that journalists take seriously the responsibility to inform the public not only of the politics of an issue, but also its substantive content?

I want us to find our way to national reconciliation. To do so, there must be a real dialogue not only among politicians, journalists and academics, but among citizens about what is necessary for our future. I know that many Albertans support the idea of recognizing Quebec's distinctiveness, and I hope that their voices will also be heard in the public debate. And I hope that papers like the *Herald* will become forums for this kind of substantive national discussion.

Quebec's Reasonable Request

THE *CALGARY HERALD*, AUGUST 3, 1996

I was pleased that my recent guest column in the *Herald,* "Fears about distinct society status are unfounded," (July 18) was successful in generating debate in the form of a quick reply from my Reform colleague, Stephen Harper.

Harper even praised me for having "quite forcefully" challenged some of the myths eating away at Canada. I take issue, however, with his charge that my editorial was "blatant propaganda" that engaged in "myth-making" of its own. ("Myth-breaker Dion peddles own propaganda," July 27). Harper is praising me for challenging myths within Quebec but dislikes it when I challenge them elsewhere in Canada.

In my piece, I wrote that a constitutional recognition of Quebec's differences "would not involve a change in the balance of power or even a major change in judicial interpretation" – a fact that has been confirmed by former Supreme Court Chief Justice Brian Dickson. Instead, I argued that it "would be a way for all Canadians to express solidarity with Quebecers in their effort to preserve a vibrant and dynamic Francophone society in North America."

Harper contended that Quebec already enjoys recognition of its distinctive character in many of Canada's laws and institutions. He also argued that many Quebecers overestimate the dangers facing the preservation of Quebec's Francophone character within Canada. To both these I can only agree and I never miss an opportunity to make these points in debate and discussion within Quebec – despite accusations from separatist leaders that I am engaging in propaganda.

I also believe, however, that a constitutional recognition of Quebec's distinctive character would be an important and positive message of support by all Canadians toward a population that accounts for only two per cent of an overwhelmingly English-speaking North America. How would Harper feel if Alberta were the only English-speaking province in a continent of 300 million Francophones and French was the

---

Article in the Calgary Herald

international language of business and the media? Wouldn't a simple recognition of Alberta's efforts to preserve its English-speaking heritage be the least he would want from fellow Canadians?

Harper displayed a deep suspicion of Quebec society. The loaded terms he used such as "xenophobic" and "ethnic nationalism" remind one of the way some Quebec separatists have referred to "Les Anglais" as "redneck" and "reactionary" The simple fact is that Quebec society is as open and accepting as Canadian society as a whole. Polls show that Quebecers are as tolerant toward visible minorities as are other Canadians. Their language laws, although admittedly not perfect, are more liberal and flexible than those that exist in other progressive multilingual democracies such as Switzerland, Belgium and Finland.

Quebecers form a society that reflects the tolerance existing in the rest of the country. The divisive consequences of separation would dramatically damage this spirit of tolerance in Quebec and significantly weaken it elsewhere in Canada, for generations to come. It would create a resentment and suspicion within a citizenry that today lives in admirable harmony.

Recognizing Quebec's distinct character, on the other hand, would go a long way toward reducing the linguistic and cultural insecurity (real and imagined) that helps give Quebec separatism its appeal. It would send a strong message to Quebecers that other Canadians see them as a vital part of our national fabric that we must not lose.

Finally, Harper charged that those who support the recognition of Quebec's distinctiveness are only "so-called" federalists and even implied that they are not "loyal Canadians." Engaging in this type of negative rhetoric brings us no closer to national reconciliation. The only way we can avoid the tragedy of the breakup of our country is to continue to improve our federation and to challenge the myths and false ideas that misrepresent Canadian reality. We must undertake this task with determination and frankness – in English and French.

Canadian Diversity and
the Recognition of Quebec
TORONTO, NOVEMBER 26, 1996

It was very important for me to accept your invitation to talk to you, here at Holy Blossom Temple, about the main reason I feel Canada must remain united. I am especially pleased that representatives of Quebec's Jewish, Greek and Italian communities are here with us in Toronto to share in that discussion.

The main reason that I believe that Canada must stay together has more to do with what is universal about Canada than with what is unique and specific to our country. It is certainly true that those things which symbolize our uniqueness, such as our flag, our national anthem, and the majestic beauty of our vast territory, fill our hearts with pride. And yet, the real reason that Canada is a jewel for humanity is that our country is perhaps the most humane country in the world, where the universal values of freedom, tolerance, and respect for differences are perhaps most respected. At the risk of contradicting my Prime Minister, I'll admit that I don't know whether Canada is "the best country in the world". But I think it would be difficult to find another country where each human being has a better opportunity to be considered as a human being, whatever his or her origin or religion, than here in Canada.

Some have said that Canada is an artificial country. If by that they mean that Canada has overcome so-called natural distinctions of race or ethnicity, to achieve what is truly universal among human beings, we should take this as a great compliment.

It is especially fitting that I talk about the search for universal values at an event organized by the Jewish, Greek, and Italian communities, for in human history it was in Jerusalem, Athens, and Rome that many of these ideals were expressed. Not only have your cultures contributed much in ancient times to the building of human civilization, but your particular communities have played a major part in the building of Canada, and of the two great cities of Montreal and Toronto. There

---

Speech to the Jewish, Hellenic, and Italian Congresses

are 970,000 people of Italian, Jewish, and Greek descent in Toronto and Montreal combined. Neither Montreal nor Toronto – nor Canada itself – would be imaginable without your communities. You, who find your roots in three of the great ancient civilizations, contribute to our pluralistic search to make Canada a model that can serve as a universal ideal.

"I should regard it as a great misfortune for mankind if liberty were to exist all over the world under the same features," wrote Alexis de Tocqueville. The Canadian ideal is a way to avoid this misfortune. Canadians know that the quest for what is right, just and good must be pluralistic. They know that it is by drawing on the best part of each culture, each individual, each regional or historical experience, that we come closer to what is best in civilization. Canadians know that equality must not be confused with uniformity.

In that sense, the Canadian ideal is the ideal of all humanity. If Canada were to break up, we would send a terrible signal to the other countries of the world. Most countries face severe challenges in trying to adapt to cultural diversity in an era of globalization when diverse populations mingle more than ever. Canada's break-up would not encourage the cultural majorities in these countries to show tolerance, openness and trust towards their minorities. On the contrary, many of them would say: "Don't try to be tolerant, democratic and decentralized, as the Canadian federation was, because you'll be signing your own death warrant."

The secession of Quebec would be especially tragic, since Canada's spirit of tolerance, which we all value, emerged precisely from the need for the French and English to find ways to live together and get along. It has not been easy, and many injustices were committed in our history. But the early history of Confederation must be judged in comparison with the 19th century attitudes elsewhere. At that time, many countries, including France and the United States, had policies of cultural assimilation, notably through a "one-size-fits-all" system of mandatory education.

From the very beginning, Canadian history has been marked by a greater openness to difference, a greater spirit of tolerance than most other countries. That initial experience between the British and French in early Canada led them in turn to give a better reception to their new fellow citizens from every continent. Today, we project our spirit of openness beyond our borders by acting as a generous country, a citizen of the world, as we have seen in the recent Canadian response to the crisis in Zaire.

We must not only preserve this Canadian spirit of tolerance, but we must continually improve on it. We must remember that intolerance is always present and has been a part of our history. Recently, the unfortunate affair of Quebec's Lieutenant-Governor, who admitted to youthful ideological errors during the last war, has reminded the people of my province of a past we would rather forget. Those Canadians in other provinces who may have been tempted to lecture Quebecers should read Abella and Troper's book, *None Is Too Many*, to see how widespread racism was in all of Canada at that time. Let us not forget that it was not until the 1960s that our immigration policy was purged of racial criteria.

The reason I am so opposed to Quebec's secession from the rest of Canada, and that I want to fight against it with every means democracy gives me, is certainly not because I believe that Quebecers are less tolerant than other Canadians. No, it is because I am convinced that secession would put tolerance at risk. There is a great contrast between the tolerance of Quebec society and the intolerance of the secessionist option. Understanding this contrast may hold the key to our unity debate.

First, let me talk about the tolerance of Quebec society. In my work as an academic, I have been struck by the extent to which Quebecers cherish the same universal values as other Canadians. If you ask Quebecers their opinion on interracial marriages, for example, you will see the same degree of openness you see elsewhere in Canada, an openness that is generally greater everywhere in Canada than in the United States or Europe. If you observe the day-to-day life of Montreal, you will see that, in spite of geographic distance, that great multicultural city shares the same culture of tolerance as Toronto, Calgary or Vancouver, in contrast with most American cities.

You know that I've spent my whole life immersed in the Quebec academic community, so you won't be surprised to learn that most of my Quebec friends are sovereignists, or at least have been tempted by the sovereignist option. I know that those men and women share the same universal values that have brought us here today. It is because my sovereignist friends share those same values that we need to dialogue with them and explain that secession would jeopardize the kind of open society that they prize.

The reason I oppose secession is that its very dynamic would destroy, for a long time, the spirit of tolerance in Quebec society and would damage that spirit in the rest of Canada. Secession is the type of divisive issue that can plunge the most tolerant of populations into intolerance. This can be seen even now, when secession is merely a possibility, rather than a reality. Since the referendum, which made secession seem a more realistic possibility than it had appeared before, we have seen a worsening of the language debate in Quebec which has shaken the consensus that had prevailed in recent years. Secession is the only issue that is causing an unhealthy split between Francophone and non-Francophone Quebecers. We cannot let this mistrust take over the entire political arena. And yet, that is exactly what would happen in the event of an attempted secession, especially if it were to occur in an atmosphere of confusion about the rules and in violation of the rule of law.

We must consider why the secessionist option divides Quebec Francophones, whereas other Quebecers massively reject it. The fact that non-Francophone Quebecers do not want secession is not because they reject Quebec society. Non-Francophone Quebecers consider themselves to be full participants in Quebec society. But they do not want secession because they do not want to give Canada up.

Indeed, why should they give it up? Some Francophone Quebecers believe there is an advantage in doing so: the advantage of becoming a majority. When they say: "We want to be a majority," it is clear that "we" does not include non-Francophone Quebecers. Jacques Parizeau's famous speech about "money and the ethnic vote" is the explicit proof of that: "If you want to stop talking about Quebec Francophones, we'll speak for ourselves: 60% of us voted Yes, so that's that!" After such a speech, Jacques Parizeau no longer had a political future in the Quebec and Canada of today. And yet, that's the state of mind in which this man would have launched his attempt at secession if the Yes side had won.

Wherever secessionist movements arise in the world, their proponents are members of a specific ethnic, linguistic or religious group, which wants to change existing borders to create a new state in which that group forms the majority. The minorities living in that same region almost never support these secessionist ambitions, unless the existing state is oppressive and authoritarian. This is obviously not the case in Canada. Secession cannot be justified in Canada except by the particular, identity-driven considerations of a specific group. That is why Quebec secession is a project which favours exclusion, and would breed intolerance and division among communities that are now living in harmony.

I'll say it again: the risks do not stem from a feeling of intolerance that is allegedly greater among Quebec Francophones than among other Canadians. Rather, it is secession itself and the break-up of Canada which would breed discord, disturbing suspicions, and feelings of rejection.

Secession would weaken the strong ties of solidarity that unite all Quebecers above and beyond our linguistic or ethnic differences, as well as those equally strong ties that unite Quebecers with our fellow citizens in the Atlantic provinces, Ontario, and Western and Northern Canada. Our universal values impel us on the contrary to strengthen those ties of solidarity. I want to help my fellow citizens, be they Aboriginal people, Newfoundlanders or Ontarians, to express their own way of being Canadian, and to build a better future for their children. I want to help the Jewish, Italian, Greek and other cultural communities throughout Canada. And I want other Canadians to help me to strengthen Quebec society so that the blend of our different cultures makes us better and stronger. But to do that, we have to stay together. We have to reach out to one another, rather than listen to the voices of division and animosity.

Because secession is the problem, not Quebec society, and because that society is such a remarkable element of the Canadian reality, we should recognize Quebec for what it is: a fundamental characteristic of Canada, which we all want to support, because it enriches all Canadians, something which we do not want to lose.

The fact is that, while non-Francophone Quebecers massively reject secession, a great many of them support recognition of Quebec within the Constitution of Canada. They consider themselves to be a part of Quebec society, and wish to remain in Canada, and see no contradiction between these two aspirations. Although they are excluded by the secessionist option, which is driven by goals they do not share, they feel strongly that Quebec society is theirs, because they are helping to strengthen it, along with their Francophone fellow citizens. In its very distinctiveness, Quebec society belongs as much to them as it does to Francophones. After all, non-Francophone Quebecers are the only minority in North America which lives with a Francophone majority. They want to help their Francophone fellow citizens to flourish in this English-speaking continent while ensuring their own rights are respected as well.

If Ontario were surrounded by a Francophone North America, all Ontarians, Anglophones and Francophones, would be in a distinctive situation that would have to be recognized as such by other Canadians.

Canada has already recognized the French language and Quebec's distinctiveness in many ways. The Official Languages Act and constitutional protections for the French language and Quebec's civil code are good examples of this. These were controversial at the time they were introduced, but are now accepted as part of Canada's identity. A further recognition of Quebec's distinctiveness would take the form of an interpretive clause in the Constitution, such as the existing section 27 of the Charter, which recognizes the multicultural heritage of Canadians. Today, after fifteen years under the Charter, nobody would say that this clause has endangered the rights of a single Canadian. Why should recognition of Quebec be any different?

Recognizing Quebec as a fundamental characteristic of Canada would not have the effect of giving Quebecers more powers, privileges or money than other Canadians. Nor would it violate the Canadian Charter of Rights and Freedoms. Rather, it would formalize a convention that already exists, under which our judges are expected to take account of the specific context of Quebec in an English-speaking North America when they rule on issues that affect the province, as former Supreme Court Chief Justice Brian Dickson has recently explained.

The purpose of constitutional recognition of Quebec's distinctiveness is thus not to give Quebec more powers. I have made that very clear, both in Quebec and elsewhere in Canada. Those in Quebec or other provinces who want more powers for their provincial government should submit a list of those powers and explain, on a case-by-case basis, how that transfer of responsibilities would improve public service. That is the only acceptable way to proceed. No federation in the world would agree to put in the Constitution a sort of grab bag that could modify federal-provincial responsibilities without having any idea in advance of how that might occur.

I do not see any valid reason for not recognizing Quebec's distinctiveness in the Canadian Constitution. Some people tell me, "Stéphane, don't make a big thing about it, it's been tried in the past, people don't want it." That's a defeatist attitude which I feel insults Canadians' intelligence. Fatigue and resignation are never good advisors in private life, and they are even less so in public life, when the fate of a country is at stake. We should remember all the major reforms of the past, such as votes for women, compulsory education, and progressive taxation, which were resisted for a long time before gaining public acceptance.

I am also told that the word "distinct" is not the most suitable, because it has in English a sense of superiority that is not found in French. I happen to like the expression in French, "Société Distincte," perhaps because its initials are the same as mine! More seriously, I like the idea of recognizing Quebec as a society, because the word "society" by definition includes all of its members. But the form of the wording chosen is less important than the content of the message that Canadians in all parts of the country would be sending to Quebecers. They would be saying: "We admire the way that you Quebecers, Francophones and non-Francophones alike, are dealing with your specific situation in North America, and we want to show our solidarity with you in your effort to express this Canadian reality, which enriches us all." If Canadians made this gesture clearly, without any haggling, without seeing it as an opportunity to bargain for something else in return; if they did so because it is right and good in and of itself, they would be taking a giant step toward national reconciliation and unity.

Prime Minister Jean Chrétien and his government have recognized Quebec as a distinct society by a resolution in the House. They have made a commitment to work to convince Canadians to entrench the recognition of Quebec in the fundamental law of our country. Some premiers have also taken steps in that direction, as has the leader of the federalist forces in Quebec, Mr. Daniel Johnson. It is clear, however, that constitutional recognition of Quebec must first be popular among Canadians. This reconciliation must be made in people's hearts, not just on a piece of paper signed by politicians.

The representatives of the Greek, Italian and Jewish communities who are here today want to convince their fellow citizens to recognize Quebec's difference. That doesn't mean they agree with everything that is happening in Quebec – far from it. But they do know that Quebec society, to which they belong, expresses in its own way the Canadian ideal. They are asking all Canadians in the other provinces and territories to say loud and clear that they do not want Quebec to be absorbed into a monolithic, English-speaking Canada, but that they want to be in solidarity with Quebec, in the same way that Quebec, by its very nature, helps them to define themselves as Canadians facing a powerful American culture to the south.

We are very much against secession precisely because we are very much for a vibrant Quebec society. Through secession, Quebec society would be renouncing not only Canada, but also the best part of itself. And we are also very much for constitutional recognition of Quebec precisely because we are very much for a strong Canada. This issue is greater than all of us. In the next century, cultural assimilation and cultural separation will be more impractical and morally unacceptable as solutions than ever before. The only solution is the cohabitation of cultures, and its name is Canada. Thank you for giving me the opportunity to express that conviction to my fellow citizens, at this defining moment in our history.

Francophone Communities Outside Quebec: At the Heart of the Canadian Ideal

SUDBURY, ONTARIO, DECEMBER 13, 1996

Linguistic duality has built our country. It has allowed us throughout our history to build bridges between Canadians. It has helped our federation to become a universal example of tolerance, openness and generosity.

I want to talk about that linguistic duality with you, about the great wealth it represents, the advantages it gives to all Canadians and the tolerance it fosters, and the need to strengthen that tolerance. I want us to examine together the current situation of Francophone minorities outside Quebec, without whom our linguistic duality would no longer have the same meaning. I hope that our examination will be neither complacent nor defeatist. We will also look at the realities you have to deal with and the assets at your disposal.

I am especially pleased to be talking about the importance of the future of our linguistic duality today with members of the Franco-Ontarian community, which constitutes the strongest French-language minority in the country. The Institut Franco-ontarien, which is celebrating its 20th birthday, is reflective of your community: courageous, determined, an example for all Canadians.

Linguistic duality: a source of dialogue and tolerance

Our official languages, one of Canada's strengths, are among the most widely spoken languages in the world. They greatly contribute to Canada's economic, social, cultural and international success.

French and English are recognized languages of the United Nations and NATO. French is the official language of no fewer than 33 countries, and English, 56. Some 800 million people in the world speak English, and 180 million speak French. Canada is a member of both the Francophonie, which includes 49 countries and governments, and its Anglophone counterpart, the Commonwealth, which comprises 50 countries.

Speech to the Institut franco-ontarien

In this era of market globalization, Canada's bilingual character facilitates trade ties with all those countries. In a highly competitive market, a bilingual work force is an asset that can make all the difference.

According to Jean Laponce, a political science professor at the University of British Columbia and the University of Ottawa: "Having English and French as its two dominant languages makes Canada unique among democratic industrialized states, the very states that are at the core of the world communication system."

Linguistic duality does not only help to create economic wealth. It also lays the foundations of a tolerant society. Linguistic duality has helped us greatly to show more solidarity and openness to diversity. That spirit of tolerance, which we all cherish today, stemmed precisely from the need for the English and French to find ways to take advantage both of their respective identities and of the complementarity of their cultures. It has not always been easy, there have been dark pages in our history and many injustices committed against some communities, such as the unfortunate passage of Regulation 17 in Ontario in 1912.

The early history of our Confederation, however, must be judged against attitudes prevailing elsewhere in the 19th century. The linguist Jacques Leclerc prepared an overview in 1986 of linguistic situations throughout the world, based on an analysis of some 6,000 languages and 170 sovereign states. According to Leclerc, "In the 19th century, centralizing authoritarianism, which consists of unilaterally imposing a single language throughout a territory and ignoring linguistic pluralism ... was the order of the day."

The values of tolerance which we now feel are essential were simply not at that time. A number of countries then, including France and the United States, had active policies of cultural assimilation, notably through a "one size fits all" system of mandatory education. Fortunately, Canada rejected that system. We can see today how much our linguistic duality gives us a clear advantage as human beings in comparison with citizens of unilingual countries.

The close proximity of another language encourages us to become open to a whole cultural universe. Language is a means for transmitting cultural and social values. Learning a second language such as French allows Anglophones to incorporate cultural elements and values from other parts of the world, such as Switzerland, Haiti or Cameroon. As the writer Antonine Maillet so eloquently puts it, "Every time you look at the world and life and humanity through the key, which is language, you discover another profile, another vision of the same world ... So learning another language makes you bigger, gives you a wider vision."

The cohabitation of our two linguistic communities has helped us to welcome with greater tolerance and openness our fellow citizens from all continents. In that respect, Canada's bilingualism and multiculturalism, rather than conflicting with each other, complement and mutually strengthen each other. That is why it would be so regrettable for Canada to break up because of its linguistic aspect, when it is that very aspect that has helped it so much to become a model of openness celebrated throughout the world.

We must preserve and continually improve that spirit of tolerance. For if intolerance were to prevail today against linguistic duality, an essential aspect of our country, it would turn on our multicultural component tomorrow, and we would thus lose the soul of Canada.

Indeed, it is to preserve tolerance and openness that I am so opposed to secession, the very dynamic of which is a source of division. Secession is the kind of divisive issue that can plunge the most tolerant populations into intolerance. The threat of secession is not only creating an unhealthy split between Quebec Francophones and Quebec Anglophones, but is also aggravating tensions between Canadian Anglophones and Francophones outside Quebec. Some of you may have some experience of this. Secession would have serious consequences not only for French-language minority communities, which would be cut off from the only majority Francophone society in North America, but for all Canadians as well.

The situation of French outside Quebec

That Francophones outside Quebec account for only 3.6% of the Canadian population overall obviously does not make things any easier for them. Some disgruntled observers conclude from that that there is no longer any future for them, and that assimilation is inevitable. To back up their pessimism, they always trot out the same series of statistics comparing mother tongue and language spoken at home. And, indeed, Statistics Canada data do indicate that, outside Quebec, French is the language spoken most often at home for 3.2% of Canadians, whereas mother-tongue Francophones represent 4.8% of the population. The same situation can be seen in Ontario: whereas Francophones represent 5% of the province's population, 3.2% of Ontarians speak French most often at home. But those numbers have to be looked at in the proper context! The indicator of language spoken most often at home does not, in and of itself, make it possible to conclude that there is assimilation. Someone living in an English-speaking city with an English-speaking spouse is likely to use English at home more often. That doesn't mean, however, that that person no longer uses French or is not passing that language on to his or her children.

It is true that the relative demographic weight of Francophones outside Quebec is dropping: from 7.3% in 1951 to 4.8% in 1991 for Canada not including Quebec, and from 7.4% to 5% in Ontario during the same period. That drop is due in large part to a lower birth rate and the strong attraction of English for immigrants. And yet, despite that drop in the relative demographic weight of Francophones outside Quebec, and despite the "no future outside Quebec" doomsayers, the actual number of Francophones outside Quebec, based on mother tongue, rose from 721,000 to more than 976,000 between 1951 and 1991, an increase of 35.4%. In Ontario, for example, the total number of Francophones also continues to rise, from 341,000 in 1951 to more than 503,000 in 1991, an increase of 47.5%; by comparison, Quebec Anglophones have seen their numbers increase by only 12.2% during the same period. That increase is especially visible in urban regions: Statistics Canada reports higher numbers of Francophones outside Quebec in 19 out of 20 metropolitan regions in Canada between 1986 and 1991.

Nevertheless, beyond Statistics Canada data and quantitative indicators, the living proof of the vitality of your Francophone communities is, in fact, their very vitality itself. No matter where they are, be it in Ontario, New Brunswick, Alberta or elsewhere in Canada, your communities display remarkable energy and great determination, as evidenced by your cultural, social and economic institutions. Your contribution to Canada is invaluable.

No matter what the writer Yves Beauchemin may have to say, the Franco-Ontarian community and Francophones outside Quebec are far from being "warm corpses"! The very opposite is true. One need only think of your institute, created by a handful of idealists 20 years ago, which is a haven for Franco-Ontarian research. The many literary awards garnered by Franco-Ontarian writers are a testimony to your vitality. In 1996, the poet Andrée Lacelle won the Trillium literary award for her collection *Tant de vie s'égare*. In 1993, François Paré won the Governor General's Award and Radio-Québec's Signet d'or award for *Les Littératures de l'exiguïté*, and Daniel Poliquin took the Signet d'or for *L'écureuil noir*. In 1988, playwright Jean-Marc Dalpé won the Governor General's Award for his play *Le Chien*, and Michel Ouellette received the Governor General's Award for *Frenchtown* in 1994. And there are so many others, such as Patrice Desbiens, Andrée Christensen, Roger Levac and Paul Savoie ... More and more Franco-Ontarian authors, writers, poets, novelists and playwrights are known not only in Ontario and elsewhere in Canada, but also beyond our borders.

The Toronto French Book Fair has been going strong since 1992. French-language publishing companies are becoming increasingly numerous, such as Prise de Parole (Sudbury), Les éditions du Nordir (Hearst and Ottawa), Les éditions du Vermillon (Ottawa), and Les éditions David (Orléans). And let's not forget the professional theatre companies, such as the Francophone theatre company of Sudbury and the Théâtre du Nouvel Ontario founded here in Sudbury 25 years ago, and the numerous Francophone festivals such as Ottawa's Franco-Ontarian festival, LeFranco, which is the foremost French-language cultural event of its kind in North America.

That same vitality can be seen at the economic level as well. Francophones own more than 7,500 stores, businesses and companies in Ontario. The Francophone business community is coming closer together: in particular, the Chambre économique de l'Ontario, which was established four years ago, not only links businesspeople within the province, but also fosters contacts with other Francophone organizations in Quebec and the other provinces. The first Forum of Francophone Businesspeople and Elected Municipal Officials in Canada was recently held in the Beauce region of Quebec, attracting more than 200 participants from across Canada to discuss ways to maximize opportunities for doing business in French in Canada and abroad. Francophone entrepreneurship outside Quebec accounts for 348 Francophone cooperatives, with $3.9 billion in assets, $327 million in investments and 20,000 Francophone entrepreneurs.

Realities you have to deal with and assets at your disposal

Francophone communities outside Quebec need to be vibrant and dynamic, because the realities of today constitute a major challenge:

– Secularisation, which has transformed the social structure and facilitated interlinguistic marriages.
– Communications, in which English is dominant everywhere, from television to the Internet.
– A falling birth rate, which cannot be offset by immigrants, who are naturally attracted by the language of the continent.
– Urbanization, which has made it more difficult to forge community ties and has attracted young people to large Anglophone cities.

And yet, you are not unequipped to deal with those realities. First and foremost, as I have said, you have your extraordinary vitality. Moreover, you can count on the values of tolerance and respect you have been able to develop alongside the Anglophone majority. Those values are certainly being tested today, by the host of reactions that the threat of secession is generating in the country. Nevertheless, the vast majority of your English-speaking fellow citizens want to help you and are proud of their country's Francophone dimension.

When you appeal to their hearts and their finer feelings, Canadians are generous people. According to a new book by Angus Reid entitled Shakedown: How the New Economy is Changing Our Lives, more than 85% of Canadians "believe that English and French Canadians can live harmoniously under one flag." Another poll (Compas, May 1995) indicates that three out of four Anglophone Canadians want their children to learn French.

A second asset is that more of your Anglophone fellow citizens now speak French than ever before in the history of our Confederation. According to Statistics Canada, close to 2.8 million young Canadians were enrolled in French or English second-language programs in 1995, 77.2% in French. Those classes are yielding tangible results: the proportion of bilingual 15- to 25-year-olds rose from 16% to 23% between 1981 and 1991. The highest rate of bilingualism is found among Anglophones in the 10 to 14 and 15 to 19 age groups, at 14.8% and 16.7% respectively. A record 313,000 young Anglophones are now in French immersion school, compared with 38,000 in 1977. That means there are now 10 times as many French immersion students as there were 20 years ago!

A third asset you have is the charters. Your rights have never been better established than since the introduction of the Official Languages Act, the Canadian Charter of Rights and Freedoms, and the Constitution Act, 1982. Since the Constitution Act, 1982, French-language educational services have been more available. Francophone school management is a fact of life in New Brunswick, Prince Edward Island, Alberta, Saskatchewan, Manitoba and Yukon, and is close to being introduced in Nova Scotia. It is unfortunate that Francophone communities in some provinces have to go to court to have their rights respected. The federal government will continue to support the full implementation of your rights in all provinces and territories.

Finally, you have another asset, which is the support of the federal government. That doesn't mean that the provinces don't have to help you, but you know that the Prime Minister and the federal government will always have a special responsibility in respect of this country's official-language minorities. It is true that you are often hurt by budget cuts. We have had to make difficult but necessary decisions to reduce the deficit, which had reached record levels, and to put our fiscal house in order. All federal departments and agencies have had to deal with budget cuts. It is impossible to spare Francophones outside Quebec, but we have always sought to ensure that your communities are given equitable support.

The federal government's support to official-language minority communities takes account of the sociological context. You, as Francophones outside Quebec, are a minority in your own province, a minority within Canada and a minority within the English-speaking North American continent.

Our policies seek to help you in four ways. First, through support for official-language education. Next, through support to your communities themselves, through equitable representation of Francophones within the public service and federal institutions, and finally, by availability of federal services in French.

Since 1970, in accordance with the recommendations of the Royal Commission on Bilingualism and Biculturalism, the federal government has financially assisted the provincial and territorial governments so as to give members of official-language minority communities the opportunity to study in their own language and to enable young Canadians to learn French or English as a second language. Those two elements – minority-language instruction and second-language education – correspond to our vision of Canada. Through the Official Languages in Education Program, some 161,000 Francophone elementary and secondary students can study in their own language in some 700 Francophone schools outside Quebec. In addition to giving young Canadians the opportunity to learn French or English as a second language, it has supported the development of existing institutions such as the University of Ottawa, and has also made it possible to expand the network of Francophone post-secondary institutions. Collège Boréal in Sudbury, Collège des Grands-Lacs and Cité collégiale, institutions that did not exist only a few years ago, will help to advance knowledge of and use of French among Canadian young people.

Our government also provides direct support to official-language minority communities through Canada-community agreements. The agreements were initiated in 1988 with Saskatchewan's Francophone community and enable communities to make decisions that affect their development and reflect the needs of their members. The Canada-community agreement with Ontario, the last to be signed, will provide more than $18 million to Ontario's Francophone community and will help it to set development priorities. Through the Department of Canadian Heritage, the federal government supports official-language minority community media such as TFO, the French-language service of TV Ontario, as well as weekly newspapers.

The federal government has very specific obligations under the Official Languages Act, particularly with respect to equitable participation by members of official-language communities in federal institutions. The federal government is continuing its efforts to ensure that participation of federal employees reflects the presence of the two linguistic communities. Francophones have maintained their presence despite the reduction in the size of the public service. As of March 31, 1996, 29% of federal employees were French-speaking and 71% were English-speaking. We know that Francophones make up 25.2% of Canada's population and Anglophones, 74.3%.

We also have obligations pertaining to the availability of federal services in French. The situation is not perfect. In his 1995 annual report, the Commissioner of Official Languages noted that the Ontario public was experiencing proportionally more frequent problems than in the other provinces. Federal institutions have taken action and progress has since been made with respect to three indicators of public service: service in person, service by telephone and active offer of services. The improvements were highlighted in the latest report by the President of the Treasury Board: service in person and by telephone is now available in 98% of offices that are required to provide services in both official languages, compared with 85% and 88% in 1994 and 1995 respectively. With respect to active offer of services, the percentage of offices fulfilling their obligations has risen from 53% to 97%.

Another example is labour market agreements transferring active employment measures to the provinces. Those agreements, one of which has just been concluded with Alberta, will stipulate that all signatory provinces must provide services in French where there is a significant demand. The Government also takes official languages considerations into account in connection with privatization measures, on a case by case basis. For major privatization operations, privatized organizations have been made subject to the Official Languages Act, in whole or in part, as is the case with Air Canada, CN and Nav Canada. Under the *Act*, Internet sites of federal offices must be designed in both official languages and provide information in French and English. Guidelines will help federal institutions to understand clearly and fulfil this requirement.

Progress has been made, but there is room for improvement. In 1996, the Government published the results of the first phase of an audit on service to the public that was conducted between January and March 1995 in some census areas. The Government intends to continue its audits.

Your federal government is providing you with support, a framework and tools, but your vitality comes first and foremost from within yourselves.

Conclusion

Our linguistic duality has fostered the emergence of a tolerant society which we must strengthen. Canada itself is a major challenge which we must never take for granted. And your communities are at the heart of the Canadian challenge. You are the very essence of the Canadian ideal. It would be very difficult to find your equivalent elsewhere in the world in this century, when the number of languages spoken is getting smaller, rather than larger, for the first time in the history of humanity.

While there are now only 20 million Europeans who speak a minority language in their own country, compared with 50 million at the turn of the century; while there are now 20,000 people in Ireland who can speak Irish, compared with 6 million of their ancestors in the 18th century; while there are now only 25,000 Austrians who speak Slovenian, compared with 100,000 in 1880; while there were only 7,000 Germans who spoke Friesian in 1925 and there are even fewer today, whereas there were 52,000 two centuries ago; and while a paltry 1% of the Welsh population knows Welsh, whereas two thirds of the population spoke Welsh in 1840, in this country called Canada, there are now and still will be in the next century strong Francophone communities outside Quebec who speak French. In the next century, they will still express an irreplaceable facet of the culture and history of our country. They will become stronger, because this is Canada, the country of tolerance.

Which Canada do we want to prevail: that of Regulation 17, or that of the Canadian Charter of Rights and Freedoms; that of Francophone communities outside Quebec left to their own devices, or that which supports them; that of French not recognized in federal institutions, or that of the Official Languages Act?

The Canada that will prevail is the Canada of openness and tolerance, the Canada of the Canadian Charter of Rights and Freedoms, the Canada of official languages, and the Canada of the Franco-Ontarian community.

Renewal and the Role of the Métis

OTTAWA, FEBRUARY 14, 1997

I am pleased to be here today on behalf of the Honourable Anne McLellan, Federal Interlocutor for Métis and Non-Status Indians, and to have the opportunity to participate in the Métis National Council policy conference. This conference, of course, is one of the key elements of the bilateral process between the Privy Council Office and the Métis National Council. The bilateral process provides an important forum for the Métis National Council to discuss issues of mutual interest with federal government departments, and assists the Council in facilitating its work with those departments.

Your conference provides a timely forum for you to discuss various issues that governments are currently examining in the context of the renewal of the federation. It is also timely in that it follows fairly closely upon the release of the Final Report of the Royal Commission on Aboriginal Peoples. I trust that you will have the opportunity over the next few days to have interesting discussions on many of the vital issues that confront us today.

In the past year, I have travelled much across Canada. I have come to appreciate as never before the vastness of our country and the invaluable contribution of our many diverse groups and communities, including that of the Métis people, to the edification of Canada. In my remarks this morning, I would like to say a few words about something we should all learn more about, which is the historic role of the Métis people in building our country, as well as the important continuing role the Métis have in strengthening national unity.

I would also like to address the renewal of the federation, and the significant role that the Métis people are playing in this endeavour. In that context, I would also like to discuss some notable developments that have occurred over the past few years in areas such as self-government for Métis and off-reserve Aboriginal people.

Speech to the Métis National Council

Working together toward national reconciliation

The Métis people have left their imprint on the evolution of Canada, particularly the West, in a truly unique way. Indeed, the history of Canada would be much different without the contribution of the Métis people. With their remarkable adaptation of European and Indian languages and cultures, the Métis were logical intermediaries in the commercial relationship that arose from the development of the fur trade and the opening of the West.

The Métis of our early history were one of the principal determinants of Canada's expansion westward, not only in their vital economic role, but also in their role of protectors of that region from American incursions. The special qualities and skills of the Métis made them indispensable to our nation's development. They were traders, suppliers, freighters, couriers, interpreters, diplomats and guides.

They developed a new culture, one that is rooted in the history of Western Canada. Their "Metchif" language formed from a mixture of French, English, Cree and Ojibway languages.

They were inventors. They adapted European technology to a rugged wilderness, through innovations such as the Red River cart and the York boat, which facilitated the transport of large volumes of goods and supplies across the West to the far-flung outposts of the fur trade. The Métis developed their own forms of governance which ultimately resulted in the development of a new province, Manitoba.

Any discussion of nation-building and the Métis must of course make reference to the role of Louis Riel. As with many prominent figures in our history, Riel was a controversial figure in his day, and he has remained so. Whatever your point of view, Riel's accomplishments were numerous and they were significant. First of all, as a politician, I have to admire a man who was elected by acclamation three times to the House of Commons.

In examining Riel's controversial role in our history, I am struck in many ways by the parallels in what he faced at that time and the challenges we currently face in our efforts to strengthen the unity of our country. The population of the area of the Northwest at the time of Riel was about 12,000. It included about 6,000 French-speaking Métis, 4,000 English-speaking Métis, and 2,000 others from different nations. These individuals represented several different languages and cultures and several different religious views. In many ways, the Northwest of Riel's time was a microcosm of Canada as we know it today, with our many cultures, languages and traditions.

Louis Riel was an eloquent defender of Métis rights, as well as those of all members of his community, whether Aboriginal or non-Aboriginal,

Anglophone or Francophone. He and his followers drew up a list of rights that protected not only his own people, but all of the settlers living in the Northwest Territories at that time. This is a remarkable contribution, especially when we consider the similarities between that list of rights and our own Charter of Rights and Freedoms, which came over one hundred years later.

Riel's list of rights, of course, became the basis for his negotiations on the terms of admission of Manitoba into Confederation, the Manitoba Act, which provided for certain guarantees for Métis people, including schooling and religious rights, as well as recognition of French and English language rights. Unfortunately, many of the achievements of the Manitoba Act were destined to be short-lived.

In the ensuing decades, the execution of Riel and the dispersement of the Métis people throughout the Northwest, along with the subsequent denial of language and religious rights in Manitoba, had a dramatic impact on the entire nation. Indeed, as a Quebecer, I am struck by how closely the destinies of Quebec and the Métis people are linked. Had Manitoba and Canada evolved in the vision of Riel and his followers, there would likely have been a much stronger Francophone presence in Manitoba, and perhaps in all of Western Canada. This would have affected the evolution of the Canadian federation, and may have avoided the sense of isolation from other parts of Canada that many Quebecers feel today.

That being said, we must look forward to the future. As Louis Riel said to his followers in the Northwest prior to the passing of the Manitoba Act: "Let us hope that the lessons of the past will guide us in the future!" Despite differences of language, religion and lifestyle, the Métis and the other settlers of the Northwest learned to live together in a bilingual climate. In our struggles of today, we need to take inspiration from this early chapter in the history of our nation. We need to be reminded of the words of Sir Wilfrid Laurier who, in 1886, very aptly described the lesson we need to draw from history. In condemning the Government's actions with regard to the Metis people, Laurier stated: "Had they taken as much pains to do right, as they have taken to punish wrong, they never would have had any occasion to convince those people, that the law cannot be violated with impunity, because the law would never have been violated at all."

How true this is today! In order to avoid the bad one must promote the good. This is the approach the federal government is taking in the measures it is putting forth to address Métis concerns. I will be speaking about some of these measures later in my speech.

The Métis people have always worked to build and to strengthen this great country, and that role is as important now as it has always been.

Throughout the 1980s and 1990s, the Métis people have been growing stronger and are continuing to make a valuable contribution to the evolution of our nation. Métis men and women today distinguish themselves in many fields of endeavour, such as business, education, law, medicine, and the arts.

I know how much you want to continue to play a strong role in our country's future. Indeed, your former president, now the Lieutenant-Governor of Manitoba, Yvon Dumont, and your current president, Gerald Morin, have spoken out on many occasions about the desire of the Métis people for a strong and united Canada. Let us not forget the legacy of the early Métis nation-builders, as we continue to build this nation with the Canadian values of tolerance, justice, fairness, cooperation, sharing and generosity to all people.

Building stronger relationships

There are, of course, many aspects to building a nation, particularly in such a complex federation as Canada. As many of you may be aware, one of my key roles as Minister for Intergovernmental Affairs has been to coordinate the federal government's efforts in renewing and modernizing the Canadian federation. The Liberal government's vision is of a federation where the different orders of government work together to ensure Canadians receive the best possible range of services. To that end, I have been working with my colleagues and with the provinces and territories to clarify the roles of the different orders of government.

As you know, all governments today are facing difficult fiscal, economic, and social changes. But we have to deal with change in constructive and innovative ways if we are to ensure that all Canadians receive the programs and services and opportunities that underpin our social and economic future together. In some areas, we are building new relationships with the provinces and territories to ensure that our activities are complementary. We are working with the other orders of government to clarify our roles, to untangle them if necessary, and to ensure that we are working well together. In some areas, such as job training, we are withdrawing, recognizing that the provinces and territories are closer to the people who need these services, and therefore best able to adapt job training to their needs. In all cases, we are looking for new ways to ensure we are better able to respond to the needs of Canadians. I am happy to note that many of the issues which we as governments are addressing are issues that you have on your agenda for today and tomorrow – issues such as social policy renewal, economic development and training, and the environment.

In meeting the challenges ahead, the federal, provincial and territorial governments cannot operate in a vacuum. While we are continuing to work with the provinces, we are also working with you. That is why the Prime Minister has asked us to ensure that the rights and interests of Aboriginal peoples are respected, and that the Aboriginal people have a voice in these endeavours. To that end, senior federal ministers, including Minister McLellan and I, have met on several occasions with the representatives of the national Aboriginal associations, including your president, Gerald Morin. These meetings have been extremely positive and have provided a valuable input to our work. As you may be aware, the focus of the follow-up work arising from the First Ministers' Meeting is on sectoral initiatives led by sectoral ministers. As such, I have encouraged Aboriginal leaders to pursue their concerns directly with the federal ministers who have the lead responsibility for specific initiatives to renew the federation.

The Métis National Council has been involved in regular discussions on renewal of the federation with officials from various departments, and, in her role as Federal Interlocutor, Minister McLellan and her officials will continue to ensure that you can work with the lead federal ministers on the various initiatives. In key areas, such as social policy renewal and the environment, officials from the Métis National Council have been meeting regularly with federal officials, thus ensuring that the views of the Métis Nation are taken into account. The feedback that I have received on these meetings, from both Aboriginal groups and federal departments, has been extremely positive. The input of the Métis National Council and its members is important to the development of these new relationships we are pursuing, and I look forward to your continuing participation in these efforts. At the same time, I would encourage you to take your views to the provinces, which also have a key role to play in the renewal of the federation.

Building our relationships with Métis

I often point to the flexibility of our federation as one of the key strengths of our federal system. It is flexible enough to adapt and evolve when faced with new challenges and new contexts. It is a flexibility that also allows us to respond well to the evolving aspirations of its different citizens, provinces, regions and cultures. Our approach to the renewal of the federation builds on this flexibility.

Our commitment to building effective relationships and finding innovative solutions is also the spirit which animates the federal approach to the implementation of the inherent right to and the negotiation of self-government for all Aboriginal peoples, including Métis, which was announced by the Honourable Ron Irwin and the Honourable Anne McLellan in August 1995. The federal approach to self-government is flexible enough to take into account the unique circumstances of the Métis people.

Rather than focussing on abstract discussions of self-government, the federal approach focuses on what works, to achieve the progress that we all want to attain in this important area. The federal approach contemplates various practical ways of implementing self-government for Métis people, including the development of institutions providing programs and services, the devolution of programs and services, and forms of public government. I believe the federal approach will ultimately result in the Métis people having control over self-government institutions, and correspondingly over the programs and services which are key to your future.

Of course, no one has the formula for exactly how self-government for Métis people will look in the future. But, by working together through tripartite self-government processes, we will find out what works most effectively to provide Métis people with the tools they need to build stronger, healthier communities. With its emphasis on practical progress, I am optimistic the federal framework provides a solid foundation for progress to be made on self-government, which will allow Aboriginal people to exercise their full social and economic potential.

Earlier, I spoke about the importance of improving collaboration between governments. Like the renewal of the federation, the negotiation of self-government is a challenging undertaking that will require the long-term commitment of all involved. Working together effectively is the key to the success of the self-government initiative. All parties need to be involved – Aboriginal people, the federal government, the provinces, and the municipal governments.

Turning to some specific sectoral initiatives, I believe the federal government has taken some bold, pro-active steps in the area of federal programs and services. As you are aware, in the area of post-Pathways, the Métis National Council has signed a national framework agreement dealing with labour market training. I understand that some Métis National Council affiliates have already negotiated regional bilateral agreements under this framework, and that others are underway. This is an important step toward self-government.

I would also like to mention the Aboriginal Procurement program, the Aboriginal Justice strategy, and the Aboriginal Veteran's scholarship fund. These programs all offer evidence of the continuing benefit of governments working together with Aboriginal groups, including Métis people, to develop programs and services that meet the needs of your community. Some of them are of course at an early stage of development, and we will require your continued input to make them work.

Conclusion

In conclusion, I am reminded of a quotation from the Prime Minister, who said "Our federation should be responsive to our common needs and diversity. It should show respect for each other and our institutions. It should involve partnership and dialogue with our governments and citizens."

As you progress through your conference, and address the individual issues that confront you, I invite you to keep in mind your necessary role in keeping our country strong and united, and in fostering the dialogue to which the Prime Minister was referring. I am confident that you will meet this responsibility with the same vigour and dedication that has always characterized the contribution of Métis people to Canadian society.

You have a continuing important role to play in the future of this country. The strength of the Métis Nation helped build this country and the strength of the Métis Nation will help bring it united into the 21st century. I wish to join Minister McLellan in expressing my best wishes for a successful meeting. Thank you.

Respecting the Balance of Equality and Diversity

THE *FINANCIAL POST*, NOVEMBER 7, 1997

To the Editor:

Your columnist Rafe Mair, while offering me kind words personally, says that my "wide-eyed innocence" has led me "to badly misread British Columbia and probably Alberta as well" with regards to the acceptability of the Calgary Declaration in those provinces. While I appreciate the friendliness he has shown me, both in his column and on his radio show, I want to be clear that my support for the Calgary Declaration is not motivated by any kind of naïveté.

First, the Calgary Declaration is not a constitutional amendment. It is a statement of principles about the kind of Canada we want. In particular, it shows how Canada is built on a balance of respect for the equality of citizens and provinces and respect for the diversity of people and cultures.

I don't think that many Canadians have difficulty accepting that an important part of Canada's diversity is the unique character of Quebec, as the only society in North America with a French-speaking majority, culture, and civil law. Where they have difficulty is with the suggestion that if we recognize this within the Constitution, it may somehow give Quebec powers or privileges that other provinces will not have.

I think these fears are unfounded. Even in the distinct society clauses of the Meech Lake and Charlottetown Accords, the recognition would have been in the form of an interpretive clause – a guide to the courts for making decisions about the grey areas of our Constitution. Mr. Mair says I do not realize "that this is why there was such a fuss in the first place."

Frankly, I don't think the fuss was over the idea of an interpretive clause, as I don't think most Canadians were aware of what an inter-

---

Letter to the Financial Post

pretive clause is and what weight it would have in guiding the courts. There was a non-derogatory clause in both Meech and Charlottetown making clear that distinct society would not have reduced the powers of either Parliament or any provincial legislatures. And as I have pointed out before, even on Rafe Mair's show, many jurists, including former Chief Justice Brian Dickson, have stated that the courts already consider Quebec's linguistic and cultural uniqueness in formulating their decisions, so formalizing this recognition in the Constitution would not be a major departure from current legal practice. The fears surrounding "distinct society" had little to do with the legal technicalities of an interpretive clause, and much to do with the phrase becoming a black box into which people could project their fears of Quebec gaining special status and powers unavailable to others.

The Calgary Declaration, however, makes it clear that this cannot be the case. The recognition of Quebec's uniqueness does not detract from the equal status of the provinces. And in the event that an interpretive clause conveys some advantage to one province, Calgary makes it clear that the same right must be made available to the other provinces as well.

As to whether I have misread public opinion in B.C. and Alberta, I cannot say. But current polls show that about two-thirds of citizens in both B.C. and Alberta support the Calgary Declaration, levels very close to those in the rest of Canada.

In the event that there is a federalist government elected in Quebec, and an interpretive clause based on all of the principles included in the Calgary Declaration is proposed as a constitutional amendment, there will have to be referendums under B.C. and Alberta law in order for their legislatures to pass the amendment. Furthermore, acceptance by B.C. and Alberta is necessary for the Parliament of Canada to pass such an amendment under Bill C-110. So if Mr. Mair is correct about public opinion, and the current approval level melts away as the debate unfolds, then there will be no constitutional amendment.

However, I remain confident that Canadians would easily accept a recognition of Quebec's unique character combined with a clear statement on the equality of citizens and provinces in our Constitution, as these are a true reflection of widely held Canadian values. Canadians believe, as Alberta's Premier Ralph Klein has said, "in a Canada where all provinces have equal status but a Canada that allows Quebec to protect those things that make it such a unique part of our national character ... a tolerant and diverse nation where we are all equal as Canadians, no matter where we live, but where the word 'equality' is not used as a blanket to smother diversity." Perhaps the greatness of Canada has been that we have been better able to reconcile these values of equality and diversity than any country on earth, and I don't believe that Canadians will hesitate when the time comes to enshrine these values in our Constitution.

Sincerely,

Stéphane Dion

On the Harmonization of
Federal Legislation with Quebec Civil Law

MONTREAL, NOVEMBER 24, 1997

I am happy to open this Conference on the Harmonization of Federal Legislation with Quebec Civil Law. Your deliberations will provide us with food for thought on a topic that is of close interest to the legal community in Quebec and in Canada as a whole. I intend to devote my opening address to the concept of bijuralism and the advantages it brings to Canada.

Canada: A bijural country

Without a doubt, Canada has one of the most respected legal systems in the world. That well-earned reputation is clearly due to the excellence of our law faculties, the exceptional quality of our judges and the wisdom of their decisions. But it is also due to the coexistence of two great legal traditions of the Western world, civil law and common law.

For Canada can in fact be proud to be one of the rare bijural countries in the world. As early as 1774, the Quebec Act maintained in force French laws and customs with respect to property and civil rights in the province. The Constitutional Act, 1791 and the Union Act, 1840 did not modify the rights recognized in 1774. And when the Canadian federal union was created, this legal duality was confidently entrenched. Indeed, the Constitution Act, 1867 provides that private law is an exclusive provincial jurisdiction, which has allowed Quebec to make the Civil Code of Lower Canada the framework of its civil law, while the other provinces could continue to be governed by common law. That duality is also reflected in the requirement that superior court judges in Quebec be selected from members of the bar of that province. The same is true for the Supreme Court of Canada, for under the Supreme Court Act, three of its nine judges must be from the Barreau du Québec. The bijural character of our legal system is thus entrenched in the very heart of our basic law. In that and many other respects, Que-

Speech at a symposium in Montreal

bec enjoys a degree of autonomy that is uncommonly high, and much higher than that of many other federated states.

The civil law tradition is not only an essential characteristic of Quebec society, as the premiers of nine provinces recognized once again in the Calgary Declaration, but it is also an asset for Canada as a whole.

Bijuralism certainly poses some particular challenges, which you will be studying in the course of your deliberations. But it is an undeniable richness for those who know how to use it and benefit from it. In the words of Mr. Philip Simpson, a British lawyer who works with the Court of Justice of the European Communities [translation]: "the existence of two independent legal systems within a single nation-state does not inevitably lead to conflict; on the contrary, such coexistence can be advantageous for all."

Absolutely: Canada has every reason to be proud of its two great legal traditions, and it has a duty to do everything in its power to ensure that they flourish and complement each other. Civil law cannot but benefit from its interactions with common law, and the reverse is also true. In that respect, it is wonderful that more and more Canadian jurists are mastering our two legal systems, a development which promotes the teaching of common law in French and the learning of civil law in English. In so doing, not only are our jurists expanding their horizons and honing their skills; the entire legal community is forging closer ties, and all Canadians are the winners.

Our bijuralism is not only advantageous in our mutual relations among Canadians. It also facilitates access to other countries. We thus gain a better understanding of the laws in force in the countries with which we are intensifying our relations, the vast majority of which are governed by legal systems stemming from common law or civil law. As points of contact between very diverse legal cultures multiply, that is an appreciable competitive edge. Indeed, in this era of economic and market globalization, mastering the two most widespread legal systems in the world is more than ever a substantial asset. For example, the fact that most South American countries are governed by legislation inspired by civil law gives us in our relations with them an advantage over our neighbours in the United States.

Our bijuralism obliges us to develop expertise in solving problems relating to the juxtaposition of rules of law stemming from different traditions. We can help other countries to benefit from that experience we have acquired. The Government intends to make Canada a leader in that field.

Bilingualism allows Canada to be a member of both the Francophonie and the Commonwealth. The varied cultural origins of the Canadian population also give us many footholds in the world. Our opening to the Pacific and the Atlantic bolsters our cultural and commercial exchanges. In the same way, our bijuralism gives us a window on the world, and the Government of Canada wants to work actively to promote that fundamental characteristic of Quebec society, which is shared by all of Canada.

Respecting the civil law tradition

As Professor Morel of the Faculty of Law of the Université de Montréal has noted [translation], "The complementarity of federal law and civil law, however natural it may be ... must be constantly maintained and reaffirmed, if not reinvented, to remain alive."

More than ever, then, we must do all we can to develop this important aspect of Canadian diversity. Prime Minister Jean Chrétien believes deeply in the advantages of that diversity, which is why he moved the resolution adopted in 1995 by both Houses of Parliament recognizing that Quebec society is distinguished in particular by its civil law tradition and calling on "all components of the legislative and executive branches of government to take note of this recognition and be guided in their conduct accordingly."

Turning words into action, his government developed the means to capitalize on this richness. First, the Department of Justice adopted in June 1995 a policy on legislative bijuralism, which reflects its desire to make laws clearer and for an interpretation that is more accessible to all Canadians. The Department of Justice also made a commitment at that time to draft both versions of all bills or regulations relating to private law, also taking account of the terminology, concepts, notions and institutions specific to Canada's two private law systems.

The coming into force of the Civil Code of Quebec in 1994 was the catalyst of the harmonization project. The scope of this project, which seeks to bring Quebec civil law and existing federal legislation more into step, is without precedent in Canada's legal history. This initiative, which has now been underway for more than four years, is based on close cooperation between the departments of justice of Canada and Quebec and has benefited from the vital contribution of the academic community.

The objective is ambitious. It is not only to bring about terminological changes, but in particular genuinely to take into account the bilingual and bijural nature of Canada. While the harmonization project is designed first and foremost to allow Quebecers to recognize themselves better in federal legislation, it will also be an opportunity to ensure that there is not too much discrepancy between the common law in various provinces and the concepts imparted in federal legislation. All Canadians will benefit, because the end result will be clarification and a legal corpus that is more respectful of their own institutions.

My colleague, the Minister of Justice, the Honourable Anne McLellan, will give you an initial overview in a few moments of what has been done so far. I would simply like to underscore the scope of the task. Of some 700 federal laws that have been examined by jurists in the Department of Justice, just over 300 have been earmarked for a more in-depth review. In the bill to be tabled by June 1998, laws with the clearest links to civil law and having a greater effect on citizens will be harmonized.

Once that phase of the project is completed, the Department will proceed to harmonize more complex legislation in the fields of securities, property, family and civil liability. More extensive studies will also have to be conducted with respect to laws that present more specific difficulties, such as the Divorce Act and the Interpretation Act. There is thus much work to be done. This is obviously an undertaking that will be spread out over several years.

I am therefore proud to announce today, in Montreal, that the Government of Canada has decided to provide, for the harmonization of federal legislation with Quebec civil law, initial funding of over $7,418,839 for this large-scale project: $3,931,193 for the 1997–1998 fiscal year and $3,487,646 for the 1998–1999 fiscal year. The Department's needs will have to be reassessed in two years, to enable it to proceed with and complete its project.

Conclusion

We have long known that the unity of the state does not necessarily go hand in hand with uniformity of legislation. In The Spirit of Laws, Montesquieu wrote, 250 years ago [translation]: "If citizens follow laws, what matter if they follow the same." Montesquieu could have been Canadian. If there is one country that knows that equality is not synonymous with uniformity, it is certainly ours.

Quebec is governed by a legal system that is specific to it and whose existence is protected by the Constitution. Its private law tradition is an essential component of its specificity and also an element of Canada's diversity. The Honourable Charles Gonthier, Justice of the Supreme Court of Canada, has given this eloquent description of the importance of the Civil Code: "It thus appears that as a fundamental building block of the Quebec identity, the Civil Code also constitutes an original and characteristic component of the Canadian identity ... This Code is more than a mere legal instrument. It is truly a social statement."

The project to harmonize federal legislation with Quebec civil law is an inevitable necessity. It will be a considerable task, and the Department of Justice of Canada has the good fortune of being able to count on one of the most skilled legal communities in the world to bring this enterprise to fruition. Common law and civil law will both be enriched by it, and all our citizens will reap the fruits of this labour. I wish you productive deliberations and stimulating exchanges.

The Canadian Ideal

JERUSALEM, JUNE 28, 1998

Canadians are polite, modest folk. At least, that's the reputation we have with Americans. Our neighbours to the south claim that, to find the Canadian in a packed elevator, all you have to do is step on everyone's toes, and the person who says "sorry" is the Canadian. As for our reputation with the French, did you hear the one about the Canadian tourist who gets lost in Paris? Instead of asking, "Where's the Eiffel Tower?," he phrases the question in a typically Canadian way: "Excuse me, but I'd like to go to the Eiffel Tower," to which the traffic cop replies: "Be my guest!"

So you can understand how much this major conference goes against my Canadian sense of modesty, seeing that it has attracted an impressive number of participants from many countries, who will spend the next three days studying important aspects of Canadian life: the education system, the economy, literature, history ... Nevertheless, I would like to take this opportunity to thank the Israel Association for Canadian Studies and the Halbert Centre for Canadian Studies.

The Israelis also have their own joke about Canada, which wins over our sense of modesty. When God asked Moses, "So where do you want your promised land?", Moses meant to answer: "Canada." But as everyone knows, the liberator of the people of Israel had a speech impediment, so when he stammered: "Can ... Cana ... Cana ...," God impatiently answered: "Canaan? Okay, that's where you're going!"

Canada is obviously not a promised land, but I'm proud nevertheless to see that my country has sparked the interest of so many researchers like you from around the world; that so many human beings of all origins and from all continents have chosen Canada as their adoptive country; that so many others dream of moving to Canada: even the French, who supposedly are people of good taste, as well as the Australians and the Americans, choose Canada as the country where they

Speech before the Israel Association for Canadian Studies, Hebrew University of Jerusalem

would most like to live other than their own (*Paris Match*-BVA, February 12, 1998; *Canada and the World*, Angus Reid, 1997).

All of you have your own reasons for specializing in Canadian studies. Just as all those who have chosen to immigrate to Canada have had their own reasons. For my father-in-law, who is Austrian by origin, it's because he read Jack London books as a child!

I too, in a way, have chosen Canada, even though I was born there. I've chosen the cause of a united Canada, to the point of accepting Prime Minister Jean Chrétien's invitation to leave academia and work alongside him for Canadian unity. Today, I'd like to talk about the reasons I have chosen Canadian unity, and about the important place that my society, Quebec, occupies among those reasons.

Why Canadian unity?

I'll begin with a quotation from a former president of this country, Chaim Herzog. In a speech to the House of Commons on June 27, 1989, he was too generous to Canada: "You are an outstanding model of coexistence between individuals of different cultures and backgrounds who live here in a climate of mutual tolerance and respect for their original identity."

We are not that model of tolerance that President Herzog and many other foreign observers have celebrated. This idea of a "model of tolerance" has to be handled with great care, because contexts vary greatly from one country to another. For example, Canada's geostrategic limitations are nothing compared with those weighing on Israel. Moreover, there are still far too many instances of intolerance in Canada. But President Herzog was basically right: Canada has no meaning if it does not continually come closer to that model of tolerance it is associated with, and it is that quest that is its true greatness.

The main reason I believe that Canada must stay united has more to do with the universal than with the specific. To be sure, our flag, our national anthem, the majestic beauty of our vast land, all these manifestations of our Canadian singularity fill our hearts with pride. But the real reason that Canada is a jewel of humanity is that our country is one of the most humane countries in the world, one where the values of freedom, tolerance and respect for differences are the best observed. There are few countries where human beings have a better chance to be considered as human beings, whatever their origin or religion.

"I should regard it as a great misfortune for mankind if liberty were to exist all over the world under the same features," wrote Alexis de Tocqueville. The Canadian ideal seeks to avoid that misfortune. Canadians know that the quest for what is true, just and good must be plural; they know that by drawing on the best of each culture, each individual, regional or historical experience, we come closer to what is best in civilization. Canadians know that equality must not be confused with uniformity.

Some people say that Canada is an artificial country. If they mean that Canada has triumphed over so-called natural differences of race or ethnicity, and has come closer to what is truly universal in human beings, we should take their criticism as the greatest of compliments. The philosopher Johann Herder, who wrote that "the most natural state is one nationality with one character," might also have found Canada quite artificial. I'm not all that concerned about whether my country is a "natural state," but I know that a country gains in humanity when it draws on the best of what the Canadian philosopher Charles Taylor, a Quebecer, calls "deep diversity."

Allow me to summarize some of the reasons I'm proud to be Canadian.

Canada was a pioneer of democracy. It is an exceptional and admirable fact that, since 1792, my country has almost always been governed by a political regime comprising an elected assembly. March 11, 1998, marked the 150th anniversary of responsible government in what was then the Province of Canada. (Nova Scotia marked the same anniversary on February 2 of this year.) On that occasion, an historian many of you know, Ged Martin, a professor at the University of Edinburgh, wrote, "In the crucial combination of mass participation, human rights and self-government, Canada's history is second to none in the world."

I can think of no achievement of which a country could be more proud. Canadians can take pride that they have never had an empire and have never sent troops abroad in the 20th century for reasons other than defending democracy and peace. They invented insulin, proposed the United Nations peacekeeping force – during the Suez crisis in 1956, to be exact – and drafted the initial version of the Universal Declaration of Human Rights, which, as Eleanor Roosevelt predicted, has become the "international Magna Carta of all men everywhere." Just recently, Canada fulfilled its role as a good global citizen by undertaking a vast worldwide initiative to ban antipersonnel mines.

I am also proud of my country because it has remained faithful to its original ideal. George-Étienne Cartier, one of the best-known "Fathers" of our Confederation, said that Canada should be an English- and French-speaking "political nationality," formed of several different populations, proud of their identities, and united around common objectives: "In our own Federation we should have Catholic and Protestant, English, French, Irish and Scotch, and each by his efforts and his success would increase the prosperity and glory of the new Confederacy." (February 7, 1865)

Canada has maintained its Francophone character in a North America dominated by English, despite the wind of assimilation that has been blowing in the world at a time when, for the first time in the history of humanity, the number of languages spoken has decreased rather than increased. Canada was the first country in the world to introduce a multiculturalism policy, and it is still a pacesetter in that respect, as noted by UNESCO in a recent report. According to the polls, the vast majority of Canadians agree that cultural diversity strengthens Canada.

I am proud that our major cities – Montreal, Toronto, Vancouver – have managed to contain racism, which plagues so many other large cities in the world. For that reason alone, those three cities deserve to remain in the same country, despite the geographic distance that separates them. A study by the Corporate Resources Group of Switzerland ranks them among the metropolitan areas with the best quality of life in the world. Vancouver came in second, Toronto fourth and Montreal seventh.

I'm sure you're familiar with Kipling's line that: "East is East, and West is West, and never the twain shall meet." If there is one city in the world that can make a liar out of Kipling, and successfully combine the Far Eastern and Western civilizations, it is surely Vancouver. I want to live that experience alongside my fellow citizens from Vancouver, because I know that their chances of success, and those of my city, Montreal, are better if we all stay together within one generous federation. The constituency that I represent in the House of Commons, Saint-Laurent-Cartierville, on the Island of Montreal, is itself an example of a plural, harmonious community, a genuine mini-United Nations, composed of more than 50 different cultural communities, including a Jewish community.

Canada's Jewish community now numbers 350,000, including 90,000 in Montreal and 7,200 in my constituency (according to the 1996 census). The arrival of the first Jews in Canada dates back to the early 1750s in Montreal and Halifax. Canada's first synagogue was also established in Montreal, in 1777.

The first Jew elected to Parliament in the entire British Commonwealth was Ezekiel Hart, who was chosen in 1807 by voters in Trois-Rivières, the majority of whom were Francophone Catholics, to represent them in the Legislative Assembly of Lower Canada. Unfortunately, he was unable to take his seat, because the law prohibited non-Christians from taking their oath of allegiance on the Bible. It wasn't until 1832 that Jews obtained full civil and political rights, which was still some 25 years before such measures of justice were taken in the United Kingdom.

Canada's Jewish community has been an active participant in the quest for the Canadian ideal. The Hebrew University of Jerusalem, the venue of this conference, is surely aware of that, since it awarded an honorary doctorate to the distinguished legal scholar, Bora Laskin, Chief Justice of the Supreme Court of Canada from 1970 to 1984, who made a remarkable contribution to promoting individual rights and freedoms.

I am proud that the Jewish community in my country feels both intensely Canadian and very close to Israel. That is the case with 83% of Montreal Jews, according to a 1991 study. Sixty-one per cent of Toronto Jews and 70% of Montreal Jews have visited Israel, compared with 31% of American Jews. Free trade between Canada and Israel will further strengthen these ties, which benefit both countries. And those benefits will not just be economic. The two countries will learn from each other on an issue crucial for both of them: the harmonious integration of populations of different languages and cultures.

There are those who say that openness to cultural diversity has fostered a ghetto mentality which weakens the very idea of a common sense of belonging to Canada. I believe that the very opposite is true. The vast majority of immigrants to Canada instantly develop a deep attachment to their new country. They enthusiastically devote their talents to its service and educate their children in Canada. Because Canada has seen diversity as a strength, it has averted the rise of xenophobic political movements that now poison the life of too many democracies. Canada has two official languages, which are international languages. Its diversified population gives it a cultural foothold on every continent. Its Civil Code and common law enable it to share the legal traditions of the vast majority of countries in the world. It is positioned geographically between Europe, the United States and Asia. For all these reasons, Canada is better positioned than ever to make its mark on the next century, in this global world where mastery of different cultural registers will be more of an asset than ever before.

Unfortunately, learning mutual respect and openness to others is never an easy exercise. There are many dark pages in Canadian history that I am not proud of, such as demonstrations of intolerance against Aboriginals and Francophones. I am ashamed that my country took in so few Jews before, during and after the Second World War. I will never forget that it waited until the 1960s to purge racist criteria from its immigration policy.

And yet the Canadian ideal was able to advance despite these errors, partly because, from the very outset, the British and French had to learn to live together: first to tolerate each other, then to respect each other, and eventually to help each other. That learning process, which has often been difficult, has made us more disposed to welcome new citizens from every continent. To separate now, especially along Francophone and Anglophone fault lines, to undo that which has united us from the start, would be much worse than the economic decline predicted by the vast majority of economists: it would be a moral defeat. We Canadians have learned too much from our history not to see that working together within a single country makes us all better citizens.

I say this as a Canadian and also as a Quebecer, proud of my Quebec identity and convinced that it is essential to Canada as a whole.

Quebec and the Canadian ideal

I am proud of Quebec, a dynamic, predominantly French-speaking society which we have built on a continent where English is dominant. Since the beginning of Confederation, Quebec has never been as Francophone as it is today, with 94% of its inhabitants able to express themselves in French.

The federal and provincial language laws passed in the 1960s and 1970s have helped the cause of the French language. The language laws in force in Quebec are more liberal and respectful of the minority linguistic community than those passed by other multilingual democracies such as Belgium and Switzerland. When they are applied in a spirit of openness and conciliation, they help Francophones and Anglophones in Quebec to live together in trust and harmony.

I want to talk a little about the tolerance of Quebec society. In my academic research, I have been struck by how much Quebecers cherished the same universal values as other Canadians. If you ask them for their opinion on interracial marriages, for example, you will see the same degree of openness as elsewhere in Canada, an openness generally greater than that in the United States or Europe. As Michael Adams, the head of a major polling firm, has written, on the basis of a series of opinion polls: "French and English Canadians have far more in common with each other in terms of values than either group has with the Americans." (*Sex in the Snow: Canadian Social Values at the End of the Millennium* (Toronto: Viking, 1997), p. 195)

I say it again: look at Montreal in its day-to-day life, and you will find that, in spite of geographic distance, that great multicultural city belongs to the same culture of tolerance as Toronto, Calgary and Vancouver.

Some Quebecers wrongly believe that they have to renounce Canada to remain Quebecers. We need to show them all the common values that unite all Canadians, beyond language barriers. We need to convince them that to strengthen solidarity among Quebecers, they need to strengthen, in the same spirit, their solidarity with other Canadians, rather than breaking it. As a Quebecer, I want to help my fellow citizens in the Atlantic provinces, Ontario, Western and Northern Canada to express their own way of being Canadian, and to build a better future for their children. I want to help the Jewish community and other communities throughout Canada. And in return, I want to accept the help that other Canadians are giving to us Quebecers, so that the alliance of our different cultures makes us better and stronger, as George-Étienne Cartier wanted. To do that, however, we have to stay together, rather than listening to the voices of division and rancour.

And now I'll tell you why I am very confident about Canadian unity. It's not just because, as you are no doubt aware, Quebecers' support for even the vague concept of "sovereignty-partnership" has dwindled to around 40% in the polls. It's also because Quebecers are increasingly supporting Canadian unity because they think it's good for Quebec to be in Canada, whereas it wasn't that long ago that their choice was motivated in particular by the fear of the negative consequences of separation. This increased valuing of the Canadian ideal can be seen in a number of polls, and I've also heard it from people first-hand.

Being both a Quebecer and a Canadian is a wonderful opportunity. Every Quebecer must be able to say: "I am a Quebecer and a Canadian, and I refuse to choose between the two identities." In the same way that Jewish families in my constituency tell me they feel deeply that they are Jews, Quebecers and Canadians. They feel both rooted in Montreal and close, in spirit, to Israel.

Conclusion

I'm sure you can answer this question: What contribution have Jewish thinkers made to humanity? First there was Moses, who said that everything is law. Then Jesus preached that everything is love. Then Marx roared that everything is struggle. Freud diagnosed that everything is sex. Finally, there was Einstein, who commented: Well, you know, everything's relative.

Allow me to transpose those premises to the debate on Canadian unity.

Everything is law. Precisely because the debate on the unity of a country is something extremely sensitive and difficult, governments must set an example by committing themselves, without any ambiguity, always to act completely frankly, peacefully, legally and clearly. Whatever happens, the debate must take place respecting the rule of law and democracy for all. It is important that there be a clear legal framework. This is why the Government of Canada has taken the initiative of asking the Supreme Court to clarify for all of us the legal status of a unilateral attempt at secession by the Government of Quebec.

Everything is love. You know that in Canada, we often talk of the "*two solitudes*" to describe the difficulties between Francophones and Anglophones. We have forgotten that this expression is taken from a letter by Rilke, who was trying to express love, rather than isolation. "*Love consists in this, that two solitudes protect, and touch, and greet each other,*" wrote the poet. Canada is not an endless constitutional squabble. Canada is, fundamentally, a principle of caring between different populations united around common objectives, a principle of caring that we must be conscious of not only in an ice storm. Improving the federation must be guided by this principle of caring, so that the federal government and the provinces work together more, while respecting their different roles.

Everything is struggle, or, more properly, *everything is conviction.* Canada is not an emergency cord to be pulled on once every fifteen years, one week before a referendum. The Canadian ideal must be defended on a permanent basis and with conviction. Canadians must be shown how much they owe their enviable quality of life to their being together, and that, united, they will be better able to fight unemployment and poverty. And this work of conviction must be effected through dialogue, never through exclusion.

Everything is sex, or, to make another slight modification, *everything is passion.* Cool-headed economic analyses of the advantages of Canadian unity certainly have their place in this debate, but it has been proven that they are not enough. We need to talk about Canada, and Quebec within Canada, with passion, with the passion of reason. Once again, I don't mean frenzied flag-waving so much as heartfelt promotion of the universal values we are all seeking.

Everything is relative, or at least, *let us be aware of the relativity of things.* We need, at the same time, respect for the law, clarity, straight talk, caring, conviction and passion. All these ingredients are needed so that Canadians can prove to the world that their ideal, which is also, as I think I have shown, the ideal of humanity, is possible on this planet.

SECTION 4

The Dangers of Secession in Democracy

Speech on a Motion by the Opposition

Mr. Speaker, having had the honour of being elected by the citizens of Saint-Laurent-Cartierville is particularly relevant to what I am about to say in my maiden speech in the House of Commons.

I will never be able to express my gratitude sufficiently to the constituents of Saint-Laurent-Cartierville for having chosen me to represent them. This diverse and harmonious community, inhabited by over 50 different nationalities fully integrated into Quebec society, intends to exercise its right to remain in Canada.

I dedicate what I am about to say to all the young people I met during my election campaign in March 1996. Sometimes speaking in French, sometimes in English, and often in one or two other languages, a sign of how well equipped they are for the next century, these young people sadly told me that they were not sure their future lay in either Saint-Laurent or Montreal.

They belong in Montreal and to the surrounding area; that is their home. And rather than leave, they must convince their fellow Quebecers that belonging to more than one group is a source of strength, not a contradiction. They must convince their fellow Canadians in other provinces that recognizing the distinct nature of Quebec is not a threat to Canadian unity, but, on the contrary, a wonderful way to celebrate one of Canada's fundamental characteristics.

The theme of this first speech will be democracy, which the opposition invites us to consider this May 16, 1996, by presenting the following motion: "That the House endorse the declaration of the Prime Minister of Canada, who stated in Straight from the Heart, in 1985, 'If we don't win, I'll respect the wishes of Quebecers and let them separate.'"

This quotation is taken out of context by the Official Opposition. It goes back to 1970, and was repeated by Mr. Chrétien in 1985. In the same passage, the current Prime Minister also said: "We'll put our faith in democracy. We'll convince the people that they should stay in Canada and we'll win."

We'll put our faith in democracy. This reliance on democracy is an invitation to us to consider the meaning of the word, and to ponder the teachings of the classics. Let us begin with that great prophet of democracy, Alexis de Tocqueville, and I quote: "I consider unjust and ungodly the maxim that, in matters of government, a majority of the people have the right to impose their will."

Tocqueville is saying that democracy cannot be limited to the rule of the majority, because it also includes the rights of minorities, and of the smallest minorities, and of the smallest minority of all, the individual, the flesh and blood citizen.

The second classical author I call on is Jean-Jacques Rousseau: "The more important and weighty the resolutions, the nearer should the opinion which prevails approach unanimity."

What Rousseau is setting out here is not obviously the rule of unanimity, which clearly is impracticable. What he is showing us is that the more a decision threatens the rights of individuals, the more irreversible it is and the more it involves future generations, the more stringent must be the procedure democracy selects for the adoption of this decision.

This brings me to the fine quote of Montesquieu linking democracy tightly with universal solidarity. And I quote: "If I knew of something that could serve my nation but would ruin another, I would not propose it to my prince, for I am first a man and only then a Frenchman, because I am necessarily a man, and only accidentally am I French."

Tocqueville, Rousseau, Montesquieu. With these three French authors, no one can accuse me of distancing myself from Francophone tradition. In fact, however, the principles these three set out are universal and have guided constitutional democracies in establishing their rules of law. These principles are the reason that the supremacy of law is a vital component of democracy.

Let us apply these principles to the issue dividing us in Canada: secession. It is defined as a break in solidarity among the citizens of a common country. This is why international law in its great wisdom extends the right of self-determination in its extreme form, that is the right of secession, only in situations where a break in solidarity appears de facto to be incontrovertible.

Let us quote, in this regard, the five experts who testified before the Bélanger-Campeau Commission. I quote: "Legally, Quebec's eventual declaration of sovereignty cannot be based on the principle of the equality in law of peoples or their right to self-determination, which permits independence only to colonial peoples or to those whose territory is under foreign occupation."

The secessions that have taken place to date have always arisen out of decolonization or the troubled times that follow the end of totalitarian or authoritarian regimes. It is not simply a matter of chance that no well established democracy with a minimum of ten years of universal suffrage has ever faced secession. Such a break in solidarity appears very hard to justify in a democracy. International law and democratic principles encourage the people to remain united, not to break up.

While democracy infers that a group of people cannot be forced to remain within a country against their will, it also sets strict rules, which, under the law, maximize the guarantees of justice for all. That is what we learned from near-secessions that have taken place in stable democracies. It may be a good idea to review the procedure by which Switzerland, a fine example of democracy, managed to separate the Jura from the canton of Berne while being fair to all. We could also look at how the USA intends to consult the Puerto Ricans on their political future. Closer to home, we might consider the approach taken recently by Canada to transfer title, in all fairness, on lands in the north.

Now it is the time to calmly set, under the law, mutually acceptable secession rules. Not two weeks before a referendum. The Government of Canada does not deny in any way the right of Quebecers to pull out of Canada, if such is their explicit wish. However, the Government of Canada does object to the Quebec government's plans to unilaterally set and change as it pleases the procedure according to which this right will be exercised and expressed. A unilateral declaration of independence would fly in the face of democracy and the rule of law.

What is not known is whether the secessionist leaders are able to enter a calm, level-headed and reasoned discussion process. The coarse language used recently by the Premier of Quebec, who compared Canada to a prison, or Quebec's Minister of Finance, who compared the Canadian government to former totalitarian communist governments, is an insult to the memory of the East German and North Korean people who were killed trying to escape totalitarian prisons. Separatist leaders must get a grip on themselves and make responsible statements. Otherwise, they should be prepared to call every constitutional democracy a prison, as well as the separate entity they want to make of Quebec, whose territory they consider indivisible and sacred.

With mutually consented rules in place, Quebecers could then examine with some clarity the argumentation used by secessionist leaders to try to convince them to break their ties of solidarity with their fellows citizens of the Maritimes, Ontario and Western Canada. It is my belief that Quebec will find this secessionist argumentation very shaky.

Exploitation cannot be used as an argument to justify secession, when the Canadian federation is one of the most generous for have-not regions. Neither can self-determination, or the lack of it, be used as an argument, as few other federal components in the world benefit from as much autonomy as Quebec does within the Canadian federation.

The only argument secessionist leaders could put forth is the fact that, according to several established criteria, Quebecers could be considered as a people and that each people must have its own state. This idea that any group of people that is different from the others must have its own state is terribly untrue.

The flawed equation "one people, one country" would blow up the planet. Experts have estimated at around 3,000 the number of human groups with a recognized collective identity. But there are fewer than 200 states in the world.

Letter to Mr. Lucien Bouchard

AUGUST 11, 1997

Translation from French

Mr. Lucien Bouchard
Premier of Quebec
J Building, 3rd Floor
885 Grande-Allée East
Quebec City, Quebec
G1A 1A2

Dear Premier:

The open letter you recently sent to the Premier of New Brunswick, Mr. Frank McKenna, was brought to my attention, and I read it with interest. I will consider it as a contribution to public debate about the procedure by which Quebec might eventually become an independent state, an issue of great importance to Quebecers and other Canadians.

Your argument is based on three rules that you claim are universally accepted: that a unilateral declaration of independence is supported by international law; that a majority of "50% plus one" is a sufficient threshold for secession; and that international law rejects any changes to the borders of the entity attempting to secede. We are convinced that such assertions are contradicted by international law and state practice.

Let me start with the question of a unilateral declaration of independence. The Government of Canada has always maintained that if Quebecers expressed very clearly a desire to secede from Canada, then their will would be respected. As you know, this position is highly unusual in the international community. Most countries do not allow constituent parts to secede under any circumstances. For example, the constitution of the French Fifth Republic, that of General de Gaulle, provides that "La France est une République indivisible," while the United States Supreme Court has found that our neighbour forms an "indestructible union."

The Government of Canada has never contested the right of the Government of Quebec to consult Quebecers on their future, but it has affirmed that the provincial government cannot have a monopoly on the establishment of a fair process that might lead to secession. There is no democratic country in the world where the government of a province or other constituent entity has been allowed to determine these procedures unilaterally.

The vast majority of international law experts, including the five experts consulted by the Bélanger-Campeau Commission, believe that the right to declare secession unilaterally does not belong to constituent entities of a democratic country such as Canada. If you believe otherwise, then I invite your government to ask the Supreme Court of Canada for the opportunity to submit your arguments on these questions as part of the present reference.

Quebecers and other Canadians should reflect on this fine statement by the Secretary-General of the United Nations, and I quote: "If every ethnic region or linguistic group claimed statehood there would be no limit to fragmentation, and peace, security and well-being for all would become even more difficult to achieve."

Canada is the last place in the world where identity-based fragmentation should be allowed to prevail. In the eyes of the world, this country symbolizes better than any other the ideal of how different people can live together in harmony in a single state. In this regard, let us listen to President Clinton, who said, and I quote: "In a world darkened by ethnic conflicts that literally tear nations apart, Canada has stood for all of us as a model of how people of different cultures can live and work together in peace, prosperity and understanding. Canada has shown the world how to balance freedom with compassion."

Many others have said the same thing about Canada. I will give just one other quotation: "Canada is a land of promise and Canadians are people of hope. It is a country celebrated for its generosity of spirit, where tolerance is ingrained in the national character. A society in which all citizens and all groups can assert and express themselves and realize their aspirations."

These words, which have the ring of truth and could have come from Sir Wilfrid Laurier or Pierre Trudeau, were pronounced on July 1, 1988, by the then Secretary of State, the Hon. Lucien Bouchard.

The Canadian government's priority is to help Quebecers and other Canadians achieve reconciliation. They must speak to one another, stay in closer contact, clear up misunderstandings, find ways to make their federation work better, and celebrate Quebec's distinctiveness within Canada. They must achieve reconciliation, not only as fellow citizens but also as inhabitants of this poor planet. Let us bet on democracy.

Therefore, if the amendment put forward by the Hon. Member for Berthier-Montcalm is deemed to be in order, I, seconded by the Hon. Member for Simcoe North, move: "*That the motion be amended by deleting the words 'in 1985' and by substituting for those words the following:* 'In the 1970s and in 1985 as outlined on page 150 of his book *Straight from the Heart*: 'We'll put our faith in democracy. We'll convince the people that they should stay in Canada and we'll win.' "

Turning to the "50% plus one" rule, it should be noted that it is customary in a democracy to require a consensus for serious, virtually irreversible changes that deeply affect not only our own lives but also those of future generations. Secession, the act of choosing between one's fellow citizens, is one of the most consequence-laden choices a society can ever make.

It is no accident that all instances of secession effected through referenda have been supported by a clear consensus. It would be too dangerous to attempt such an operation in an atmosphere of division, on the basis of a narrow, "soft" majority, as it is commonly called, which could evaporate in the face of difficulties.

If I had enough space, I would cite a series of examples from other countries in which a referendum verdict that was too uncertain was not acted on, for decisions much less important than the break-up of a country. But let us confine ourselves to your secession project.

In the white paper that led up to Quebec's Referendum Act, it is noted that, because of the consultative – and not decisive – nature of referenda, "it would be pointless to include in the law special provisions requiring a certain majority vote or rate of participation." When the bill was tabled on April 5, 1978, its sponsor, Mr. Robert Burns, spoke of the "moral weight" of a referendum won on the basis of "a clearly and broadly expressed popular will." You yourself acknowledged on June 15, 1994, that an attempt at sovereignty with a slim majority would adversely affect "the political cohesion of Quebec." And on September 12, 1992, in the case of a simple constitutional referendum (on the Charlottetown Accord), Mr. Bernard Landry linked the legitimacy of a "yes" vote to obtaining a substantial majority in Quebec.

As to the question of territorial integrity, there is neither a paragraph nor a line in international law that protects Quebec's territory but not Canada's. International experience demonstrates that the borders of the entity seeking independence can be called into question, sometimes for reasons based on democracy. For example, you are no doubt aware that France insisted on partitioning the island of Mayotte from the Comoros at the time the latter gained independence because the residents of Mayotte unequivocally expressed their desire to maintain their link with France.

Even the most prominent secessionists do not agree that Quebec's borders would be guaranteed if secession were being negotiated. When he was a professor of international law, Mr. Daniel Turp stated his belief that, in the event of Quebec separation, Quebec's Aboriginal peoples would have the right to remain in Canada if they so chose. During the recent federal election campaign, Mr. Gilles Duceppe also pointed to the special geographic position of Quebec territory occupied by Aboriginal peoples and suggested the issue might be referred to an international tribunal.

Neither you nor I nor anyone else can predict that the borders of an independent Quebec would be those now guaranteed by the Canadian Constitution.

These are crucial questions which, so that they can be better debated on their substance, require your government to choose between two contradictory positions. In effect, you are saying simultaneously: 1) that the procedure leading up to secession is a purely political matter, in which case the established law is not relevant; and 2) that the established law demonstrates you are right and those who contest the procedure you intend to follow are wrong.

If you hold the first assertion, you must alert our fellow citizens that you are prepared to plunge them into a situation of anarchy, outside the legal framework, which is not done in a democracy. If, on the contrary, you hold the second assertion, you must produce the rules of law that support your position and agree that our reference to the Supreme Court is a constructive and necessary exercise of clarification, whether or not its outcome is in your favour. One thing is certain: you cannot continue to deny the relevance of law while invoking it when it suits you.

The Government of Canada is convinced that Quebecers will never choose to renounce the deep-rooted solidarity that unites them with other Canadians within this great federation, which we must always strive to improve. Our being together gives us one of the best qualities of life in the world. We acknowledge, however, that the spirit and practice of democracy must be respected in all circumstances, even the very unlikely and sad prospect of Canada's partition.

Reconciling secession with democracy is such a difficult undertaking that no well-established democracy has yet attempted to do so. These grave questions cannot be avoided if you persist in your project of secession. Our fellow citizens expect their elected representatives to debate these issues in a calm and level-headed manner. This debate on the procedures that would apply concerns us as Quebecers first and foremost, because an attempt at secession in an atmosphere of confusion would profoundly divide our society; but it also concerns Canadians as a whole, all of whom would be affected by the break-up of their country.

Yours sincerely,

Stéphane Dion

Letter to Mr. Bernard Landry

AUGUST 26, 1997

Translation from French

Mr. Bernard Landry
Deputy Premier and Minister of State
for the Economy and Finance, Quebec
12 Saint Louis Street, 1st floor
Quebec City, Quebec
G1R 5L3

Dear Deputy Premier:

The citizens who have elected us are entitled to have us discuss the procedures of secession frankly and thoroughly. I was therefore delighted that you wrote on behalf of your government in response to my own letter of August 11. I hope that this beginning of a dialogue between us marks the end of your government's regrettable attitude of seeking to discredit your critics so as to avoid a debate of substance.

Now that both our letters have been the subject of widespread media coverage, and many of our fellow citizens have had time to familiarize themselves with their contents, permit me to go a little further.

For my part, I am not accusing you of being a poor democrat. I am simply reproaching you for not adequately considering your arguments. Above all, I note that you have not responded to my three objections regarding the process you plan to follow to make Quebec an independent State. I shall review those three objections in the order in which you raised them in your letter: majority rule, the question of territory and the consequences of a unilateral declaration of independence.

First, I noted that in all cases of secession where a referendum has been held, it has always been to confirm the existence of a clear consensus. You have not denied that fact. Rather, you have maintained that a simple majority in a referendum in Quebec would be sufficient to declare independence, citing the processes that resulted in the creation of the Canadian federation and in Newfoundland's entry into Confederation. You conclude that it would be absurd if it were more difficult to leave Canada than to enter it. It is in no way absurd.

Human societies consistently ensure that more care is exercised in dissolving than in creating an association. Democracies do this at all levels of social life. For example, the laws are drafted in such a way that it is easier to get married than to get divorced, and to create corporations in law than to dissolve them. The United States Congress is considering passing legislation that would offer statehood to Puerto Rico on the basis of a referendum result of " 50% plus one," on the condition that it clearly be a definitive, irreversible entry into a federal union that proclaims itself to be indestructible.

Democracies set more stringent requirements for separation than for union because the risks of injustice are much greater in the case of separation. In effect, a just way needs to be found to break the ties of solidarity and allegiance forged over time, while dividing up the assets that have been jointly acquired. It is better to ensure that populations truly wish to break up before embarking on such a step.

Today, all of Canada belongs to Quebecers and to other Canadians. Quebecers are entitled to the assurance that they will not lose Canada unless they have very clearly renounced it. Our governments would be acting irresponsibly if they tried to negotiate a break-up without solid confirmation that this is truly what Quebecers want.

Second, I pointed out the absence of any legal basis on which Quebec's borders would be inviolable while Canada's borders would not be. There again, you did not contradict me.

Instead, you are asking that any possibility of modifying Quebec's borders in the event of negotiations on secession be excluded a priori. The Government of Canada is against partitioning Canadian territory, and is thus against partitioning Quebec territory. It may be, however, that in the difficult circumstances of negotiating secession, an agreement on modifying borders would become the least unfavourable solution. Our fellow citizens must be aware that such things can happen.

Third, I noted the absence of any legal principle, international or otherwise, that would create a right to a unilateral declaration of independence in a democratic country such as Canada. According to almost all the experts consulted, there is no legal foundation of this type. It would appear that you have not been able to find one either. We have referred this precise question to the Supreme Court because it is important to have the opinion of the highest court in the country. We believe that the position we are defending before the Court is in accordance not only with international law, but also with international practice.

You point out that Canada and the international community have recognized the emergence of many new States since the Second World War. You ask why the Government of Canada does not state that it is prepared in the same way to recognize a unilateral declaration of independence contemplated by your government in the event of a breakdown in negotiations whose framework you had established alone. The answer is that no government in Canada can commit itself to recognizing a secession in advance, in the abstract, without knowing its concrete conditions. This position seems to us to be the only reasonable one and is in accordance with normal international practice, under which no constituent entity of a state should be recognized as independent against the will of that state. Since 1945, no state created by secession has been admitted to the United Nations without the approval of the government of the predecessor state.

Without the support of the Canadian government, a declaration of independence by your government would not be recognized by the international community. Other countries would regard your attempted secession as a Canadian matter to be dealt with in accordance with our democratic and legal traditions. You well understand that Mr. Parizeau's "great game" of diplomacy last time would not have changed this.

The international community's dislike of unilateral declarations of independence is not legal quibbling. It is a condition of the system of legal and orderly government without which our societies could not function. Imagine the chaos that would ensue if your government unilaterally told Quebecers that they must ignore the courts, the Constitution, the federal government and the international community, and henceforth recognize only your authority, your laws, your regulations and your taxes. Your unilateral declaration of independence would divide Quebec society in an utterly irresponsible manner. It would be a complete departure from the democratic traditions of our society. It is very dangerous in a democracy for a government to place itself above the law but nevertheless require the obedience of its citizens.

We must avoid such a situation at all costs. You desire the independence of Quebec. I want to preserve the unity of Canada. I am convinced, however, that we are both concerned that our disagreement be resolved in a peaceful and orderly manner, respecting human rights.

Mr. Deputy Premier, you think that being a Canadian prevents you from fully being a Quebecer. I think that being both a Quebecer and a Canadian is one of the most fortunate things that life has given me. You want to choose between Quebec and Canada and to force me to choose, although I have no wish to do so. At the very least, I am entitled to insist on a process that is clear, legal and fair not only to me, but also to the seven million human beings who are both Quebecers and Canadians, and to the other twenty-two million human beings who enjoy the good fortune of having Quebec as part of their country.

If we are all to agree on such a procedure, we must discuss it calmly and in a level-headed manner, as our fellow citizens wish us to do.

Yours sincerely,

Stéphane Dion

Letter to Mr. Bernard Landry

AUGUST 28, 1997

Translation from French

Mr. Bernard Landry
Deputy Premier and Minister of State
for the Economy and Finance, Quebec
12 Saint Louis Street, 1st floor
Quebec City, Quebec
G1R 5L3

Dear Deputy Premier:

A man of action such as yourself needs to have accurate information.

Yesterday, you described my assertion that no state created by secession has been admitted to the United Nations without the approval of the predecessor state as a "fundamental historical error." You claimed that, "to use one example out of fifty," Germany recognized Slovenia as an independent state within hours of its declaration of independence.

Here are the actual facts on Slovenia:

On December 23, 1990, the Slovenian government held a referendum on a crystal-clear question: "Should the Republic of Slovenia become a sovereign and independent state?" The "Yes" side won, taking 95.7% of the valid votes cast, and voter turnout was 93.3%.

– On June 25, 1991, Slovenia declared its independence.
– On November 29, 1991, the Arbitration Commission appointed by the European Community concluded that the Socialist Federal Republic of Yugoslavia was in the process of dissolution.
– On December 5, 1991, the President of the Socialist Federal Republic of Yugoslavia, Mr. Stipe Mesic, resigned, declaring that the Republic no longer had any legitimacy.
– On December 16, 1991, the Ministerial Conference on European Political Cooperation called on all Yugoslav republics that so wished to submit their request to be recognized as independent states.

– On December 23, 1991, Germany officially recognized Slovenia, thus six months after the declaration of independence.
– On January 15, 1992, Canada and the European Union recognized Slovenia.
– On May 22, 1992, Slovenia was admitted to the United Nations, not against the will of the Socialist Federal Republic of Yugoslavia, but after the Republic had ceased to exist.

In short, despite the almost unanimous support of its population, Slovenia had to wait until the international community had determined that the dissolution of the Yugoslav federation was irreversible before obtaining international recognition.

The case of Slovenia shows how difficult it is to obtain international recognition. Our fellow citizens have the right to know that.

I am at your disposal to talk about the forty-nine other cases of international recognition you had in mind.

Yours sincerely,

Stéphane Dion

Why a Quebecer Wants to Keep
British Columbia as Part of His Country

VANCOUVER, OCTOBER 17, 1997

I want to tell you why, as a Quebecer, I want to keep British Columbia as part of my country. I want to tell you why my nine-year-old daughter, Jeanne, should grow up with B.C. still a part of her future. I want to tell you why I will fight against the separatist leaders in Quebec who want to take British Columbia away from me.

Your province is not some alien place to me, three thousand miles from my home. B.C. is part of my country, and it is a part of my country that I am very proud of. When I look at your history, your culture, your innovations that have improved all of Canada, I know that it is worth fighting as a Quebecer to stay in a country that includes British Columbia.

Your history is a record of growth and progress that makes one of the great stories of exploration and pioneering in the world. We know that when Captain Cook came to these shores he found a sophisticated culture that had been thriving here for thousands of years. We know too that the settlers who followed Cook and Vancouver and Juan de Fuca also achieved great things in this land.

There were only 12,000 colonists when British Columbia voted to join Confederation in 1871. They could not have imagined that, 126 years later, the province would have a population of just under 4 million drawn from every corner of the globe. Who would have guessed when William Van Horne announced that Canadian Pacific Railways would extend its line a few miles from Port Moody to Vancouver, that he was laying the tracks for one of the great cities of the world?

It is amazing what you have achieved within Canada. This story is part of my history too as a Canadian. But perhaps your greatest achievement is not how you have overcome mountains and rivers, but how you have succeeded as human beings in reconciling diversity. Like Montreal, Vancouver is a multicultural community where people of many different backgrounds have learned to get along. Of course, just

---

Speech to the Canadian Club of Vancouver

as there have been difficulties between English and French in Montreal, so too in the past there have been tensions in this city between different groups.

But lessons were learned, and now both our cities are tolerant communities. While we should not forget the sad episodes of our past, such as the Head Tax laws that once faced Chinese immigrants, today we can celebrate that the Vancouver area has given Canada its first federal Cabinet ministers of East Indian and Chinese origin, in my colleagues Herb Dhaliwal and Raymond Chan. I also applaud the work of my colleague Hedy Fry as Minister responsible for Multiculturalism. You may have seen the recent study commissioned by Canada Immigration which showed that Vancouver was rated as the most tolerant and welcoming city in Canada towards immigrant groups. This is an achievement that you can all be proud of.

While it is a cliché for politicians travelling West to come to B.C. and praise your mountains, it is not your mountains but your people that most make me want to keep B.C. as part of my country. B.C. has given Canada many great figures in our national life, from Emily Carr to Bryan Adams. And it would be impossible to over-estimate the impact of Terry Fox's courage and heroism on Canadians' sense of ourselves. I am sure that B.C. will give us many more outstanding Canadians in the future, and I want to share in the pride of being their fellow citizen as well.

British Columbia doesn't only have a great history, but a great future. When Prime Minister Jean Chrétien came to Vancouver two weeks ago, he said "I have seen the future and it is working here in British Columbia." Who can tell what we will accomplish together in the 21st century?

While Vancouver was the end of the line for people travelling West when the CPR was built, today it is just the beginning, as Vancouver is indisputably Canada's gateway to Asia Pacific, where much of the economic growth of the future will come from. Here again, your multicultural diversity will be an asset more than ever in the global markets of the next century.

As a political scientist and now as a politician myself, I have come to admire British Columbia's innovations in the field of public policy. B.C.'s reforms to its income support system for children have provided an inspiration for the integrated, national approach to child poverty that the federal government and the other provinces are now pursuing. As a father, I am proud that the new National Child Benefit your premier helped champion means that children across Canada will be waking up to brighter futures. Our government recently endorsed pharmacare as a long-term national goal, so once again a B.C. program can provide a model for all Canadians. These are concrete examples of how our federal system works. I want B.C. to stay part of my country so that it can continue to bring its own perspectives to bear on the challenges we face together.

Your history, your culture, your innovative solutions to our national problems, the potential you represent for the future. These are all aspects of my country that I value, and that I will try to prevent anybody from taking away from me. We must all work together for a stronger Canada and a stronger B.C.

Working together for a stronger B.C.

Working together means cooperating as individual citizens, in the private sector, in community groups, but also as governments. Different levels of government must work together with the community to solve our common problems. And in fact, while there is often more attention paid to the problems between the federal and provincial governments than to our successes, there are many areas where the governments of B.C. and Canada have been able to work together constructively. I want to share with you four examples of fruitful collaboration.

Transportation has always been crucial to the B.C. economy, from making the completion of the CPR a condition of joining Confederation to making "man in motion" the theme of Expo '86. In keeping with this, the federal government has done much in recent years to improve B.C.'s transportation policies and infrastructure. Vancouver is now a major transportation hub for the continent – and the departure point for all Team Canada trade missions to Asia. The "Open Skies" Agreement means 8,000 more flights a year for Vancouver International Airport, which is now the number two airport in North America for Pacific destinations.

I was very pleased to assist my colleague David Anderson with the sterling work he did in keeping Canadian Airlines flying. Canadian is the most important carrier for Western Canada, but the restructuring facilitated by the federal, Alberta and B.C. governments is good for all the country.

Or take B.C.'s role in the Asia-Pacific. As I mentioned, B.C.'s role as Canada's gateway to Asia is a benefit to the whole country. Naturally, by its location and population, B.C. has gained much from Asia-Pacific trade. But the role that the federal government has played in opening Asian markets to B.C. business is important to recognize. B.C. businesses have benefited greatly from the Prime Minister's Team Canada missions to Asia. Canada's hosting of the APEC summit in Vancouver will inject some $23 million into your city's economy in one week. And in the longer term the summit will raise your already considerable international profile.

Consider also the field of immigration. British Columbia has often stressed that federal policy must consider B.C.'s unique immigration patterns, which are connected with your Asia-Pacific location. So this spring, Premier Clark and Prime Minister Chrétien shook hands on a new deal for immigration settlement, so that B.C. will get a fair share of settlement funding. As the Premier said, the agreement was "a win both for Canada and for B.C." And just two weeks ago, responding to B.C. concerns, Finance Minister Paul Martin and Revenue Minister Herb Dhaliwal announced a delay in the foreign assets reporting requirement, removing a major irritant to business immigrants.

Finally, even in the area of fisheries, which sometimes seems to be only a source of acrimony between Victoria and Ottawa, we should not forget the important progress we have already made. In April, we signed an agreement that will increase cooperation between the two governments, the salmon industry and stakeholders in the management and conservation of this resource. Premier Clark said the signing represented "an historic day for British Columbians" and "more proof that cooperation between our two levels of government can bring real gains for us all." Three months later, the two governments signed a memorandum of understanding to jointly review the status of the West Coast fishery and their respective roles and responsibilities in managing it.

The challenges we must face together

I could mention other fields – labour market training, the Softwood Lumber Agreement, funding for technology research – where B.C. has benefited by constructive federal-provincial cooperation, but now I want to deal with some of the challenges we face. Two areas that stand out are the fisheries issue, forever in our headlines, and what actions our governments can take to deal with B.C.'s slowing economy.

We must make sure that the fishermen of British Columbia get a fair share of the salmon catch compared with their American counterparts – and ensure that there will still be enough salmon around to sustain the fishery twenty, fifty, a hundred years from now. We must find a long-term solution.

At times, the fact that all of us share these goals is obscured by the debate over the best way to reach them. Yes, the federal government and its B.C. counterpart do not always see eye to eye on tactics. But British Columbians are also divided amongst themselves on the best approach to take. Some clearly favour aggressive action such as that taken by blockading the Malaspina ferry. Others, including many representatives of your tourism industry, publicly favour a more diplomatic, constructive approach. But we all want to get the best possible deal for B.C. fishermen and their families.

Tough talk and threats may make waves, but they don't make progress. I for one applaud the solid work my colleague David Anderson and Prince Rupert Mayor Jack Mussallem have done to restore the Alaska ferry service. It means millions of dollars in business activity are going back into Prince Rupert – dollars vital to the local economy and the families who depend on it. And I also applaud what former UBC President David Strangway is doing to get talks on the Pacific Salmon Treaty back on track for British Columbians.

While the fisheries issue is a challenge, it is being played out against the backdrop of the broader challenge of ensuring growth in the B.C. economy. Some sectors of your economy are performing well: small businesses are being rapidly established and self-employment is up 15.3% over the last twelve months; retail sales are doing reasonably well outside Vancouver; and emerging manufacturing and knowledge-based industries are strong performers. But the fact that the plastics and computer services sectors are performing well is of little comfort to a sawmill worker in the Cariboo who has lost his job because his mill was sold.

It would be wrong to assume that B.C. has been experiencing boom times in recent years. We know that the economic cycles of B.C. are not identical to those of Ontario or Quebec. We know the need for a strategy to address the challenges of the B.C. economy. That is why the governments of British Columbia and Canada are working together to maximize the benefits your province gets as our gateway to Asia-Pacific. It is why we are working together to restructure the fishery. It is why we came to an agreement on job training that will tailor programs to the specific retraining needs of unemployed British Columbians. It is why we are supporting innovations in technology, helping to finance the Ballard fuel cell and basing Canada's national particle physics research lab at UBC.

Separation is not an option

We have made progress together. But I know there are still areas of disagreement. I know that British Columbians sometimes get frustrated with a federal government that is 3,000 miles away physically, but can seem at times even further away in terms of its understanding. I can understand the frustrations this causes for many people, including some of your political figures, which brings me to the remarks made two weeks ago by Senator Pat Carney.

When I came into politics almost two years ago, I knew I would have to fight against separatists in all kinds of places. But I never thought I would face a threat from that hot bed of revolution, the Conservative Senate caucus. I did not mean, to paraphrase Senator Carney's recent speech title, "to turn a nice lady like her into a separatist." I know that Senator Carney has worked hard for her province and her country, and I am sure that if she were asked she would say that she is proudly 100% Canadian. But I should explain to you why I reacted so strongly to her words, even though I know there is no serious support for the idea of separatism in this province.

To understand me, you need to know that I came into politics not only to fight separatism, but also to fight separatist blackmail. Those who say "give this or that thing to my province or else we will break up Canada" commit a serious moral error. Nobody should threaten his or her fellow citizens in this way, and this is not the way to discuss things and make progress in a democracy. In a country as democratic, as tolerant, as rich, and as successful as Canada, there is nothing to justify either secession or the threat of secession. Nothing in Quebec, or in any other province or territory of Canada.

Perhaps because Canada has been talking about separation for so long, we sometimes lose sight of how dangerous and wrong the idea of secession is. Secession is a political act in which some people reject some of their other fellow citizens. The Quebec separatist says, "I will not have any more ties with British Columbians or other Canadians except for those of cold economic self-interest. Only with Quebecers will I have ties of national solidarity."

In a democracy, we should not threaten to desert some of our fellow citizens: we should try to embrace and help all of them. Democracy is a principle that requires solidarity and not rupture, and it is very difficult to reconcile secession with democracy. The letters that I have written to the government of Mr. Bouchard were intended to highlight this difficulty. It is not just a coincidence that international law doesn't recognize the right of secession except in a colonial situation or situation of violent oppression, which is to say in situations where the rights of citizenship do not exist for all.

Secession is an extreme solution, one of the most divisive acts possible in a society. This is why in Quebec I am fighting not only secession, but also the tactic of using secession as a threat. Secession is too serious to use as a bargaining chip.

You, the people of British Columbia, are very attached to Canada. As Prime Minister Chrétien has said, it's here that one sees the biggest Canadian flags flying in the wind. But when I said recently that the current difficulties of the salmon industry don't justify secession, some people interpreted that as a lack of respect and sensitivity on my part towards the people of British Columbia. It is as if I am showing a lack of respect because I am so committed to British Columbia's remaining part of my country. This is absurd, and it is precisely this absurd attitude that we must fight together everywhere in Canada.

As your federal Minister of Intergovernmental Affairs, I am very aware of the importance of salmon to this province. In fact, one of my first memories of B.C. was when my friend Professor Donald Blake of UBC invited me to go with him on a salmon fishing trip. While sports fishing is important to many British Columbians, it is your commercial fishermen who face the toughest challenges today. Working to get an agreement with the United States on the Pacific salmon fishery that is fair to British Columbians is one of the items at the top of our government's agenda.

I share your frustration that the issue has not yet been resolved, though I do not believe that confrontation will produce the results we all want. Coming as I do from a city which is no stranger to the anguish unemployment brings, I can readily sympathize with the fishermen in your coastal communities who are losing not just their jobs, but their way of life. The issue goes beyond that. Salmon swim not only in your ocean and rivers, but also in the very soul of your province.

But I repeat: there are no issues in any province that justify secession, or even the threat of secession. No Canadian should feel threatened with the loss of his or her country. We must all, in every province, renounce using the threat of break-up as a political weapon.

This threat is not a very effective weapon in any case. Take the debate over constitutional recognition of Quebec. If you say to Canadians outside Quebec that they must recognize Quebec's distinctiveness or Quebec will separate, support for such recognition falls well below 50%. But if you ask people whether they recognize that the unique character of Quebec, its language and its culture, is a great Canadian value, a fundamental part of our Canadian identity, the vast majority of Canadians outside Quebec will agree.

If you explain that we can reconcile the diversity of Canada, including Quebec's uniqueness, with the principles of equality of citizens and the equal status of the provinces, support for recognizing Quebec is even higher. Just look at the popular support for the principles of the Calgary Declaration. An Angus Reid poll shows that 73% of Canadians, including no less than 70% of British Columbians, think that the premiers' national unity initiative is "a positive step in the right direction." And a new Environics poll shows that around 70% of Canadians – including 68% of British Columbians and 68% of Quebecers – support recognizing the unique character of Quebec in the Constitution, as long as any advantage this may give to Quebec is made available to the other provinces.

It is because Canadians judge that the principle of equality in diversity is good in and of itself that they support the Declaration. It is in this spirit that I urge citizens to participate in the consultation process that Premier Clark and his colleagues have launched to discuss the Calgary Declaration. This is an initiative that will help keep Canada together so that, as Quebecers and British Columbians, we can continue to share this marvellous country.

Conclusion

I truly want B.C. to remain part of my daughter Jeanne's country. I want her to see the sunlight filtering through the trees in the Carmanah Valley or the morning mist while crossing on the ferry to Vancouver Island, and to know that these special places belong to her. I want her to have opportunities that extend from the Atlantic to the Pacific and beyond. I want her to experience the exuberance and dynamism of Vancouver and its people, and know that they are part of her country. I want her to feel the pride that comes from having Rick Hansen as a fellow citizen. In short, British Columbians are a vital part of Canada. And I do not want Lucien Bouchard – or anyone else – to take this away from her.

Those of you here today who have children are as determined as I am to pass a united Canada on to them. So I would urge you, as British Columbians and Canadians, to ask yourselves why you want to keep Quebec as part of your country. Think about it. Then share your conclusions with your friends. You might even want to share them with your politicians and even with your self-proclaimed leaders, the radio talk show hosts.

I want your voice, the voice of the citizens, to be heard across Canada, so that Quebecers and other Canadians will know that British Columbians want to build a stronger, more united Canada for the 21st century that includes Quebec, B.C., and all the other regions of this country working together as partners, as fellow citizens, and as friends. This is my Canada, this is our Canada, this is the Canada that we will keep together.

Letter to Mr. Jacques Brassard

Mr. Jacques Brassard
Minister for Canadian Intergovernmental Affairs, Quebec
875 Grande-Allée East, Room 3.101
Quebec City, Quebec
G1R 4Y8

Dear Mr. Brassard:

The difficulties in dealing with secession within a democracy are real and serious. They require a respectful and thorough discussion which your government has postponed for too long. For this reason, I was pleased that you volunteered to pick up this debate which your Deputy Premier, Mr. Bernard Landry, started last summer.

You have chosen to raise only one aspect of the problem, namely the delineation of borders, so it is on this that I will respond. This issue is, perhaps, the most difficult, sensitive and troubling of all those raised by the prospect of Quebec's secession. It requires careful examination.

You are pursuing a line of reasoning that seems on its face to be self-contradictory, namely that Canada's territory is divisible while Quebec's is not. In so doing, you advance both legal and moral considerations which are questionable or erroneous. Let us begin with the legal aspect.

You are right that a province's borders cannot be modified without its legislative consent under Canadian law. This protection originated in the Constitution Act, 1871, and was carried over into the amending procedures contained in Part V of the Constitution Act, 1982. Nor are you mistaken in saying that the borders of an independent Quebec would be protected by international law. You neglect to mention, however, that they would be as protected "as Canada's are today," as is made clear on page 385 of the official French version of the report written by the five experts on whom you base yourself almost exclusively.

You seem to believe that the borders of Canada as an independent state are not protected because it is a federation of which one of its components, Quebec, could be described as a "people." A federation is no less an independent state because it gives wide autonomy to its component parts. International law provides the same guarantee for the external borders of a federation as it does for those of unitary states. Canada is no more divisible than is France under international law. As we have indicated in our factum in the Reference before the Supreme Court, international law does not provide a right of unilateral secession to a "people," except in cases of colonies and possibly cases of extreme human rights abuses. In other cases, there is no right at international law for constituent parts of a state to secede without the consent of that state.

The critical question, then, is how Quebec could be transformed into an independent state while respecting the right of Canada to maintain its territorial integrity. Your government persists in claiming for itself the right to effect such a change unilaterally, even though you are contradicted by the vast majority of experts, including those whom you quote.

Your claim is so contrary to what the Government of Canada believes to be established law that one can only assume that it is your awareness of this weakness that lies behind your refusal to test its validity before the Supreme Court. Yet, recourse to the courts is a legitimate means to resolve questions of law in a democracy. The country's highest court is not being asked whether or not secession has political merit, but rather whether your government has the right to effect secession unilaterally.

You believe that you would be able to obtain international recognition without Canada's consent. Since the Charter of the United Nations was signed in 1945, many new countries have been admitted to the United Nations but *no* country outside the colonial context has become a member against the will of the state from which it separated. Unless a reason can be found which would render this state practice applicable to all countries except Canada, we can reasonably predict that the international community would not recognize your government as an independent state until *after* Canada had given its consent.

On November 12, you suggested that it would be enough for your government to exercise "effective authority over the territory of Quebec" after a unilateral declaration of independence to achieve international recognition. You advance a very troubling scenario which is fraught with risk and is almost certainly doomed to fail.

First of all, even the "effective control" of territory by a secessionist regime does not in itself lead to recognition by the international community. The "Turkish Republic of Northern Cyprus," Chechnya and Katanga are all examples of unilateral declarations of independence that were effective on the ground but that failed to receive the support and recognition of the international community.

Second, what does your talk of "effective control" mean? How would you exercise such control following a unilateral declaration of independence which was not accepted by the Government of Canada? What would you do faced with the many citizens who would claim their right not to lose Canada on the basis of such a procedure? If they chose to respect existing laws and contest unconstitutional ones, you could not accuse them of civil disobedience because your government itself would be outside the legal framework. The prospect of even a secession which conforms with international practice and Canadian law is difficult and agonizing enough for Quebec society, without having your government exacerbate matters by threatening to act in such an irresponsible manner. And yet you know full well that democracy and the rule of law go hand in hand.

You invoke the collapse of Yugoslavia as a valid precedent to provide a legal argument for your proposed unilateral declaration of independence. However, in so doing, you confuse secession and the total disintegration of a state. Yugoslavia was a case of disintegration, in which the state itself had ceased to exist. The Arbitration Commission which you quote reached this conclusion only after finding that the Yugoslav governmental institutions no longer met the minimum requirements for participation and representation inherent in a federal state, that four of the six constituent republics had expressed a desire to become independent, and that the central authorities had proven themselves to be incapable of ending the civil war. It was in those extreme circumstances that a principle of the inviolability of borders, *uti possidetis*, was invoked in relation to Yugoslavia's constituent republics.

Take the example dear to your Deputy Premier, that of the former Yugoslav republic of Slovenia. From the day that Slovenia was recognized as independent, its borders were as protected by international law as Canada's. But Slovenia became independent through the disintegration of the state to which it belonged, which has nothing to do with the secession that you are contemplating. As long as Canada exists as a state, its Constitution, which represents the source of legal authority for both our governments, applies.

The Government of Canada accepts the possibility of Quebec's becoming independent. But such a break-up of the country could only occur after Quebecers had very clearly expressed their desire to renounce Canada and after the conditions of secession had been established. You cannot predict the results of any negotiations any more than I can. However, it can be predicted with certainty that they would raise difficult issues for Quebecers and other Canadians, including, perhaps, the issue of territory. Canada would be legally entitled to withhold its consent to secession until it was satisfied with the conditions of this secession.

Let me turn now to the moral dimension of the boundaries issue.

Clearly, a proposal to partition a country gives rise to moral problems, because it invites its citizens to break their ties of solidarity. Once engaged, there is always the risk that a break-up may be done according to bonds of race, language or religion. That is one reason why many very respectable democracies have explicitly or implicitly prohibited secession in their constitutions.

In Canada, we see things differently. We believe that our country would no longer be the same if it were not based on the voluntary adhesion of all its components. That is why there is no major political party, either in Quebec or in the country as a whole, that says it is prepared to keep Quebecers in Canada against their will.

But nor would Quebec be the same if its unity were based on coercion. Just as it would be difficult to hold populations in Canada against their will, it would also be difficult to oblige them to renounce Canada against their will. That is why Quebec's territory cannot be considered to be sacred once it is accepted that Canada's territory is divisible. And that is why you, Mr. Brassard, should clearly disavow the statements you have made on at least three occasions with respect to the use of the police as a means to subject populations to your secession against their will.[1]

You argue that Quebec's territory is indivisible because it is inhabited by only one people. There is a sense in which Quebecers constitute a people, but there is also a sense in which there are several peoples in Quebec or only one people in Canada. It is better to reject exclusivist definitions of who we are and see our multiple identities as an incomparable collective richness. Above all, we need to remember that it is always dangerous to attach greater importance and moral weight to the collective representations one gives oneself, such as the notions of "people" and "nation", than to flesh-and-blood citizens. As Renan wrote, "Man belongs neither to his language nor to his race; he belongs to himself above all, because he is above all a free and moral being."

I entered public life to help Quebecers and other Canadians remain united and not to negotiate their break-up. But if it were ever to come to that, the universal democratic values that we hold dear would have to continue to guide us all. In such difficult circumstances, we could not then exclude the possibility that modifying borders might appear as the least undesirable democratic solution. Borders sometimes change when new states are born. Since 1945, such changes have occurred peacefully following referenda (e.g., The British Cameroons, The Federal Islamic Republic of the Comoros) or negotiations (e.g., Zambia, Czechoslovakia).

The highly democratic country of Switzerland adopted a series of referenda to resolve the difficult issue of determining the borders of the new canton of Jura which was being created out of the existing canton of Bern. The procedure that Switzerland followed was by no means a simple one, but no one can describe it as undemocratic. On the contrary, it attests to Switzerland's desire to satisfy as many of its citizens as possible.

Our governments too, like Switzerland, could be obliged to find arrangements that would not impose secession on populations that do not want it. If you had won the last referendum, we would have been forced to deal with this issue when no one was prepared. You are certainly aware of the three referenda held in Northern Quebec just prior to October 30, 1995, in which over 95% of those Aboriginal voters who were consulted opposed Quebec secession or rejected having their territories removed from Canada.

The surest way to divide Quebecers among themselves is to ask them to renounce Canada. No one has a clear understanding of what would have to be done to overcome those divisions in the case of a negotiated secession, including whether we would have to modify borders. You say that this would risk dividing Quebec along ethno-linguistic lines. But it is your proposal of secession that is creating that problem, with its focus on taking the only province with a Francophone majority out of Canada. In Quebec itself, separation is massively rejected by non-Francophones, while Francophones are deeply divided by it. Your proposal of secession is the only issue that is creating a deep ethno-linguistic division in Quebec. It is depriving our society of all of the cohesive force it would otherwise have.

It is precisely because the territorial issue raises a sensitive and difficult problem that you cannot continue to invent rules of law that do not exist. Of course, there may be good reasons against moving borders, and especially against creating enclaves. I underscored these arguments each time I met with groups and citizens who call for their municipalities to remain in Canada under all circumstances. I asked them to redirect their energies toward promoting the advantages of a united Canada. But other arguments based on solid democratic underpinnings can be made to support changes to borders. Therein lies a dilemma which merits a substantive debate and which ought to be taken seriously.

In summary, if ever Quebec were to separate from Canada, modifying its borders would assuredly pose real problems, but that does not mean to do so would be excluded *a priori*. Your government is mistaken in claiming that the law protects Quebec's territory but not Canada's and commits a moral error when it proposes to force populations to renounce Canada against their will.

Your government should pursue the debate on the various difficulties in reconciling secession with democracy. And you should do so in full respect of the democratic values of those who disagree with you, without questioning their loyalty to Quebec.

Yours sincerely,

Stéphane Dion

NOTE

1 *Le Devoir*, April 30, 1994, page A4; *Le Soleil*, February 15, 1996, page A1; *Globe and Mail*, January 30, 1997, page A4.

Beyond Plan A and Plan B:
The Two Debates on Canadian Unity
MONTREAL, DECEMBER 3, 1997

Ladies and gentlemen of the media, thank you for this opportunity to summarize how the Government of Canada views the Canadian unity issue. I believe it is important this evening that we deal with the substance of the debate together, beyond the notions of Plan A and Plan B. With Mr. Bouchard, those two notions have become prefabricated slogans, impediments to serious reflection. You know the extent to which "Plan B" is synonymous with "attacks" against Quebec in the incantations of the PQ leader.

And because he and his ministers are short on arguments, they prefer to put down those who speak up. That's the response they have given to my letters.

So let's go beyond Plan A and Plan B. The truth is that the many questions raised by Canadian unity and Quebec's future can be classified into two debates. The first deals with the comparative advantages of a united Canada and an independent Quebec. The second deals with the procedure through which Quebec could be transformed into an independent state. So, 1) why Canadian unity; 2) how that unity could cease to exist. These are two different but related debates, because how secession would be attempted would have effects on the consequences of secession.

It would thus be a mistake to see those two debates as contradictory, opposed to each other, Plan A and Plan B. Both are necessary and must be advanced together, in the same spirit of clarification.

1. *Why Quebec ought to stay in Canada*

Quebecers ought to stay in Canada because the country they have built with other Canadians is indisputably a success in the world. And Quebecers and other Canadians owe that success to their being together. That, in its most simple form, is the argument that the Government of Canada is making to Quebecers and all Canadians.

Speech to the Montreal Press Club

And yet, we are aware that the argument of Canada's success, however true, is not enough. We must also win the battle of identity. Most Yes supporters are prepared to admit that Canada is a success. But they see sovereigntism as a way to affirm their Quebec identity. Convincing them that they don't have to choose between Quebec and Canada is undoubtedly the most important issue.

Let us begin with the tangible achievements of Quebec within a united Canada. From that viewpoint, there is an error in perspective that must be corrected, which depicts the existence of a separatist movement as proof that Canada is a failure. That false perspective leads some people to conclude that Quebec ought to leave Canada, while others believe that Canada must have one "last chance" to reform itself from stem to stern so that it finally becomes acceptable to Quebecers.

I believe that the very opposite is true. I feel that the Canada that Quebecers have achieved with other Canadians is a success that will be even more striking when the separatist ideology is no longer harming our cohesion. The changes we are making are not designed to make Canada acceptable: it already is. They are designed to improve a country that is an overall success but is far from perfect. When governments put public finances back in order, strengthen the economy, launch new initiatives to combat child poverty, harmonize federal legislation with the Civil Code, or amend the Constitution with respect to education, they are not making an already acceptable country acceptable, they are making it better.

This is not an argument for the status quo. This notion of status quo is meaningless. A federation is continually evolving, and it must be ensured that it does so in the best interests of citizens. Progress has been made in the past two years, and the first ministers will continue that impetus at their meeting on December 11 and 12, which will deal with the social union.

Commenting on that upcoming first ministers' meeting, Mr. Bouchard had this to say on Saturday to his supporters: "I've seen the agenda. They want to talk primarily about social policy. That's funny, because according to the Constitution, social policy is our jurisdiction."

It is certainly misinterpreting the Constitution to say that the Government of Canada has no role whatsoever in social and health matters. Mr. Bouchard would be quite unable to find a single modern federation where the federal government is not involved in either social policy or health. Mr. Bourassa didn't have the same ideas on those matters as Mr. Trudeau, but he never denied that the federal government had a role to play. As far back as 1970, he called for "a primary responsibility" for the provinces in the area of social policy and acknowledged [translation] "the key role of the federal government in ensuring an acceptable standard of living for all Canadians."

Similarly, today, there are differences in approach among Messrs. Chrétien, Romanow, Klein and Johnson, but those differences are inevitable, and often healthy in the quest for better policies for citizens.

Mr. Bouchard and his ministers tell us that this federation is paralysed by endless conflicts between the federal government, the Quebec government and the other provincial governments. In fact, such tensions exist in all federations. Difficulties must not overshadow successes. Let's take the example of job training. As long as that issue was being disputed, many saw it as proof that the Canadian federation was irreparably dysfunctional. Now that a solution has been negotiated by Mr. Pettigrew and Ms. Harel, people have no more to say about it, except to repeat Mr. Bouchard's comment that it took 31 years to see any movement. That statement is too often accepted at face value, including by federalists. Canada obviously didn't sit on its hands for 31 years before taking an interest in job training. Federal-provincial agreements have been signed which, while perhaps not perfect, could not have been all that bad, since Canada is second in the world in terms of labour force competitiveness, according to the most recent index of the International Institute for Management Development (IMD).

In short, Quebec society and Canada form a whole which works well and which has every interest in staying together. There are abundant arguments to convince more and more of our fellow citizens to turn away from the independence parties. Those arguments must be highlighted by our actions and our words. All my colleagues in the Chrétien government are active on that front, because Canadian unity affects all aspects of our collective life and must not be relegated to a dry discussion on the Constitution.

That being said, there is another battle to be fought, the battle of identity. Many Quebecers are well aware that Canada is a success, but they don't feel at ease in a country where most of the inhabitants don't speak their language and don't have the same cultural references. That uneasiness with identity is a widespread phenomenon in this global world at the dawn of the next century.

We can already tell them that French is not threatened in Quebec. In point of fact, Quebec has never been as French as it is now, with 94% of its population able to speak the language. Outside Quebec, we must not throw in the towel: Francophones are better educated than before and enjoy more rights, cultural resources and their own institutions. Separation would mean "they'll have a hard time," as Jacques Parizeau admitted on November 25 in Edmonton.

But identity is not just about insecurity. Above all, it is about self-affirmation. That is the main issue, in my opinion. We Quebecers are also Canadians. And we are both Quebecers and Canadians not just because we understand that is in our best interests. It is because those two identities are a part of us, and we are proud of them. We should therefore vote accordingly. It isn't normal that 49% of Quebecers voted Yes in the last referendum, when a poll only a few months before indicated that 80% (including 61% of Yes supporters) were "proud to be both Quebecers and Canadians." It is not normal for Yes support to remain above 40% when recent polls indicate that a much smaller proportion of Quebecers define themselves as Quebecers rather than as Quebecers and Canadians (25% according to CROP, February 1996; 17% according to EKOS, March 1997).

We must succeed in clarifying this question of identity at all costs. The independence project not only seeks to take Quebec out of Canada. It also seeks to take Canada out of Quebec, to strip us of our Canadian identity. We would still be Quebecers, but we would no longer be Canadians.

We are a people, Mr. Bouchard thunders day after day. We can easily agree that Quebecers are a people. It's simply difficult to deny that the Cree are a people, or that Canadians are a people. It's all a matter of definitions: sociological, ethnic, political. The real question is whether we are a people in the exclusive sense given to the word used by the PQ, whereby we would be Quebecers but not Canadians.

Of course we are Canadians. We have put too much into this country to take ourselves out of it. Sure, it would be desirable for our own identity to be given greater recognition. But Quebec is currently recognized as a Canadian province, and its provincial government occupies, more completely than the other provincial governments, the extensive areas of jurisdiction it has under the Constitution. The rights of the French language are recognized more than ever since the Constitution Act, 1982. The specificity of Quebec society is taken into account in court rulings, as recognized by former Supreme Court Chief Justice Brian Dickson. In my opinion, there is not a single judgment based on the Canadian Charter of Rights and Freedoms that went against the interests of Quebec society. The federal government has initiated an unprecedented harmonization of its legislation with Quebec's Civil Code, so that federal institutions speak the legal language of Quebecers and our country gets the greatest benefit from its bijuralism. The Constitution will probably soon be amended so that school boards can be organized along lines more in keeping with the specificity of modern Quebec.

It would be desirable, in addition, for Quebec to be recognized as a society, a more inclusive term than people. You know that since the

Calgary Declaration, an initiative was launched to recognize the unique character of Quebec society, which would go hand in hand with equality of status of the provinces, in accordance with the principle that equality is not synonymous with uniformity. That would be a great addition. But there again, that addition would not make Canada acceptable: it is already an indisputable success.

There is no reason to deprive ourselves of Canada. And the Government of Canada's plan is to prove that there is no reason.

2. How secession could be effected

"It is up to the Quebec people to decide its future, not nine judges," Mr. Bouchard roars. Who is saying otherwise? The Government of Canada has obviously not asked the Supreme Court to decide on the merit of secession. It has asked it whether Mr. Bouchard and his government, by virtue of their majority in the National Assembly, would have the right to effect secession unilaterally. You understand how important it is for the Government of Canada that Mr. Bouchard's distorted description of the Supreme Court reference not become the standard language of the media.

The issue before the Court is not Quebec's right to self-determination. It is the Bouchard government's claim that it can effect independence unilaterally. That distinction, which is too often overlooked, is crucial. Allow me to explain why.

We Quebecers may one day want to stop being Canadians. That would be a grave error in my opinion, but I do not deny that it is a possibility, although I do believe it is improbable. In fact, no one can or should deny that this is a possibility.

We in Canada accept secession as a possibility not because we are forced to do so by international law. In reality, secession is not a right in democracy. It is a right only for peoples in a colonial situation or in cases of extreme violation of human rights. That, at least, is the opinion the Government of Canada shares with the vast majority of experts. We shall see what the Supreme Court thinks about it.

We accept secession as a possibility because we know that our country would not be the same if it were not based on the voluntary adhesion of all its components. I do not know of a single major political party in Quebec or elsewhere in Canada that wants to detain us against our will.

In practice, secession would mean that we Quebecers would give up Canada to make Quebec an independent state. Federal institutions would no longer be operative in Quebec's territory.

Well, that is the essential point: the Government of Canada is also a government of Quebecers. It would no longer be so after secession. It therefore has a *duty* to us not to withdraw from Quebec's territory without the assurance that this is very clearly what we want: Canada's withdrawal from Quebec.

Would it have had that assurance the last time if 30,000 more voters had voted Yes instead of No? No one will ever know what would have happened. It is likely, however, that things would have turned out badly, precisely because the Parizeau government would have wanted to effect secession without the firm support of the population.

Research by Professor Maurice Pinard has gauged the extent to which the question chosen by the PQ government artificially swelled support for the Yes side. The question referred to a "partnership" that the chief negotiator, Mr. Bouchard, admitted on June 19 was only "bare bones." Mr. Bouchard should have told us at the time of the referendum that he was asking us to vote for "bare bones." He has promised us since then that his party would put some meat on those bones. We'll have a long wait, because the more they will want to flesh out their partnership, the more they will be divided among themselves, and the more we will see that this is something much flimsier than bare bones: it is a pipe dream. It needs saying and it needs repeating: one quarter of a population could never break up a country and then come back in force and count for 50% in common institutions. That is an absurd project.

Messrs. Bouchard and Parizeau did not tell us of the sketchy nature of their partnership during the referendum campaign. They hid from us their secret plan, the Plan O (for obligations, the French word for bonds), which sought to use $19 billion of our savings bonds in the vain hope of calming the markets after a Yes vote. They said nothing about Mr. Parizeau's "big gamble" with which he planned to force the agenda and put pressure on France, which would put pressure on the United States: a bogus plan. So Mr. Parizeau knew that international recognition is something that is very hard to come by. And yet, he told us just the opposite.

Three referenda were held in northern Quebec in the days preceding the vote on October 30. Those populations asked to stay Canadian, at a rate of over 95%. Mr. Parizeau would no doubt have said that those referenda did not accord any legal rights, because he's said so since then (*La Presse*, p. B1 1997–05–22). Legality! is the very word he would have used. Wasn't there a judgment by the Quebec Superior Court that raised various questions about the legality of the project he intended to implement following a referendum result in his favour? It is hard to guess how many Quebecers would have wanted to contest the illegal procedure by which Mr. Parizeau would have tried to deprive them of Canada, but the post-referendum difficulties would have swelled their ranks. So what would have happened if support for "sovereignty-partnership" had slipped well below 50% in the polls?

I am afraid that the PQ government would have reacted as it is reacting today to the Supreme Court reference. It would have played on emotions, trumped up indignation, looking for a "backlash" and thus making things even more confused and uncertain.

The secession debate is too often described as opposing Canada and Quebec, viewed as two monolithic blocks. Mr. Bouchard says that it is "Quebec," "Quebec democracy," "the Quebec people" that are attacked by the Supreme Court reference. And so we're all boiled down to a single being (or a single bloc). In fact, his attempt at unilateral secession would first and foremost divide us Quebecers among ourselves. Because the surest way of dividing Quebecers is to ask them to give up Canada. Mr. Bouchard would be forcing seven million people to overcome a profound disagreement without a precise legal framework in which to do so. You don't do that in a democracy.

Those who love Quebec do not want to see it plunged into such a situation. The way in which our secessionist leaders want to effect secession is completely irresponsible.

Democracy and the rule of law go hand in hand. Mr. Bouchard says that accession to sovereignty is a purely political matter, but he keeps inventing rules of law to justify the procedure he intends to follow. In fact, there are no "purely political" questions in a democracy. The law is an essential ingredient in the political life of a democracy; otherwise, things slide into anarchy. The PQ government has no right to proclaim itself to be the government of an independent state using a procedure it has established alone and an interpretation of the will of Quebecers of which it would be the sole judge. It cannot unilaterally strip us of our constitutional rights as Canadian citizens. It cannot establish alone the conditions for secession, whether they relate to the debt or to territory.

We must discuss this issue, as democrats, to find a just and fair procedure to settle the issue of secession. I cannot suggest a specific procedure today. But I must reiterate the three principles that should guide us in finding that procedure.

The first is peacefulness. Everyone, governments first and foremost, must renounce force or the threat of the use of force. I repeat my invitation to Mr. Brassard to take back unambiguously the threatening statements he has made in the past.

The second is clarity. It would be too dangerous to launch into negotiations on secession without having the assurance that it is what Quebecers truly want.

The third is legality. The legal framework must be clear and recognized, so that everyone knows his or her rights and obligations and governments are able in all circumstances to protect citizens, respect their rights and obtain their obedience.

If Mr. Bouchard would agree on those three principles tomorrow, we would have taken a giant step as democrats in this difficult debate.

Conclusion

Ladies and gentlemen of the media, this is the way in which the Government of Canada asks why and how. Why Canadian unity? How could it be ended? In both cases, we begin with the principle that Quebecers are also Canadians. We find that the vast majority of them want to stay Canadians. Our government has a duty to show them that they are right. We must work even harder to improve this federation, which already serves us so well. The Government of Canada also has a duty to Quebecers not to take Canada away from them unless they have very clearly demonstrated that this is what they want.

Above all, we must not mistake the target. The problem we face is not Quebec society: it is just as open and tolerant as the other parts of Canada. Nor must it be confused with Quebec nationalism, which can be a positive force. Nor does it pertain to our language laws, which refer to a debate which, in itself, when separatist ideology does not sow mistrust, is conducted rather better in Quebec than in most other multilingual democracies. The problem pertains specifically to the project of secession itself, which is dividing Quebec society and depriving it of all the strength of cohesion it would otherwise have.

In an atmosphere of clarity, I believe that Quebecers will never give up Canada. But if that were to happen, the sad act of secession would have to be negotiated. It would have to be negotiated peacefully, clearly and legally. But the Government of Canada has great hopes that those difficult circumstances will not come about. It has confidence in Quebec's future within a united Canada.

Letter to Mr. Claude Ryan

FEBRUARY 6, 1998

[Translation from French]

Dear Mr. Ryan:

At your press conference of February 3, you stated that the Government of Canada was wrong to go before the Supreme Court. While I do not agree with your point of view, I believe that the intervention of such a respected public figure provides all of our fellow citizens with the opportunity to deepen the understanding of a crucial issue for us all.

With this reference, the Government of Canada aims to clarify an important point: the legal aspects of a unilateral secession. We believe that Quebecers and other Canadians are entitled to this information. The decision about whether to effect secession should above all not be made on the basis of myths and false theories.

Allow me to outline the points on which we agree. We both believe that Quebecers cannot be held in Canada against their will. We also believe that they must not lose Canada without having renounced it very clearly. Indeed, you yourself have strongly criticized the referendum procedures that the PQ government used in 1980 and 1995. You have talked about "dangerous ambiguity" and "tragicomic misunderstandings" (*La Presse*, 27–05–97). This brings to mind, for example, the referendum question, which alluded to a political and economic partnership that Mr. Bouchard now describes as bare bones (*Le Devoir*, 20–06–97) and sketchy (*Le Soleil*, 19–12–97), or Mr. Parizeau's famous "Plan O," which nearly cost us a part of our savings.

Are you suggesting then, Mr. Ryan, that it would be democratic for Quebecers to lose Canada in such a "dangerous ambiguity"? Surely not, because you have written that, under such circumstances, "the federal government will feel obliged, as, incidentally, it did in 1980 and 1995, although this was not sufficiently noted, to refuse to commit itself in advance to recognizing a result obtained through an equivocal question." And you have added: "It would be pointless to claim to deny the federal government this power of reserving its reaction" (*La Presse*, 27–05–97). You suggest that the Government of Canada be involved in advance discussions on the content of the question and on the rules to be used in interpreting the result, since you agree that it would be in the public interest that these parameters be considered acceptable by both sides.

We agree on many points. The most important is our shared conviction that the country's unity could not be maintained against the clearly expressed will of Quebecers. The Government of Canada has repeated this viewpoint on several occasions, but is also of the opinion that this position is totally compatible with the view that Quebec provincial institutions do not have the right to proceed unilaterally with secession. On this point, we disagree.

You state that secession is a political and democratic, rather than a legal, question. Certainly democracy is paramount, but the law is essential for democracy. The law is necessary in order for political action to take place democratically and not in anarchy.

If the PQ government were to pull off a referendum victory through trickery and by means of an ambiguous procedure and question, the Government of Canada believes that it would have a duty not to consent to it. It would continue to use peaceful means to discharge its responsibilities, and thus would enable Quebecers to enjoy fully their rights as Canadians, in spite of the unilateral attempt at secession. This is what the Government of Canada would consider as its duty, insofar as it would have the right to do so. Presently, this right is denied by the Government of Quebec. Since only the Court can confirm that the Government of Quebec would have no basis in law to make an attempt at unilateral secession, it seems that our initiative before the Supreme Court is entirely logical, legitimate and honourable.

This debate goes well beyond legal niceties. Even a secession which were to take place within a legal framework would pose enormous problems. If it were true that unilateral secession has no legal basis, it would raise practical difficulties that would be even harder to overcome. These can be classified into three categories.

1 Quebecers would be divided among themselves. There is currently a great deal of talk about the Quebec consensus, without analysing its scope more closely. The "right of Quebecers to decide their own future alone" has become a knee-jerk slogan. There is certainly a consensus that Quebecers must be able to effect secession if that is very clearly their will. But there is no consensus in favour of the PQ procedure for effecting that secession, at least none that seems to me to include Claude Ryan.

Many Quebecers would claim the right not to lose Canada in confusion, without a recognized legal framework. The Government of Quebec would be ill positioned to require those citizens to respect its laws, since it would have positioned itself outside the legal framework. We Quebecers would not want to see our society plunged into such instability.

2 From a practical point of view, the active cooperation of Canadians in other provinces and of the federal government is necessary to effect secession. This would be the first time that a modern democratic state would be undertaking a break-up after experiencing many decades of universal suffrage. There would be countless practical problems to be resolved, such as dividing the debt, the question of territory, and transferring taxes. A common and concerted effort would be indispensable for ironing out the numerous difficulties. Such an effort could be obtained within the legal framework, because there is no first minister, no government, no major political party in this federation that wants to keep Quebecers against their very clearly expressed will.

3 We believe that it is very unlikely that a unilateral declaration of independence would win international recognition. As you will understand, it is not possible for me to develop this point here, since it is part of our arguments before the Court.

In short, while Quebecers must not be kept in Canada against their will, neither must they lose Canada without having very clearly renounced it. These two considerations cannot be respected unless governments act in accordance with the Constitution and the law. After it had been clearly established that Quebecers no longer wanted to be Canadian, secession would be negotiated within the legal framework. This is the only practicable scenario if one wishes to effect secession while avoiding chaos or, as you put it, "impasse".

I support the Supreme Court reference as a Quebecer who wants assurance that neither I nor my fellow citizens will lose our identity and our full rights as Canadians in confusion, without a legal framework to overcome our divisions, in a dangerous ambiguity that is unacceptable in democracy.

Yours sincerely,

Stéphane Dion

Respect for Democracy in Canada
MONTREAL, MARCH 18, 1998

"Canada was born, 121 years ago, as the result of a process that drew on the sources of dialogue, negotiation, and openness" [*translation*].

Lucien Bouchard, July 1, 1988

Today, as I have the pleasure and the honour to be the guest of the Students' Association of the Faculty of Law of the Université de Montréal, I have many memories of the 11 years I spent teaching political science just a stone's throw away, at Lionel Groulx Hall – I won't comment on the name of the hall ... They are fond memories, because I believe that I have always succeeded, with your help, in overcoming an even greater barrier than political partisanship, namely, academic rivalry. There is little love lost between the noble disciplines of law and political science. A jurist once told me that, outside the rule, there is only anecdote, and so political science is the science of anecdote ... but I won't tell you what political scientists have to say about jurists! I prefer to think back happily on the law students I have known who have ventured into political science, on your library, in which I have spent many long evenings, and on your professors, including the one who now sits across from me in the House of Commons, Professor Daniel Turp.

I would also like to pay special tribute to another of your professors, André Tremblay, speaking as one pro-democrat to another. Because democracy, of course, is what we will be talking about today: respect for democracy in Canada.

I will affirm that the history of Canadian democracy, even with its shortcomings and its darker pages, compares favourably with the progress of democracy in other countries. There are few histories closer to the democratic ideal than the history that Quebecers have written with other Canadians. Of course, Canada can learn from other democracies; for example, we cannot boast of the most democratic Senate in

---

Speech to the Faculty of Law, University of Montreal

the world! In general, however, democratic progress has been achieved in better conditions here than elsewhere.

March 11 marked the 150th anniversary of responsible government in Canada. On this occasion the historian Ged Martin, a professor at the University of Edinburgh, wrote: "In the crucial combination of mass participation, human rights and self-government, Canada's history is second to none in the world." I can think of no achievement of which a country could be more proud.

If we were fully aware of this, we would have no doubt celebrated the 150th anniversary of responsible government in Canada as loudly as the French rightly celebrated, on January 13, 1998, the 100th anniversary of Émile Zola's article "J'accuse."

We must understand the extent to which parliamentary democracy is for humanity a very recent and still incomplete victory. When I was a university student in the late 1970s, Eastern Europe, almost all of South America, a large part of the Mediterranean region and Asia all lived under authoritarian or totalitarian regimes. Even in democracies, parties advocating the dictatorship of the proletariat found a wide audience. Here in Canada, leftist theories hostile to parliamentary democracy were making inroads in the labour movement and in our universities ... even our law faculties.

The wave of democratization that has swept through the last two decades of this century is one of the most extraordinary phenomena in the history of humanity. Millions of human beings now enjoy democratic rights that their parents never had. This must make us, as Canadians, see how lucky we are to belong to a country that has been a pioneer of democracy.

1. The advance of democracy in Canada

A pioneer of democracy is an apt description of our country. It is true that elected assemblies were established in Virginia in 1619 and in Massachusetts in 1634, but we followed, with Nova Scotia in 1758, Prince Edward Island in 1773, New Brunswick in 1785 and Lower and Upper Canada in 1792. It is an exceptional and admirable fact that, since 1792, our country has almost always been governed by a political regime comprising an elected assembly.

Those assemblies were elected by limited suffrage, in accordance with rather rudimentary procedures. Expanding the franchise and cleaning up electoral practices turned out to be difficult achievements for all fledgling democracies. There again, the Canada of the 19th century was a leader.

Census-based suffrage was established in Canada following essentially the same rules as in Great Britain, but because our social structure was more egalitarian and property less concentrated, suffrage was in fact less restricted in Canada.

The powers of the first elected assemblies were much more limited than those of parliaments today. Here again, Canada was at the forefront of reform. As I said earlier, the system of responsible government in Canada is now 150 years old, one of the oldest in the world. Specifically, it was on March 11, 1848, that Louis-Hippolyte Lafontaine became the first Prime Minister of Canada – which was then known as the Province of Canada – after the coalition of reformer parliamentarians in the two Canadas that he led with Robert Baldwin convinced the Governor General to appoint a Cabinet that had the support of the majority of the assembly. From that moment onward, the legitimate link between government and governed was established. Responsible government had also been established in Nova Scotia a few weeks earlier. Those elected assemblies had powers that were quite extensive for that period, especially since, because we have never had a real aristocracy, our non-elected upper chambers did not have the same influence as those in Great Britain.

It would have been far preferable if the colonial authorities had consented to responsible government without a single drop of blood being spilt, that is, without the rebellions that were put down in Lower and Upper Canada, as Quebec and Ontario were then known. On the whole, however, the victory of democracy was achieved here under much more peaceful conditions than elsewhere, without the need for bloody revolution to abolish royal despotism or civil war to abolish slavery.

As well as their democratic dimension, the rebellions of 1837–38 in Lower Canada had a national dimension, to which the Durham Report's advocacy of the assimilation of French-Canadians reacted. But it must also be realized that the emerging liberal democracies of the 19th century considered active homogenization of their populations and linguistic assimilation to be the standard to follow, in particular by means of a one-size-fits-all public education system. In the words of the linguist Jacques Leclerc: [translation] "The centralizing authoritarianism which consists of unilaterally imposing a single language throughout a territory and ignoring linguistic pluralism ... was standard practice in the 19th century."

Today, we tend to forget just how recent the value of linguistic and cultural pluralism is in democracy. Even the liberal and progressive thinkers of the last century tended to see assimilation as a necessary condition for equal opportunity for individuals. Durham, for example, while certainly a staunch imperialist, a narrow-minded advocate of assimilation, un "mange-Canadiens," was also, and here is the paradox, a liberal enamoured of equal opportunity, who was nicknamed "Radical Jack" at home and supported the right to vote, public education and land reform. His report recommended that responsible government be established in Canada. In the same era as Durham, one of the great thinkers in the history of liberalism, Tocqueville, sought the means to assimilate Algerians into French civilization.

What is exceptional in Canada is not that assimilation was sought, but that it was not achieved. The union of the two Canadas by which Durham hoped to assimilate French-Canadians instead paved the way for the alliance of Baldwin and Lafontaine. The English Protestant and French Catholic populations laid the foundations for agreement, rather than scrapping, as they had hitherto done too often wherever historical circumstances had brought them together. Without that agreement, who knows what would have become of the French fact in Canada? There have been and still are too many Francophone Canadians who have lost their language, but it would be difficult to find a country with a better counterbalance to the forces of assimilation, in today's world where, for the first time in the history of humanity, the number of languages spoken is decreasing rather than increasing.

We must always place ourselves in the context of the time. For example, one might feel that it would have been better if the Constitution of 1867 had been put to a referendum, rather than simply being approved by the Parliament of the Union. But the fact remains that the parliamentary system that prevailed in the united Canada in the 1860s "was in some respects in advance of any other in the world at that time" (S. J. R. Noël, *Patrons, Clients, Brokers Ontario Society and Politics, 1791–1896* (Toronto: University of Toronto Press, 1990), p. 174). Even today, there are too few countries which, like Canada, were born in their modern form from an act of Parliament rather than an act of violence.

2. Five conclusions drawn from our history

If I had the time, I would continue this retrospective on our history to try to explain why Canada is seen throughout the world as a country which is one of the most respectful of democracy and universal values. But it is time to sum up and to each draw our own conclusions about the birth of our democracy. Here are five conclusions that I propose.

1 *Let us never forget that the advanced democracy Canada has inherited from its history is also a Quebec achievement.* It didn't come about

against us or in spite of us, it came about with us. We can be proud of that. It is in this democracy that we have developed our own culture and our own spirit. We shall never know what might have happened if Canada had remained under the French regime. Perhaps Napoleon would have sold us to the United States at the same time as Louisiana to bankroll his European wars, and we would have been swallowed up in the "melting pot". But history is not made of "what ifs". It is in Canada, with mutual assistance between Quebecers and other Canadians, that Quebec society has flourished with its own character.

2 *Let us remember that we have learned from our history tolerance and respect for opposing opinions.* Especially since we are involved in one of the most difficult debates a society can have, that of secession, we must steer clear of impugning motives, demonizing opponents and voodoo politics.

That leads me to some comments on the Supreme Court reference. I will never say of those of you who disagree with the reference that you are bad democrats. I simply think that you seriously underestimate the difficulties posed by trying to reconcile secession with democracy. As fellow democrats, allow me to outline the viewpoint of the Government of Canada.

It is customary in democracy that when there is a major disagreement not only of substance, but also about the legal procedure that ought to be followed to resolve that disagreement of substance, the parties turn to the courts to obtain the necessary legal clarification. That is exactly what the Government of Canada has done in this case. It has not asked the judges to decide in the people's stead whether secession is the right choice. It has asked them whether an attempted unilateral secession by the Government of Quebec would have a legal basis, as that government claims, or would not, as the Government of Canada claims. This is a purely legal question, to which the answer, in the circumstances, will clarify the democratic debate.

The fundamental question in this case is as follows: if the Government of Quebec proclaims itself the government of an independent state, do citizens and other governments have a legal obligation to consider it as such? If, as the Government of Canada believes, the answer to this question is no, from the perspective of both domestic and international law, this is something that it is better to know as soon as possible. There are few things more dangerous in democracy than a government that places itself outside the legal framework yet still demands obedience of citizens.

As law students, you well know that the rule of law is essential to democracy, whereby no one is above the law, especially not the lawmakers. You well know that majority rule is not the be-all and end-all of democracy, and that a simple majority obtained in a referendum does not give any government the right to annul unilaterally the constitutional guarantees that a country grants to its citizens and its minorities.

The Government of Quebec, for its part, wants to disregard the Constitution and yet demands obedience of its laws. It wants to portray secession as a purely political act which does not bind that government to the law, and yet, that secession would bind citizens and other governments to its conception of the law. In our opinion, that is just not done in democracy. Not in an exemplary democracy such as Canada, which Quebecers have built with their fellow Canadians.

With a clear and honest question and procedure, Quebecers will never renounce Canada. I truly believe this. Nevertheless, if Quebecers were to indicate very clearly that they wanted to renounce Canada and make Quebec an independent state, then the break-up of the country would have to be negotiated within the legal framework. That would be the only way to proceed if we want to respect the rule of law and democracy for all and minimize the serious risks of derailment.

3 *Let us compare with other democracies so as better to judge our own.* The hue and cry being raised about this or that situation in Quebec or in Canada as a whole is utterly surreal when compared with what is going on in other democracies. I sometimes wonder whether the way to settle the constitutional problem might not be to insert in section 2 of the Constitution: "Canada has been unfair to everyone," after which the case would be closed and we would enjoy together the benefits of our country.

Let me give just two recent examples that closely affect us Quebecers: the constitutional change of 1982 and, once again, the reference to the Supreme Court.

The events preceding the Constitution Act, 1982 can be interpreted in different ways, but the separatist leaders are dreaming if they believe that this episode from our recent history might mobilize international opinion in their favour. It is impossible to see how a constitutional change supported by every constitutional entity but one, and by almost every Quebec Member of Parliament, whose centrepiece is a charter of rights and freedoms that is admirable relative to what exists in the world, could be condemned by international opinion. On the contrary, our separatist leaders evoke incredulity when they present grievances that are so bizarre by international standards.

You know that the federal government has argued before the Supreme Court that unilateral secession is not a right in democracy.

Those who condemn that position should first ask themselves why a number of other very respectable democracies believe that their country's territory belongs to all its citizens and could therefore not be divisible. They should also ask themselves why the international community is so opposed to the idea that nations or regional communities could automatically have a right to effect secession unilaterally. I suggest that it is because it would be very difficult to determine to whom that right might be granted, that such an automatic right to secession would have dramatic consequences for the international community, with more than 3,000 human groups in the world claiming a collective identity, and that the creation of each new state would risk creating minorities within the state who would claim their own independence. On a more basic level, a philosophy of democracy based on the logic of secession would incite groups to separate rather than to work at coming closer together and understanding one another.

Rather than advocating a right to secession, the international community focuses on the rights of populations with distinct characteristics to preserve their culture and have their own institutions within a larger community. In other words, the right of self-determination translates in democracy precisely into the type of arrangements provided by our federation.

4 *We need to strengthen and improve our democracy, and the best way of succeeding is to do it together.* Together, different populations, speaking different languages and not always having the same cultural references, have learned to tolerate, appreciate and help one another. That difficult learning process has won us international recognition today as one of the countries most tolerant and open to ethnic diversity. To separate, especially along French-English fault lines, to undo what has united us from the outset, would mean much more than the economic problems predicted by the vast majority of economists: it would be a moral defeat. We have learned too much from our history not to see that sharing this generous federation together makes us all better citizens.

5 *Let us realize that our country's true greatness lies in that ability to give tangible expression to universal values.* What is most admirable in Canada has less to do with what is particular to it, such as its oft-sung vastness, than with what is universal. The Canadian ideal is that of a country where human beings have the best chance to be considered as human beings.

"Wherever I see what is beautiful, what is good, what is true, that is my country." Those words by Rousseau sum up the Canadian ideal.

We must do everything to achieve that ideal, but to do so, we must stay together. We must keep Canada united and make it even better, for ourselves, for our children, for future generations of Canadians, but also for all those human beings throughout the world who love our country as a paradigm of what the world can become.

The Practical Difficulties of
a Unilateral Secession
MONTREAL, MARCH 23, 1998

As lawyers, you know that you don't argue a case in the court of public opinion, especially if it is already being heard by the Supreme Court. So I don't intend to reiterate the arguments we have presented in the reference on the legal dimension of a unilateral secession. I want to talk about something completely different. I want to talk about the practical consequences that such a unilateral declaration of independence would entail for the citizens of Quebec.

The debate on Quebec's separation/independence/sovereignty/secession has been dragging on for more than 30 years. So you might assume that all aspects of the issue have been explored in detail. In fact, however, one essential dimension of the problem has been almost completely neglected.

The debate has in effect centred on the "why," while neglecting the "how." We've been asking ourselves "why" we should or should not become independent, without really taking the time to ask "how" that independence could be effected, that is, how could Quebec be changed from a Canadian province into an independent state.

The separatist parties certainly have a very firm thesis to that effect. Until recently, however, it had been discussed only superficially.

According to this thesis, the separatist government monopolizes the procedure through its majority in the National Assembly. Once elected, it alone determines whether accession to sovereignty requires two referenda, as in 1980, or only one, as in 1995. The means of public consultation is set and interpreted by it alone, whenever the time seems right, with a question of its own choosing. A simple majority would be enough for it to proclaim independence, and that change of status applies to the entire territory of Quebec. Negotiations with Canada can be conducted before or after the declaration of independence, with the government reserving the freedom to declare itself independent at any time if it doesn't like the way negotiations are going. It is in a position of strength, even to the point of being able to slam the door leaving behind its share of the debt, a threat that Mr. Gilles Duceppe repeated just recently.

That, if you will, is the separatist credo on the procedure for secession. Anyone who challenges that credo is branded as undemocratic, an enemy of Quebec, and so on and so forth.

But let's not let ourselves be intimidated; let's try to sort out what's true and what's false. What I feel is true is that we Quebecers will never be held in Canada against our very clearly expressed will. I feel it is inaccurate, however, to claim that only our provincial government can assess that will of Quebecers. Moreover, it is a mistake to think that that government could determine on its own what would be negotiable and what wouldn't, and dictate the terms and conditions of secession.

Even a mutually agreed-upon secession would pose tremendous practical problems. A unilateral declaration of independence would create insurmountable concrete difficulties. Permit me to examine with you why this is so.

The practical difficulties of a unilateral secession

If secession were to be attempted in Canada, it would be the first time that a well-established democracy was broken up. It would be the first attempt to remove a citizenship that confers rights as extensive as ours, from citizens who wish to keep it. It would be the first time that a secession would be attempted when there exist a charter of rights, organized groups to defend a wide variety of interests, well recognized minority rights, and fiduciary responsibilities toward Aboriginals. Never to date has it been attempted to separate such complex and elaborate public bureaucracies, with a public sector that represents almost half of the collective wealth.

One dare not imagine what would happen if the separatist government, after asking its "winning" question and pulling off a slim referendum majority in what Mr. Claude Ryan has called a "dangerous ambiguity," and after having its offer of political and economic partnership soundly rejected because it was so unrealistic, unilaterally declared itself the government of an independent state.

In a press conference on November 12, 1997, Minister Jacques Brassard suggested that it would be enough, following a unilateral declaration of independence, for his government to exercise "effective authority over Quebec's territory" for international recognition to follow. In so doing, he raised a very disturbing scenario, fraught with uncertainty and almost certainly doomed to failure.

In practice, neither Mr. Brassard nor any PQ minister has ever explained how their government could assume all federal responsibilities within all of Quebec's territory. Because that is the most concrete definition one can give of an attempt at unilateral secession: the Government of Quebec would be trying to swallow up common Canadian institutions insofar as they affect Quebec. The federal government, for its part, would believe it had a duty, in light of the above context of "dangerous ambiguity," to continue to exercise its constitutional responsibilities, because 1) Quebecers would not have clearly indicated their desire to renounce Canada and make Quebec an independent state, and 2) the secession would not have been duly negotiated.

Such an attempt by the Government of Quebec would fail for two reasons. First, the conflict of legitimacy that a unilateral declaration of independence would provoke would place Quebec citizens in an untenable situation which is unacceptable in democracy. Second, the Government of Quebec would not have the means to back up its claims and would be unable to assume all of the functions currently fulfilled by the federal government. Let's look at these two aspects of the problem in turn.

First, let's consider the moral dilemma that would face citizens. Everyone would be forced to decide for himself or herself which law, which government to obey. In democracy, citizens should not have to choose between different public authorities. Citizens filing their tax returns, public servants getting up for work in the morning, police officers conducting an investigation, lawyers defending their clients, must all know where the authority lies.

If citizens had to travel, what passport and what consular services would they use if not Canada's?

What would happen to the many Quebec citizens working in the federal public service and federal Crown corporations such as Canada Post and the CBC? In the absence of agreements with the Canadian government, would they leave their jobs and join the Quebec public service? Without agreement on transferring their pension plans, would they take the risk of the money accumulated when they worked for the federal government or Crown corporations not being transferred to their new employer?

Questions just as thorny would also be raised with respect to maintaining order. Would members of the RCMP renounce exercising the functions assigned to them by numerous federal laws, such as investigating drug and money-laundering offences? Would Sûreté du Québec officers agree to enforce laws that the federal authorities would not recognize and whose legitimacy and legality would be contested in court? And to what correctional institutions would people be sent who were found guilty of a criminal offence? For citizens who refused to obey certain Quebec laws on the grounds that they violated the Canadian Constitution, which court would they be tried in?

In such circumstances, how would you, who practise law, counsel a business operating in a field of federal jurisdiction that wanted to obtain an environmental permit or authorization, to change its corporate structure, or to settle a labour relations problem? What government would give you access to the Free Trade Agreement dispute settlement mechanisms in a commercial dispute between one of your clients and an American competitor? Surely not a government that had declared itself independent but was not a signatory to NAFTA.

And just imagine the tax nightmare for the Government of Quebec! How, in the absence of intense cooperation by the federal government, could the Government of Quebec collect source deductions for tax, employment insurance, excise tax and customs duties, payment of operating licences, fees of all kinds and various levies for the exercise of countless economic and professional activities? And if the Government of Quebec were unable to count on all of the tax revenues from Quebecers, how could it provide all the services and take over all federal programs in Quebec, such as Employment Insurance and Old-Age Pensions?

How could the Government of Quebec prevent the province's citizens from continuing to make use of the services provided by the federal government, especially since it would not have the means, expertise or human resources to provide them itself? Can one imagine that artists and businesspeople would forego the grants and loans of all kinds provided by the Government of Canada?

Just to transfer one thousand federal public servants to the Government of Quebec under the new job training agreement, endless precautions have had to be taken. And yet, both governments cooperated closely and the federal government agreed to cover most of the transfer costs. The upheaval involved in trying to integrate the federal bureaucracy into the Quebec public sector against the counsel of the federal government defies understanding. The Government of Quebec would not have the means to do it, especially in the economic turbulence provoked by its attempted unilateral secession.

Many other examples might be given of the inextricable practical difficulties that would be created by a unilateral declaration of independence: port activities, fisheries, airports, air traffic control, banking ... Our Quebec society would be utterly divided within itself, shaken by conflicting directives, in an overexcited, emotionally charged atmosphere.

Let's clearly admit it: the break-up of a well-established democracy such as Canada, whose public sector represents half of the economy, is an impossible undertaking without the willing and intense cooperation of the country's governments and citizens. If it were to be determined that Quebecers no longer wanted to be Canadians, negotiations would be undertaken within the legal framework. In that eventuality, the secessionist government would be in no position to decide alone what would be negotiable and what wouldn't. Secession would be very difficult to achieve, there would be numerous pitfalls and risks of derailment, the economic situation would be deeply disturbed, but at least one could hope to avoid chaos.

A mutually agreed-on secession could be based only on very clear support by Quebecers, recognized by all, and would have to be negotiated with concern for fairness for all. The different interests that would be expressed within Quebec would also have to be taken into account, as well as the concerns of all Canadians. I believe this is something we should all agree on, whether we are for a united Canada or for Quebec's independence.

The separatist leaders, for their part, claim that Canada would be a "prison" if it did not commit itself to recognizing a possible unilateral declaration of independence. Well, they must be prepared to describe every constitutional democracy in the world as a "prison." Many of them declare themselves to be indivisible, and none would agree to the possibility of a unilateral secession. Indeed, those leaders should also describe as a "prison" the indivisible secessionist entity into which they want to transform Quebec.

Asserting that a unilateral secession poses inextricable practical problems has nothing to do with a so-called hard line against Quebec. On the contrary, no one who loves Quebec wants to see it plunged some day into such uncertainty, which is unacceptable in democracy.

Conclusion

It would have been much more agreeable for me to talk about other topics which, for their part, touch on unity, such as the transformation of economic forces in Canada and the greatness of our common values as expressed in the Calgary Declaration. I could also have spoken enthusiastically about the initiatives of the Liberal government that have improved our federation and which I have been pleased to collaborate on, including the new job training agreements, environmental policy harmonization, and the constitutional amendment on school boards.

In two days' time, I will be speaking at the University of Ottawa about the decentralized nature of the Canadian federation and the changes we have made to the federation in the past two years. This is a topic which inspires me.

In fact, since I'm speaking to an audience of lawyers, I would much have preferred to discuss a topic that is of great importance to me: harmonization of federal legislation with the Civil Code. Our country is not only bilingual, it is also bijural, and this is one of its little-known great strengths. In our trade with South America, for example, our civil law tradition automatically gives us an edge over the Americans.

But instead of talking about these things, I have examined a possibility that is deeply repugnant to me, that of a rupture between Quebecers and other Canadians. Why examine such a possibility? Because frankness dictates that it be said that there is no consensus not only on whether or not secession would be the right choice, but also on how secession could be effected.

There is no consensus on whether it is appropriate to hold a third referendum. Nor on the question that should be asked if one is held. Nor on the majority required to effect secession. Nor on the status of territories inhabited by populations who very clearly intend to remain Canadian, especially Aboriginal peoples. On all these issues and on many others besides, Quebecers are divided among themselves, not to mention the opinions held elsewhere in Canada.

More and more voices are calling for clarifications on all these issues. As Michel Venne wrote in *Le Devoir* on March 7: [translation] "The controversy surrounding Jacques Parizeau's great game with Parizeau and the $19 billion that would have been set aside as a buffer has led many Quebecers to wonder what would have happened if the Yes side had won. Would there have been negotiations before or after the declaration of sovereignty? What would the negotiations be about exactly? At what point would Quebec turn to the international community? People don't want dates, but they do want a fairly clear idea of the process."

Mr. Bouchard should not be afraid to make these necessary clarifications; unless, of course, he is afraid that with full knowledge of the facts, without any trickery, Quebecers will never want to renounce Canada. My own conviction is that, in an atmosphere of clarity, we will never renounce being both Quebecers and Canadians. We will continue to improve further this federation that already serves us so well, by helping our fellow citizens in the other provinces and accepting their assistance in turn.

Statement in Response to the Ruling of the Supreme Court

OTTAWA, AUGUST 20, 1998

There are few decisions in a democracy that are more grave than the decision to divide a country – to establish an international border between fellow citizens who then cease to be fellow citizens. Such a decision must not be based on false information, especially when individual rights are at stake.

1. Why this reference to the Supreme Court?

Separation based on mutual agreement is accepted by Canada as a possibility, even though it is not accepted in most democracies. In the highly unlikely event that Quebecers clearly indicate that they want to renounce Canada, secession would be negotiated in accordance with the rule of law and democracy for all.

However, the current Government of Quebec has argued that international law gives it the right to effect independence unilaterally – to separate while ignoring the Canadian legal order. It has claimed that under international law it could take from us, Quebecers, our right to also be Canadians and to enjoy the full benefits that come from being Canadians in Quebec, throughout Canada and throughout the world. That is what it intended to do, after consulting us in its own fashion.

The Attorney General of Quebec made this argument in the *Bertrand* vs. *Bégin* case in the Quebec Superior Court on April 16, 1996, declaring that the process of attaining independence [translation] "is sanctioned by international law, and the Superior Court has no jurisdiction in this respect". The federal government disagreed with this extraordinary claim and had no choice but to challenge it by intervening before the Quebec Superior Court. After the Superior Court determined that the case could proceed and the Attorney General of Quebec decided to withdraw, the Government of Canada referred the issue to the Supreme Court.

The Government of Canada maintained that the Government of Quebec could not rely on international law as a basis to unilaterally put an end to the obligations and responsibilities of the federal government toward Quebecers. It was convinced that, on moral as well as legal grounds, it could never give up its constitutional responsibilities to Quebecers unless it was persuaded that this was clearly their wish. And from a strictly practical point of view, separation without agreement seemed impossible.

The Government of Canada was convinced that its responsibility toward all Canadians compelled it to defend the interests of all Canadians under all circumstances, even the extremely painful circumstances of a separation.

Thus, there were two opposing legal views: one giving the Government of Quebec a unilateral right to effect independence, and the other holding that no such right existed.

In a democracy, in the event of disagreement over a legal issue, it is usual to seek the necessary clarifications from the courts. That is what the Government of Canada has done.

Despite what may have been suggested, the Government of Canada has clearly not asked the court to usurp the will of the people. That is not its role. But it has provided us with fundamental legal clarifications on the unilateral act of secession contemplated by the current Government of Quebec.

This opinion of the Supreme Court of Canada creates no new barriers to Quebec's independence. If a government attempted unilaterally to effect independence, many resulting issues would inevitably have come before the courts. Are we to believe that no Quebecer would have gone to court to challenge a unilateral act designed to deprive him of his rights as a Canadian? It is much better to clarify these issues now, in an atmosphere of calm, rather than in the turbulent environment of a possible attempt at secession.

2. The consequences of this reference

The Court has given its opinion today. This confirms that our constitution as well as international law permit the independence of Quebec, but that the Government of Quebec does not have the constitutional power nor the right in international law to effect independence unilaterally. This means that the Government of Quebec is not in a position on its own to impose the process and terms of the break-up of Canada. It does not have the right, by itself, to take away from us Quebecers our full membership in Canada. The ruling of the Court in this regard could not be clearer.

At the same time, the Court established, as the Government of Canada has always maintained, there is an obligation to negotiate secession in the case of a "clear repudiation by the people of Quebec of the existing constitutional order." These negotiations, the Court has clarified, would deal with much more than just the logistical details of secession. "Negotiations would need to address the interests of the other provinces, the federal government, Quebec and indeed the rights of all Canadians both within and outside Quebec, and specifically the rights of minorities." This is exactly the position that the Government of Canada argued before the Court. It is the position I presented as well in my letters to Premier Bouchard and his Ministers.

Our citizens are the big winners. The citizens of Quebec have had their right to remain part of Canada confirmed so long as they have not clearly indicated their desire to leave. In addition, they have obtained the assurance that they will not be held in Canada against their clearly expressed will.

The current Government of Quebec should respect the Court's ruling and consequently reject a unilateral declaration as a means to effect independence. To act otherwise would be irresponsible on its part. It must accept the fact that unilateral secession is obviously impractical as well as illegal. Such an act would confront Quebecers with impossible choices and could plunge us into disorder.

We now know that if the Government of Quebec, after a public consultation process determined and interpreted by it alone, unilaterally proclaimed itself the government of an independent state, citizens and other governments would be entitled not to treat it as such. This would create a serious problem between the Government of Quebec and Canada as a whole, but – above all – a much more serious problem between the Government of Quebec and many Quebecers.

The current Government of Quebec should be asked how it could, contrary to the law, take Canada away from millions of Quebecers who would still consider themselves Canadian. In what court would it take legal action against citizens who refused to comply with certain of its laws on the grounds that they breached the Constitution of Canada? There are few things more dangerous in a democracy than a government that places itself above the law but continues to demand obedience of its citizens.

We must bear in mind past statements by the PQ government concerning the need to respect the law in all circumstances. For example, former Premier Jacques Parizeau said: [translation] "We are a state governed by the rule of law. Canada and Quebec are not banana republics. There is the law. There is the Constitution. There is international law. And we were all elected to uphold the law. It is said that our role as legislators is to uphold the law as it exists and amend it if it is considered appropriate to do so. But we are members of a state governed by the rule of law" (National Assembly Debates, May 19, 1994).

Or, as current Premier Lucien Bouchard said: [translation] "I believe that in a society based on the rule of law, particularly for a Premier, it is quite inconceivable to allow the threat of brutal intervention against the law" (press briefing, September 21, 1996).

Nor would a unilateral secession be supported by the international community, which has always been extremely reluctant to endorse such a destabilizing act. It is clear: unilateral separation is unworkable. Even when contemplated within a legal framework, separation is an extreme act involving endless uncertainties.

The Government of Canada is convinced that Quebecers will never give up Canada. But whatever happens, we must all respect the Court's judgement in pursuing this debate. We should all agree on this in Canada, including in Quebec, whether we are for Canadian unity or for the independence of Quebec.

The opinion that the Supreme Court has just rendered is pro-democracy. It should be respected by everyone who has the interests of Quebecers at heart.

Letter to Mr. Lucien Bouchard

AUGUST 25, 1998

Translation from French

Mr. Lucien Bouchard
Premier of Quebec
885 Grande-Allée Street East
Quebec City, Quebec
G1A 1A2

Dear Mr. Premier:

During your press conference on August 21, you expressed satisfaction in the opinion of the Supreme Court concerning the legality of a unilateral secession. Please allow me to assure myself that your satisfaction is not selective.

The Government of Canada has, of course, declared itself bound by all aspects of this ruling. You, on the other hand, only recognize its legal validity for others and not for you or your government. You praise those passages that interest you and ignore the content – however obvious – of those passages that displease you. This game of light and shadows is damaging to your project, especially given that you need the greatest transparency to succeed in the highly uncertain adventure that negotiating secession in good faith would be.

It was precisely that obligation to negotiate that pleased you. The Court tells us that a clear majority in favour of secession in a referendum based on a clear question would be sufficiently legitimate to compel all parties involved to undertake negotiations on secession in good faith and in accordance with the principles of democracy, federalism, the rule of law and the protection of minorities.

In this obligation to negotiate, you see a "winning condition" for a possible third referendum. I see it as the confirmation of a legitimate right of our fellow citizens, a right well accepted in Canada and one I have consistently promoted since I entered politics. For example, I am

quoted in *Le Soleil* of January 27, 1996, two days after my appointment as Minister, in the following terms: "If a strong majority of Quebecers unfortunately voted in favour of secession in response to a clear
question, I believe that the rest of Canada has the moral obligation to
negotiate the division of the territory."

There is, however, a point that cannot be ignored: given that this obligation to negotiate is reciprocal, it would also be binding on you,
much more so than the negotiations you had in mind in case of a referendum victory in 1995. There are three fundamental differences.

1. Negotiations conditional on clear support for secession

You can no longer claim to be the sole judge of the clarity of the question and of the majority. The Court makes the obligation to negotiate
conditional on obtaining a clear majority of Quebec electors responding in the affirmative to a clear question on secession. It leaves it to the
political actors to judge the required clarity.

The National Assembly is of course free to ask Quebecers any questions it wants. But you will appreciate that the federal government,
among others, cannot surrender its responsibility to evaluate the clarity
of a question which could result in the break-up of the country.

A question that does not address secession, or that includes other
topics, would not provide the assurance that Quebecers want to give
up Canada. In order to trigger the obligation to negotiate, which you
so enthusiastically welcome, there must be a clear response to a clear
question on secession.

During your press conference you rejected the proposal put forward
by Mr. Claude Ryan that would have given the Official Opposition in
the National Assembly a right to examine the referendum question. But
don't you believe that the opinion of the principal federalist party in
Quebec would have an influence on the Government of Canada's own
evaluation of the clarity of the question?

The Government of Canada could never undertake negotiations on
secession based on a question addressing such vague concepts as
"sovereignty-association" or "sovereignty with an offer of political
and economic partnership." The risk of misinterpreting the vote would
be too great, as many polls demonstrate.

Requiring that Quebecers be asked a clear question does not insult
their intelligence. A clear question is an essential condition of a valid
referendum in a democracy, in Quebec as elsewhere. Public consultations on attaining independence held in other parts of the world have
almost always put a clear, simple question to voters.

As for the majority required to trigger negotiations on a secession, the Court tells us that its evaluation is qualitative in nature. There is no absolute legal standard on which to rely. You draw the conclusion that the Court invites us to be content with 50% + 1, a Quebec split in two. We do not share this interpretation because the quantity is relevant to evaluating the quality.

The Court, in its 78 pages of advice, takes the trouble to link the negotiation of a secession no less than thirteen times to obtaining, beforehand, a "clear majority," three times to a "clear expression," twice to a "clear repudiation of the existing constitutional order," as well as once each to a "strong majority," to "results (...) free of ambiguity" and to a "clear referendum result."

Many important decisions in society require qualified majorities. Thus, the Court mentions the need for a "substantial consensus" and "broad support in the form of an 'enhanced majority'" in order to effect important constitutional modifications. Furthermore, the Court states that secession would require a constitutional amendment and that these modifications would be "radical and extensive."

There are no examples of a successful secession based on a slender majority obtained through a referendum. When questioned on this point you were unable to refer to a single case during your press conference, and for good reason.

The Government of Canada believes that a majority would need to be sufficiently clear to avoid any possibility of its collapsing under the pressure of the economic, social and other difficulties that an attempt at secession would undoubtedly cause. In addition, the size of the majority must be sufficient to legitimize such a radical change that would commit future generations. We must be wary of circumstantial majorities.

2. Negotiations of secession within the constitutional framework

You can no longer claim to effect a unilateral secession. Bill 1 on the Future of Quebec contemplated a one-year period of negotiation on a political and economic partnership, "unless the National Assembly decides otherwise." The National Assembly could unilaterally declare the independence of Quebec at any point. This declaration would have been perfectly legal, according to your own erroneous interpretation of international law.

After reading the opinion of the Supreme Court, no one can not know that such an attempt at unilateral secession would have had no legal basis. International law gives you no right to effect independence unilaterally while ignoring the Canadian legal order. At no point in the process would the law authorize you to take it upon yourself to deprive us, Quebecers, of our full belonging in Canada.

The Court does not rule out the possibility of your attempting a unilateral secession, but the scenario it describes bears little resemblance to the one you contemplated in 1995. The Court says that such an attempt would be without "colour of a legal right" and in a context in which Canada is entitled "to the protection under international law of its territorial integrity." The Court simply says that the chances of international recognition would be better if the Government of Quebec negotiated in good faith while its counterparts showed unreasonable intransigence. Even under such a highly implausible scenario, we can question whether the international community would overcome its well-known aversion to unilateral secessions.

A unilateral secession would be impracticable. If, regardless of the law, you decided to proclaim yourself the government of an independent state, citizens and governments would be within their rights not to consider you as such and to continue to act peacefully within the Canadian legal order. You cannot by an act contrary to law take Canada away from millions of Quebecers who would consider themselves to still be Canadians.

Any future negotiations on secession would have to take place within the Canadian constitutional framework, not between two independent states. Secession would be proclaimed only after a separation agreement accompanied by a constitutional amendment.

3. Negotiations of secession whose content cannot be predicted

You can no longer claim that you alone would determine what would be on the negotiating table. The Court does not recognize a right to secession, it establishes only the right to negotiate in good faith.

The Court explains that these negotiations would relate to much more than just the "negotiation of the logistical details of secession": "There would be no conclusions predetermined by law on any issue. Negotiations would need to address the interests of the other provinces, the federal government, Quebec and indeed the rights of all Canadians both within and outside Quebec, and specifically the rights of minorities."

The Court also recognizes "the importance of the submissions made to us respecting the rights and concerns of aboriginal peoples in the event of a unilateral secession, as well as the appropriate means of defining the boundaries of a seceding Quebec with particular regard to the northern lands occupied largely by aboriginal peoples."

Addressing the legitimate interests called into question by secession will raise the issue of the boundaries of Quebec. "Arguments were raised before us regarding boundary issues ... Nobody seriously suggests that our national existence, seamless in so many aspects, could be effortlessly separated along what are now the provincial boundaries of Quebec."

The Court warns of the difficulty of the negotiations: "No one can predict the course that such negotiations might take." This is the beginning of the black hole that the leader of the Quebec Liberal Party, Jean Charest, has always rightly warned us of.

In short, the obligation to negotiate secession, which the Supreme Court has just given a constitutional dimension, itself depends on clear support for secession, respect for the constitutional framework and a great deal of mutual good faith. If your government fails to observe these principles of clarity, legality and good faith, the constitutional obligation to negotiate no longer holds.

Negotiations on secession based on the clear support of Quebecers, conducted legally, and with a concern for justice for all: this is the only way to achieve independence for Quebec. The time for stratagems and "winning" tricks is over.

Instead of concocting the question that will snatch a few thousand more votes, do your job. Explain to us Quebecers why we would be happier if we were no longer Canadians as well; why we need a smaller country that is ours alone, rather than a larger country shared with others. If you convince us, the question and the majority will follow. The referendum will then merely confirm a visible consensus. Firmly determined to separate, Quebecers could wade through the problems of the negotiations.

If this is a tall order, it is certainly not the fault of the federal government. It is simply that it must be very hard to give up Canada, a country that you yourself described in 1988 as "a land of promise ... celebrated for its generosity and tolerance." Quebecers have contributed tremendously to building Canada and it is in working with other Canadians that they want to take on the enormous challenges presented at the dawn of the new millennium. It is up to you to prove to them, in all clarity, that they are wrong.

Sincerely,

Stéphane Dion

The International Community and
the Secessionist Phenomenon

BANFF, OCTOBER 30, 1998

Canadian unity, and the efforts made in recent years by the Government of Canada to strengthen it, are a topic of interest to other countries from a number of aspects. One aspect is the flexible type of federalism we have developed. An audience of foreign observers would surely be interested by the initiatives taken by the Canadian government to make our federation even more flexible and better able to address the varied needs of our populations, including the needs of Quebec society with its unique character.

Incidentally, the Government of Canada recently proposed the creation of a forum of federations, so that countries that have adopted this form of government can benefit from their respective experiences.

But today I am going to speak to you about another aspect of the Canadian unity issue, an aspect which I feel also has obvious international resonance. I am referring to the opinion rendered by the Supreme Court of Canada on August 20, 1998, on unilateral secession.

That opinion is a turning point in the history of the Canadian federation. It highlights, better than ever before, the difficulties that would be entailed in breaking the ties uniting Quebec and the rest of Canada. It helps all of us to gauge just how sensitive and difficult an undertaking it is to reconcile secession and democracy while respecting the rule of law. This legal clarification will strengthen Canadian unity, not because it would place new obstacles in the path of Quebec's independence, but because it reveals those obstacles that would inevitably arise in the event of an attempted secession.

Perhaps other countries whose national unity is challenged might draw inspiration from the approach indicated by the Supreme Court of Canada. That, at least, is the opinion of a number of observers outside Canada, including the Secretary-General of the United Nations. Indeed, Mr. Kofi Annan told *Le Devoir* recently, after referring to the Supreme Court's opinion: "You're talking to each other, not taking shots at each

---

Speech to the 1998 Banff Diplomatic Forum

other. Recently, other regions experiencing similar conflicts have turned to guns rather than discussions. I think you provide a lesson for the whole world" (*Le Devoir*, October 5, 1998).

As well, the newly elected president of the European Court of Human Rights, Mr. Luzius Wildhaber, one of two experts who submitted opinions to the Court at the request of the Government of Canada, has said: "That's really ideally what a court should be able to bring about, to bring rationality into a complicated discussion and to set up rules that hopefully will be acceptable to all sides." (*Ottawa Citizen*, October 11, 1998)

The Spanish newspaper *El Pais*, in an editorial last August 23, agreed with the Supreme Court of Canada's opinion that the separation of states in a democratic world must be settled by all the parties concerned, rather than unilaterally. The *Boston Globe* (September 21, 1998) has stated that the Supreme Court of Canada clarifies "what is obvious to the rest of the world – that independence is not there just for asking. Nor should it be." And the *Financial Times* (August 22, 1998), has noted: "If part of a country is determined to leave, [...] there are only two routes: violence or negotiation. Canada's Supreme Court has laid out a road map for the latter."

I believe these foreign observers are right: the Supreme Court of Canada's opinion could provide a positive example for international state practice. Before looking at how, I would like to review the way the international community has reacted so far to the secessionist phenomenon, a phenomenon that risks multiplying future catastrophes if the world does not improve its capacity for dealing with it.

1. The international community's aversion to unilateral secession

Let us imagine a democratic country – a federation, perhaps, though not necessarily – where an election in one of its regions is won by a separatist party. Let us suppose that the separatist party believes it has the right to proclaim the region's independence unilaterally on the basis of that single election win, but adds that it will hold a referendum among the voters in the region so as to acquire additional democratic legitimacy.

The party announces that if it won the referendum by a simple majority, it would negotiate with the rest of the country to facilitate the transition and to conclude what it calls a "political and economic partnership" agreement. It stipulates, however, that at any point in those negotiations, it could move to proclaim itself, unilaterally, a government of an independent state. It also says that following that unilateral proclamation, all citizens, both in the region concerned and in the country as a whole, and all governments, both at home and abroad, would be legally bound to consider it as the government of an independent state. The negotiations could continue, but they would be between two independent states.

The question I want to put to you, who have a good knowledge of international state practice, is how the government of that country ought to react to such a claim to unilateral secession by the government of one of its regions. My own assessment of the situation is that no country in the world would agree to be bound by such a process of unilateral secession.

Among the most democratic countries in the world, there are many who prohibit secession in their constitution, either explicitly or implicitly. They believe that every portion of national territory belongs to all the country's citizens, and that it could therefore not be divided.

The international community, for its part, has shown itself to be extremely reluctant to recognize unilateral secession outside the colonial context. If the complex phenomenon of international recognition could be demonstrated by a single indicator, it would be UN membership. This is due to the fact that under article 4 of the UN Charter only *states* may be admitted as a member of the UN.

On October 24, 1945, the United Nations Organization officially came into existence with 51 original members. It now has 185, thus 134 more. Most of these new members are former colonies, while others came into being with the disintegration of their predecessor state, which was no longer there to oppose international recognition of the secessionist entity.

As Professor James Crawford of Oxford University remarked in his expert report submitted to the Supreme Court of Canada:

Since 1945 (outside the colonial context) no state which has been created by unilateral secession has been admitted to the United Nations against the wishes of the government of the predecessor state. [...] Where the government of the state in question has maintained its opposition to the secession, such attempts have gained virtually no international support or recognition, and this has been true even when other humanitarian aspects of the situations have triggered widespread concern and action.

If the international community is so clearly opposed to the recognition of unilateral secession as an automatic right outside the colonial context, it is undoubtedly because it would be so difficult to determine on whom that right would be conferred, because such an automatic right to secession would have drastic consequences for the international community – with more than 3,000 human groups in the world conscious of a collective identity – and because the creation of each new state would risk creating minorities within that state that would claim their own independence.

More fundamentally, a philosophy of democracy based on the logic of secession would incite groups to separate, rather than to try to come closer together or reach agreement. In the words of former UN Secretary-General Boutros Boutros-Ghali: "It remains that if every ethnic, religious or linguistic group claimed statehood, there would be no limit to fragmentation, and peace, security and economic well-being for all would become ever more difficult to achieve."

These are valid principles and considerations. Yet at the same time, we must ask ourselves whether a democratic state could retain against its will a population concentrated in one portion of its territory that very clearly wanted to leave. We need to find some good answers to that question, because it is asserting itself, as we approach the new millennium, as one of the most crucial issues for humanity.

In fact, since the end of the Cold War, according to the Carnegie Commission on the Prevention of Deadly Conflict, the number of conflicts within states has greatly exceeded the number of conflicts between states, with no fewer than 233 ethnic or religious minorities calling for improvements to their legal or political rights.

2. The Canadian approach to the secessionist phenomenon

Between an outright ban on secession and its acceptance as an automatic right, there exists a reasonable position: the Canadian approach.

I expressed that position when I entered politics in January 1996: "In the unfortunate eventuality that a strong majority in Quebec were to vote on a clear question in favour of secession, I believe that the rest of Canada would have a moral obligation to negotiate the division of the territory" (Le Soleil, January 27, 1996).

That moral obligation, to which the Supreme Court's opinion has given legal significance, stems from the fact that a democracy such as Canada could not be what it is if it were not based on the voluntary adherence of all its components. As the Honourable Allan Rock, then Attorney General, so eloquently explained to the House of Commons on September 26, 1996, when he outlined the reasons for the Supreme Court reference:

The leading political figures of all our provinces and the Canadian public have long agreed that the country will not be held together against the clear will of Quebecers. This government agrees with that statement. This view has arisen partly out of our traditions of tolerance and mutual respect, but also because we instinctively know that the quality and functioning of our democracy requires the broad consent of all Canadians.

The obligation to begin negotiations on secession exists only if a population has clearly given its support to secession through a referendum. The referendum question must have been clearly about secession and the majority must be a clear one, so that the population's belonging to the country as a whole cannot be put at risk unless that population has clearly renounced it.

It is best not to hold a referendum on secession unless it is merely to officially confirm an observable consensus for this radical political change. Such was the case, incidentally, in the 13 instances of secession, outside the colonial context, in which a referendum has been held since 1945: the average majority obtained was 92%.

Naturally, I am not proposing such a majority threshold for Quebec. But, in Quebec as elsewhere, it is utterly irresponsible to contemplate negotiating secession on the basis of a slim majority, of a population split in two.

The majority would need to be sufficiently clear to avoid any possibility of its collapsing under the pressure of the economic, social and other difficulties that a secessionist initiative, even when undertaken under ideal conditions, would undoubtedly cause. In addition, the size of the majority must be sufficient to legitimize such a radical change that would commit future generations. We must be wary of circumstantial majorities.

Negotiations on secession must be conducted in accordance with the principles of democracy, the rule of law, protection of minorities, and federalism (in the case of a federation). These principles must be respected, so that secession is effected in the least unfavourable circumstances possible, with a sincere concern for justice for all.

This quest for justice may lead to negotiations on borders, to avoid, whenever possible, populations having to change countries against their clearly expressed will. This is a sensitive issue, which should be treated with the same sense of tolerance and democracy that leads to the acceptance of secession itself.

Secession could not be proclaimed until negotiations had produced a separation agreement, accompanied by a constitutional amendment.

Many details remain to be worked out, something the Supreme Court has wisely left to the discretion of politicians, but that is the broad outline of the Canadian approach. There is no doubt in my mind that, for Canada, this approach has a beneficial effect with regard to unity. That is because this approach introduces clarity. And indeed, if there is one thing that comes out clearly in poll after poll, it is that, with a clear question, Quebecers choose a united Canada.

The vast majority of Quebecers want to remain Canadian. They do not want to be forced to choose between their Quebec identity and their Canadian identity. They reject exclusive definitions of the word "people" and want to belong to the Quebec people and the Canadian people at the same time, in this global world where having multiple identities will be more of an asset than ever before to open ourselves to others.

It is not because of what the justices want, but because of what Quebecers want, that the Supreme Court's opinion has the effect of strengthening Canadian unity. By obliging all of us to act with clarity, the Court's opinion confronts us with the clear choice of Quebecers: a united Canada.

Despite its so clearly beneficial effects on Canadian unity, I don't doubt that the approach stemming from the Supreme Court of Canada's opinion is viewed outside Canada as very daring and liberal in the face of the universally detested phenomenon of secession. After all, as the newly elected president of the European Court of Human Rights has noted: Nowhere has there been any national court that spelled out the rules in advance of a conceivable separation.

The Canadian approach rejects the use of force, or any form of violence. The Canadian approach focuses on clarity, legality and justice for all. While it may seem idealistic in many national contexts, that is precisely because it seeks to deal in an ideal way with situations of break-up, which are always complex and sensitive.

In terms of universal values, the Canadian approach seems to me an admirable one. Its virtue lies not only in ensuring that such a painful and difficult undertaking as secession is effected in the least unfavourable way possible. Above all, the advantage of the Canadian approach is that it provides an excellent argument against secession. For it is by behaving admirably, even when beset by the most painful ills, that a country fosters in its citizens the desire to stay together. As the *Christian Science Monitor* so aptly put it (August 25, 1998): The court, in a unanimous ruling, has plotted a course that allows for separation but makes clear the gravity of that undertaking. Its clear reasoning and fair-mindedness, in themselves, should give many Quebecers yet another reason to stay within Canada.

Conclusion

Canada has worked hard to contribute to world peace and to promote democratic values. Perhaps this is in part why the international community finds it so difficult to hide its preference for a united Canada, while taking pains not to interfere in Canada's domestic affairs.

For example, UN Secretary-General Kofi Annan couldn't help telling a Quebec journalist recently: "Do not push for separation" (*Le Devoir*,

October 5, 1998). And the newly elected president of the European Court of Human Rights, Mr. Luzius Wildhaber, has said that he would see the break-up of Canada as "a personal loss" (*Ottawa Citizen,* October 11, 1998). And the former u.s. Ambassador to Canada, Mr. James Blanchard, said in a recent book that he was convinced that "the entire world" wants Canada to stay united.

And now, Canada has added another contribution, a unique and original contribution which is certainly difficult to put into practice, but is just as certainly a step in the right direction. It suggests a way to more effectively manage what is becoming the most important challenge in maintaining international order, namely the difficult reconciliation of respect for states' territorial integrity and the phenomenon of secession.

The Canadian approach consists first of highlighting the need to continually improve a country which all citizens can be proud of, a democratic and prosperous country whose varied populations can flourish with their own cultures and institutions, while working together toward common objectives.

If, despite these types of arrangements that federations such as Canada can achieve, a population were to express clearly its desire to separate, negotiations on secession should be initiated, within the framework of legality and justice for all, however numerous the difficulties inherent in those negotiations would be.

That's the Canadian approach. I am convinced that it will help Canada to stay united. I suggest it might also contribute to peace and to enlightened state practice.